The Good Retreat Guide

The Good Retreat Guide

Stafford Whiteaker

RIDER
LONDON · SYDNEY · AUCKLAND · JOHANNESBURG

For my brothers and sisters at Turvey Abbey

Acknowledgements
Illustrations by Sr Regina Rynja O.S.B., Prior of Our Lady of Peace, Turvey Abbey.
Book design and typesetting by Diana Goddard, Goddard Associates, Ludlow.
Secretarial support Audrey Lancaster and Jo Corfield.

Published in 1991 by Rider
An imprint of Random Century Group Ltd
20 Vauxhall Bridge Road, London SW1V 2SA

Random Century Group Australia (Pty) Ltd
20 Alfred Street, Milsons Point,
Sydney, NSW 2061, Australia

Random Century New Zealand Ltd,
9–11 Rothwell Avenue, Albany,
Auckland 10, New Zealand

Random Century Group South Africa (Pty) Ltd,
PO Box 337, Bergvlei 2012, South Africa

Printed and bound in Great Britain by
Mackays of Chatham PLC, Chatham, Kent

The right of Stafford Whiteaker to be identified as the author of this work has been
asserted by him in accordance with the Copyright, Designs and Patents Act, 1988.

A catalogue record of this book is available
from the British Library.

ISBN 0-7126-4551-9

CONTENTS

THE TRINITY OF SELF

The eternal triangle of every person is the mind, the body and the spirit. These three aspects of self are our life-long companions. Sometimes at peace with each other, but more often in conflict, they are perpetually in need of attention if we are to be balanced, fulfilled and to realise our own unique personal gifts.

For saint, sinner and ordinary folk, the spirit offers an immeasurable journey of discovery. It is the element of ourselves that unites us to all other life. It liberates us from the tyranny of the mind and the pitiful struggle of the body against time. In lives filled with ever-increasing noise, confusion and threatening events beyond our control, our spirit demands that we take notice of it. It is the voice within us that asks for an opportunity to think things through, to get away from it all for just a little while, and to reflect on our lives and relationships. We carry a sense of being overwhelmed by daily life. Even the happiest personal relationship may leave a faint awareness of unfocused longing. No material or private success can complete us. Our spiritual selves remain hungry for attention and persistently thirsty for growth. Can there ever have been a man or woman who has not asked: 'Who am I?'

If we are to resist the erosion of our religious and human values, we can hardly do better than to withdraw, however temporarily, from the sceptical climate that surrounds us and to contemplate for a few days the eternal truths that have been proposed by all the great world faiths about man's life and human destiny.

The factors at play in our personal growth are exceedingly elusive. They are at once subjective feelings and emotions that at first may be seen clearly, then not at all. Lao Tse, the founder of Taoism who lived in the sixth century before Christ, said that the growth principle in life is too elusive to be named or to be grasped at all. Yet, even in this mystery of self, we can experience not only visible growth but that which is hidden. We can achieve this only by allowing our spirit to flourish.

In many ways the spirit is a burden. It doesn't particularly help to be a Christian, for the Cross you are invited to carry is always with you in one form or another. The serenity of the Buddhist is the briefest reward for a daily trial of keeping to 'right-mindfulness'. In one respect or another, it is much the same for those who follow other faiths. So where does this leave all the people who do not go to church, synagogue, mosque or shrine room? And what about those who do not want to be involved in the religious rituals and admonishments reminiscent of childhood strictures? Where and how can they or anyone else working and living in these times begin some inner journey that reckons with the needs of the spirit and nourishes personal growth?

Nothing will happen until you find some peace and quiet in a place where distractions of every kind are at a minimum. Our ordinary holidays are hardly suitable. A quiet day alone at home is likely to end in the performing of some long-postponed domestic task. We must withdraw from our ordinary lives; this is why going on retreat is often a good solution.

A retreat is an inward exploration that lets our feelings open out and gives us access to both the light and dark corners of our deepest feelings and relationships. Then, we are able to put all these aspects into a context that enriches and promotes our individual gifts and personal spirituality. When we are able to reflect upon the discoveries we have made about ourselves, we grow in personal knowledge, opening ourselves to the adventure of living and to the manifest rewards of love.

This book aims to help you find just such a place in which to begin or continue this journey of discovery.

WHAT IS A RETREAT?

A retreat is simply the deliberate attempt to step outside your ordinary life and relationships and take time to reflect, pray, rest and be still. It is a concentrated time in which to experience yourself and your relationship to others and, if you are fortunate, to feel a consciousness of the eternal. For most it will be a movement away from the ego and towards peace; for many, an awakening to the presence of God in their lives.

A retreat offers a different experience for each person, whether alone or in a group. A private retreat may last from a day to many months, but most people, when they first go, find a long weekend the most suitable length of stay. Most group retreats run for periods of a day, a weekend or a week.

A retreat is not an escape from reality. Silence and stillness are a very great challenge in this age of noise, diversion and aggression. Our lives are filled with preoccupations, distractions and sound. Even after a few hours of stillness, an inner consciousness opens up within ourselves, which is an unexpected and, for many people, a rather startling experience. Modern man has difficulty with silence.

In opening up our interior self, we may find a surprising void – an empty inner space we never knew existed. Suddenly, there are no radios, televisions, friends, children, pets and the constant background of human activity. We are faced with ourselves. Then come the big questions that no one really likes to face and, yet, are the very questions that haunt our lives: 'Who am I? What am I? Where am I going? What is my life really about?' Happily, we have space and time on retreat to dwell on this awareness of our deepest fears and feelings. In these moments a retreat truly begins, for this new consciousness starts a meditation on self that is the giving of undivided attention to the spirit. Some have said that it is opening the door to God.

But it is not true that you have to be quiet all the time. Many retreats have little or no silence and there are retreat houses which can be noisy when fully booked.

In any case, if you are desperate, there will be people at hand to help you. And if the combination of silence and stillness is too much for you, you may well find that a quiet activity such as walking, sewing or painting is the best way to journey inwards. Many retreat centres offer a variety of activities.

GOING ON RETREAT

If you have never been on retreat before, you will be venturing into unknown territory. Whether you choose a monastery, a convent or a meditation centre, you may well feel apprehensive about going if you are striking out on your own. How should you behave? What should you do? If you go to a monastery, everyone seems so busy – and there will be bells ringing for prayers, for meals, for work starting and stopping. It can be confusing and strange. On top of all this, you are faced on a group retreat with the possibility of having to talk about how you feel about God, about prayer and about yourself. It is a prospect that stops many people from going on retreat. But the following steps will give you a good basis for feeling comfortable about it all.

First, select a place which strikes you as interesting in an area of the country which you think would be nice to visit. Then write an introductory letter, giving the dates you would like to stay, with an alternative time, and making it clear whether you are a man or woman. Ask if you need to bring anything special such as towels, soap or clothing and what time of arrival would be best. Finally, ENCLOSE A STAMPED, SELF-ADDRESSED ENVELOPE. Almost all places of retreat have limited financial resources and many letters to answer, so postage is a big expense. You don't have to say anything more about yourself unless it is specified in this guide. You need not declare either your faith or lack of it, your age or circumstances. If you decide to go on a group retreat, then most places have a brochure detailing what is on offer.

When you arrive, you can expect to be welcomed and made to feel at home. Don't worry about what to do next – someone will tell you what the arrangements are for all the basics like meals and worship.

A TYPICAL DAY ON RETREAT
A simple Christian day-retreat might be as follows. You arrive at your destination – say, a convent. The sister who is the guestmistress shows you to a quiet room where you meet a few other people who form a small group. Coffee is followed by a short introduction by one of the sisters or the retreat leader telling you about the place and the day's programme. From that moment until after lunch you and the others on retreat maintain silence. There will perhaps be a morning talk followed by worship or group prayer. You are not obliged to attend these if you choose not to. At lunch, you eat in silence while someone reads aloud from a spiritual work, or you may all talk, get acquainted and exchange views. Then a walk alone through a park or into the nearby countryside, followed by a talk from the retreat leader with a group discussion, ending on a sharing of thoughts and prayer.

A typical Buddhist day-retreat may have more silence and certainly more formal meditation times. But, again, you will be sharing with others in a new and gentle way.

At a New Age centre the day may well include more active sessions and draw on the spiritual practices of Eastern or tribal cultures. If you want to have time to yourself, check in advance that there are no sound-orientated work-shops in session.

WHO GOES ON RETREATS?
At a retreat centre you will meet people of all ages and from every kind of background – students, housewives, grandparents, businessmen and women, the rich and the poor. A group retreat can be fun. Even on a private retreat you are likely to meet interesting people.

Having placed yourself amongst strangers, you may meet people whom you like at once, those whom you are disinclined to know better and those who may make a nuisance of themselves – the kind of person who has a problem and cannot help talking about it to everyone and anyone. You may also meet another kind of person: someone who persists in hammering away about God and salvation or the greening of the planet in a manner that is apt to bore even the most virtuous retreatant. If cornered by either of these two types, don't be embarrassed about cutting it short. You are there for another purpose, so excuse yourself without hesitation and go away at once to your room or for a walk. On the other hand, you may find it both charitable and instructive to really listen to what the person is saying. The choice is yours.

DO YOU HAVE TO BE RELIGIOUS?
You do not have to be a Christian or Buddhist to go on a retreat, even if you go to a monastery. Men and women of all faiths and those of none go on retreat. The important factor is your positive decision to take this time for the nourishment and enrichment of your spiritual life. Access to places of the Islamic faith is a different matter and you must enquire first as to the position. While the Hindu monastery at Unity House in Buckinghamshire is open to all, you should always enquire first at other Hindu faith places of worship and study. The Inter-faith Network, whose address is listed in the guide under 'Helpful Addresses' will be able to assist you in these matters.

OBTAINING SPIRITUAL HELP
If you need to talk to someone about your life or your problems, many retreat places offer time for personal interviews of this nature. However, such talks should lead to some spiritual benefit. Those with overriding emotional and psychological problems should seek help elsewhere unless this kind of counselling by professionally trained and qualified people is specifically offered. On the other hand, if you need to talk to someone about your spiritual life and could do with some guidance, then most places of retreat will have someone who can help you. Meditation, shared prayer, group discussions and directed reading are all ways of obtaining spiritual help.

DIFFERENT KIND OF RETREATS
Retreats are not a new phenomenon. All the world's great religions have found that men and women need at times to withdraw temporarily from daily living in order to nourish their spiritual life. Moses retreated to Mount Sinai. Jesus went into the desert. Buddhists annually make a retreat. Moslems go for a day of prayer and fasting within the mosque. The Hindu withdraws to the temple or wanders alone across the land.

Private and group retreats
Private retreats are those in which you go alone as an individual. Group retreats are for those in a group and these are usually led by someone who is experienced in such matters. The group may be from a parish or consist of a number of people from different places coming together. Group retreats often have a theme or cover a particular topic or approach to spirituality. The retreat programme of the place will explain what these are.

Silent retreats

Silent retreats are an adventure into stillness. There are some especially designed to provide you with techniques to help you lose your dependence on noise and distractions so that you are not upset the first time you experience this rare exposure to your innermost feelings.

Individually selected retreats

These are structured around a particular system of spiritual exercises, such as those of St Ignatius, or based upon a defined form of meditation such as Vipassana, one of India's most ancient forms of meditation.

Traditional weekend retreats

These are the most popular form of retreat and are likely to run along the following lines. You arrive on Friday evening, settle your things in your room and go down to meet the retreat leader and the other guests. After supper you meet for a short talk about the weekend and are given a timetable. From that time onwards you will cease talking unless it is to the retreat conductor or unless a group discussion or shared prayer is held. During Saturday and Sunday there will be religious ceremonies of some nature and probably a short address to the group on subjects which help you meditate and pray. There will be times for walks, reading and just resting. It is all simple, easy and peaceful.

Theme and activity retreats

In the last few years the growth in awareness of the intimate connection between mind, body and spirit has produced a wide range of courses and study retreats that combine body and spiritual awareness in methods which spring from modern knowledge or which are based on rediscovering traditional forms of spiritual awakening. You enter an activity, such as painting or dance, through which you gather your feelings, senses and intuition together into a greater awareness of self, of others and of God.

There are a great number of ways to explore this form of retreat. Here are just a few that you may find on offer in retreat houses in this guide. Some are ancient arts and others very much of our own time.

Yoga retreats employ body and breathing exercises to achieve greater physical and mental stillness as an aid to meditation and contemplation.

Embroidery, calligraphy and painting retreats focus on awakening personal creativity. Through this opening of new personal horizons an awareness of others may develop, together with a sense of creation beyond one's own efforts and personal world.

Icon painting is creating a religious work of art as a form of prayer. It is an established Christian spiritual tradition, particularly in the Orthodox Church, and a very popular type of activity retreat. You do not have to be an artist to enjoy and benefit from such an experience. One of the best leaders of icon-painting retreats is Sister Esther Pollak at Turvey Abbey, Bedfordshire, where such a weekend is usually on offer in their retreat programme. Similar to this, but in the Hindu tradition, is yantra painting, offered by a number of yoga centres.

Music and dance have long been part of religious worship and the praise of God. The psalms call us to bring forth our songs, trumpets, lutes, harps, timbrels, and to dance. Don't worry if you can't sing very well or if you don't play a musical instrument or if you have never danced. That is not important. What is important are your good intentions, for music-and-dance retreats are a joyous encounter. They are apt to bring a gladness of heart that surprises and delights.

Nature and prayer retreats link care for the environment to your life and help you pray and become aware of the unity of all things in creation. Time is spent on observing flowers, birds and trees. They are active retreats, but ones in which stillness, meditation and prayer also play a part. They may well include 'awareness walks' in which you concentrate on seeing things freshly, learning to appreciate colour, shape and texture in order to heighten your awareness of creation at work all around you. This awareness of the inter-connectedness between all of creation is very much part of both Buddhist and New Age approaches to spirituality.

Gardening and prayer most retreat houses have good gardens, and in this form of retreat some practical work is combined with the study of plants, trees and shrubs. Along with talks and time for rest and prayer, this kind of retreat works well in developing awareness of the world around you and can bring the benefit of working happily and productively with others – not something that many people today find true of their ordinary daily job.

Renewal retreats

Christian renewal means a new awareness of the presence of Christ, a deeper experience of the Holy Spirit and a clearer understanding for the committed Christian of his or her mission in the Church. If you think this kind of retreat is for you, then discuss the matter first, if you can, with your priest or minister.

Healing retreats

Inner healing and healing of the physical body through prayer and the laying-on of hands have become prominent features of many Christian ministries today. It is often a feature too of New Age gatherings and explorations. Healing may be concerned with a physical complaint or with the healing of the whole person in order to eliminate obstacles to personal and spiritual growth. It can help us realise our own potential through prayer as healers and reconcilers. For the Christian this always involves the inspirational power of the Holy Spirit.

Contemplative retreats

The aim is to be still and, through silence and intuitive prayer, to hold yourself open to God from the very core of your being. Contemplative prayer is not an intellectual exercise, yet it is demanding and searching, even painful on occasion, as the lives of numerous saints and holy men and women bear testimony. A convent or monastery devoted to a contemplative way of life is probably the best place for you if you want to make this kind of retreat. There you will find spiritual support by joining the community in their daily round of prayer and worship. Contemplation as a way of spiritual awareness is not confined to Christianity but is part of the practice of other faiths as well.

Family retreats

At those places that have suitable facilities, a whole family may experience going on retreat together. These retreats need to be well planned and worked out so that each member of the family, from the youngest to the oldest, has a real chance to benefit from the experience. It would be difficult to find any convent, monastery, or temple in which children would not be welcomed with love and joy – but many such places simply have no facilities for children. Like it or not, restless children and crying babes are a distraction for those at prayer and for anyone seeking interior stillness. So take your children to a place that clearly states they have facilities – then you can relax and so can everyone else. Buddhist centres and monasteries often have children's 'Dahampasala' which is a school study-session held each Sunday.

Drop-in retreats

These are non-residential. The idea is that you live at home or stay elsewhere and 'drop in' to take part in the resident community's regular pattern of prayer or for a series of talks and other activities planned around a set programme. This is an increasingly popular type of retreat for those who have neither time nor resources to go away or whose commitments may prevent them from being away from home overnight. The idea of a drop-in retreat is a new idea for many Christians, but friends of a Buddhist centre or monastery normally attend on such a basis.

Day retreats

The programme for a day retreat can be very flexible. It might be a day of silence, a theme or activity centred day, a time for group discussion or talks, or for lessons in meditation technique. The day retreat is rather like a mini-retreat. It allows you to explore a number of different types of retreat during the year without taking a great deal of time away.

Preached retreats

These are traditional conducted retreats which may be limited to a group from a parish or other organisation or may be open for anyone to join in. The retreat conductor may be a clerical or lay person. Sometimes such retreats are led by a team rather than one person. Usually the retreat is planned around a series of daily talks designed to inspire and to provide material for individual and group meditation and prayer. There can be opportunity for silence, but not always. Sharing together is a feature of these retreats.

'Open door' retreats

The 'open door' retreat provides help to make a retreat in your own home while having direction and the support of a group. The idea is for a trained leader or a team of two religious or lay people to go to a private house or local church where a small group wish to meet. The group meets for a few hours each week over a number of continuous weeks. The group members make a commitment to pray individually during their days back in their own home and to hold regular prayer meetings. The leader provides guidance, materials and talks, which help all the members of the group in their meditation and reflection.

Meditation retreats

While all retreats are to a lesser or greater degree supposed to allow some time for individual meditation, there has been a growing demand for retreats specifically aimed at the study and practice of meditation. The Buddhist response to this has been excellent, creating many opportunities for learning how to meditate. In addition to weekly classes, most Buddhist centres and monasteries hold a monthly meditation retreat that is open to both beginners and the more experienced, enabling them to participate in what is considered to be an all-important practice of spirituality. In Christianity, meditation was long felt to be discursive, and the approach was to reflect in a devout way on some theme, often a biblical one. While this practice remains, there has been a worldwide revival of earlier Christian approaches to meditation which share much in common with those found in the religious traditions of the East.

'Journalling' retreats

On this kind of retreat you are introduced to the concept and practice of keeping a journal as a spiritual exercise. The idea is that, by recording your thoughts during your retreat, you are helped to relate these to your present and future life. This daily record, whether examined privately or shared in a workshop with others, draws your life into focus. The aim is to become more sensitive to the content of your life and to see the continuity of your inner self.

THE CHOICE IS YOURS

There are many other kinds of retreat than those listed above. Most aim towards self-discovery of an experiential nature. The choices grow by the year and are becoming ever more imaginative. In America, for instance, there is a swimming retreat where you join dolphins in their water world. No matter the theme or activity involved or the tradition on which the retreat is based, all of them share the aim of helping you to deepen your spiritual awareness

THE NON-RETREATANT VISIT

'Non-retreatant' is a description often used by those running retreat houses and the term is used in this guide. It refers to a person who is staying at a retreat centre for rest and relaxation during a short, quiet holiday and is not planning to attempt anything of a spiritual nature. Many places do not want visitors who only desire a holiday and this is understandable. Other places actively encourage this type of guest. Going on retreat has become so popular that some people do treat it as a cheap holiday, but that is hardly fair to those offering hospitality who in most cases are either poor themselves or are volunteers.

WAYS OF CHRISTIAN SPIRITUALITY

While there is a shared basic content in all Western Christian spirituality, the approaches to it may differ. For example, the approach of the 20th-century philosopher and theologian, Pierre Teilhard de Chardin, is quite different from that of the 16th-century mystic, St Teresa of Avila. Yet both belong to our common Christian heritage. Included in the many ways of Western Christian spirituality is the rich treasury of Orthodox traditions on which we may draw.

The use of a particular spiritual approach in the form of exercises or meditations is common. There are also a number of popular techniques for dicovering which way of spirituality might best suit your type of personality. Spiritual exercises are methods for spiritual growth. No matter how demanding, they are designed to help bring a change of heart. They are no shortcut to sanctity, as many a nun and monk has found out. No matter what form they take, spiritual practices are essentially to be pursued in a spirit of prayer rather than as an intellectual exercise.

Today such practices have come to mean every form of examination of conscience, meditation, contemplation and vocal and mental prayer. Such activities are designed to make the spirit – rather like the body in physical training – become ready and able to get rid of flab. In this way, the spirit may become open to love and to the discovery of God's will. Some religious traditions might say it is the bringing to consciousness of the unity of all creation and of the eternal. These are ambitious tasks – but then, why not? Unlike the mind and body, the spirit goes forth with unlimited prospects.

Listed below are some ways of Christian spirituality that you are likely to find widely available in retreat programmes. There are many ways to spirituality, including the traditions of Anglican, English, Franciscan, Augustinian, Dominican and Benedictine spirituality, to name but a few. Some, such as Black spirituality and those from the Orthodox tradition may be less familiar. The Charismatic Movement and Pentecostalism continue to foster a reawakening of the spirituality of the early Church and have developed an increasingly popular approach to spirituality. Most people find after a while a particular way that seems to suit them.

St Ignatius of Loyola retreats

These are based on the spiritual exercises originated by the founder of the Jesuits, St Ignatius, in the 16th century. A full retreat can last 30 days but shorter versions are available. The retreat director who is assigned to you and works with you on a one-to-one basis, provides different material from the Gospels for daily contemplative meditation. You then have an opportunity to discuss what response this has provoked within you. In the course of the retreat, you are led with some vigour to review your life in the light of Gospel teachings and to seek God's guidance for your future. Ignatian spirituality has been described as 'finding God in all things'. It is a way of spirituality that is designed for anyone, whether Christian or pagan. The satisfaction of these exercises is found not in knowledge of the Gospels but in greater understanding of the most intimate truths of self and God.

Teresian Spirituality

St Teresa of Avila (1515–82) wrote *The Interior Castle* in order to lead individuals from the beginnings of spiritual growth to the heights of mysticism. The steps she describes in this work constitute Teresian spirituality. These steps are viewed as mansions and we progress in our spiritual pilgrimage from one to the next. The seven mansions are those of self-knowedge, detachment, humility and aridity, affective prayer, the beginning of our union with God, the mystical experience or the prayer of quiet, and, finally, the last mansion of peaceful union with God. Teresian spirituality is, at once, both logical and mystical.

Chardinian Spirituality

Pierre Teilhard de Chardin (1881–1955) did not try to present an ordered way to spiritual progress although he was a Jesuit and follower of St Ignatius. Chardinian spirituality confronts the question of how to be in the world but not of it. It has a cosmic focus which eventually leads to man's love of the world coinciding with his love for Christ. In order to do this, we reconcile a love of God with a love of the world but detach ourselves from all that impedes spiritual growth. We may then strive towards a unified self which is real and true. From there, we are able to move in a state of love to serving others, widening the circle of this encounter with others, until we hold a cosmic view of everything. Thus, we are unified totally in Christ. It is a spirituality which is difficult for many. Yet it answers the problem, especially for modern man, of the contrast and conflict between action in the world and prayer to God.

Salesian Spirituality

Francis de Sales (1567–1622) believed that a person need not enter a convent or monastery to develop a deep spirituality. In his famous work *Introduction to the Devout Life*, he suggested five steps for spiritual growth. These make a progression from a desire for holiness through the practice of virtue to methods for spiritual renewal. His methods are gentle and have always enjoyed wide appeal among people living ordinary lives.

Celtic Spirituality

Recently there has been an emergence of retreats based on Celtic spirituality. The outstanding feature of this ancient Christian spiritual heritage is the overwhelming sense of the presence of God in the natural world. Rich in poems and songs, Celtic spirituality can bring an understanding of the depth of God's presence in his own creation. It is an ancient inheritance of Christian spirituality which has become newly appropriate in a time when we are concerned for the environment and the future of our planet.

PRAYER

Each faith has its own tradition of prayer. The Christian prayer, the 'Our Father', and the opening prayer of the Koran, when God is praised and His guidance sought on the 'Straight Path' are examples of an outstanding and important single prayer to which all may turn. The number of books about prayer and the manuals on how to pray are legion. They burden the shelves of libraries and religious institutions. Yet the question remains for most men and women: 'How should I pray?'

If there were a single way to begin, then perhaps the best might be the request: 'Grant me a pure heart'. This involves surrender of self, offering your vulnerability and patience up to God. A pure heart brings forth charity, hope, trust, faith and reconciliation. Here, love may be discovered and we may hold fast to that which is best in ourselves and in others. Perfect love is not possible since we are humans and, therefore, fallible. But a pure and willing heart, prepared to view all things through love, is constantly possible for anyone. We might fail from time to time to hold ourselves in this state because we are so human, yet it returns and we can go on again.

For those who have faith in God, divine love secretly informs the heart. Such faith makes prayer more instinctive than intellectual, and this prompting of the spirit may occur at any time and in any place. For the Christian, God is both the instigator and the object of such prayer.

MATCHING PERSONALITY TO SPIRITUALITY

Two popular techniques widely available to discover which spirituality may best suit you are the 'Enneagram' and the 'Myers-Briggs' methods.

The Enneagram

The Enneagram technique is intended to help you see yourself in the mirror of your mind, especially images of your personality that have become distorted by your basic attitudes to yourself. The Enneagram has a long history. It is reputed to have originated in Afghanistan some 200 years ago or perhaps in the early years of Christian influence in Persia. It then moved to the Indian subcontinent where it remained an oral tradition known to Sufi masters. Representing a journey into self, the purpose of the Enneagram is self-enlightenment. According to this system, there are nine types of human personality. These have a basic compulsion to behave in a certain way and this behaviour is maintained through a defence mechanism that avoids any change. For example, there are personality types who avoid at all cost anger or failure or weakness or conflict. The Enneagram technique leads to self-criticism which, in turn, leads to self-discovery. From there, we may gain a freedom from self which may open the way to deeper faith. Advocates of this spiritual exercise believe its careful study results in a new self-understanding and provides practical guidelines for healing.

Myers-Briggs

Isabel Myers-Briggs spent 40 years investigating personality types, building upon the research into personality done by Carl Jung. She set out eight qualities or characteristics found in each person. Myers-Briggs believed there were 16 personality types, all of which are either introverted or extroverted, and either perceiving or judging. By discovering which Myers-Briggs personality type you are, you select the form of spirituality which best suits you. The idea is that some personalities respond better and more easily to one way of spirituality than another. Here are a few examples. An intuitive personality might do better with a spirituality of hope. A person who is a thinking personality might do better with a spirituality centred on reason. The Myers-Briggs technique, like the Enneagram, is enjoying much popularity at the moment and a number of retreat centres offer it.

WHAT HAPPENS IN A MONASTERY?

The daily routine is different for monks and nuns who lead an active life such as teaching or nursing and for those who lead a contemplative life devoted to prayer and worship. Most people who have never stayed in a convent or monastery are afraid that somehow they will feel awkward and uncomfortable. Indeed, in a monastery or convent you *will* be sharing a different lifestyle. But once you understand the daily routine and discover that the oddly robed people around you are also ordinary men and women, then you will start to relax. As a guest, you may expect to be received with warmth and affection. Everyone will try to make you feel comfortable as quickly as possible.

Buddhist monasteries are usually places of training for monks and nuns although they often welcome guests. They traditionally are dependent on the generosity of their friends and visitors for all their material requirements, including food, so such places are kept as simple as possible.

Many Christian monasteries belong to 'enclosed' orders, like that of the Carmel Sisters. This means that the community members remain in their monastery separate from the world. There is usually a parlour in which you may meet the nuns from time to time, but you will not mix with them.

Monasteries are busy places with a day divided by pray and work. So if you have never been to such a place, do not expect to see the monks and nuns sitting around looking holy or otherwise, for they follow an active and tough daily routine. Having said that, you are likely to be able to find someone for a little chat and, even when silence reigns, the atmosphere is a cheerful one.

Within the monastery the basics of life are in most ways like those of the outside world. Monks and nuns must eat and sleep. They have emotional ups and downs like all of us. There are health complaints and moans about changes that take place. The religious life is supposed to make you more human, not less, and even saints have been assailed with doubts. One of the most famous modern monks, Thomas Merton, expressed anxieties about his life in community until the end of his days. The famous priest-poet Gerard Manley Hopkins was never quite settled and happy. Yet no one could doubt the great personal spirituality of these men. So remember that monks and nuns are just as human as you are and that, like you, they too are seeking God.

If you stay in a guest house, you will be awakened when you wish to get up, and if you do not feel like attending any of the daily round of prayer or meditation, no one is likely to demand that you do so. However, by joining the daily rhythm of prayer and worship, you should find that it helps enormously to sustain and nourish you during your time there. If you stay inside a convent or monastery, be prepared for the bells. These let you know when it is time to pray or work or do whatever is next on the schedule.

The following are examples of a typical day's routine in a Buddhist and a Christian monastery.

SCHEDULE AT A BUDDHIST MONASTERY
a.m.

4.00	Rising bell
5.00	Morning chanting and meditation
6.30	Domestic chores
7.15	Morning community meeting at which a hot drink and porridge is usually served
8.00	Help with preparation of meal or other light work and time to attend to personal needs
10.30	Main meal and time to rest

p.m.

12.30	Tea-break
1.00	Meditation
1.30	Afternoon work
5.00	Tea-break with an opportunity for informal contact with members of the community
7.30	Evening chanting and meditation, followed by a talk from a senior member of the community

SCHEDULE AT A BENEDICTINE CHRISTIAN MONASTERY
a.m.

6.00	Arise
6.20	First prayers and readings from scripture
7.15	Morning prayers
7.45	Breakfast

8.00	Reading and study of a religious nature
9.00	Beginning of day's physical work
p.m.	
12.00	Mass and midday prayers
1.00	Main meal of the day
2.00	Time for study and rest
3.00	Work or study
4.30	Tea and an opportunity for informal talking
5.00	Time for personal prayer, study and pursuit of special work
7.15	Light evening meal
8.00	Night prayers after which silence is maintained until the next morning

WAYS OF THE BUDDHA

The aim of Buddhism is to show us how to develop our capacity for awareness, love and energy to the point where we become 'enlightened' or fully awake to reality. Indeed, the word Buddha means 'One who is awake'. Although Buddhists do not believe in a supreme creator, since they believe that the world rises and declines in an eternal and timeless cycle, Buddhist philosophy still has worship which is central to its practice like all the major religions. There is a liturgy and scriptures that are chanted, physical acts of reverence, and inner worship of contemplating the Buddha which is often compared to contemplative Christian prayer.

Buddhism began in India some 2,500 years ago and its teachings spread throughout Asia. There is no doctrine and no need to hold to any particular beliefs. It offers a practical path for a deeper understanding of your life. There are many different groups in Buddhism. The two major ones are called 'Theravada' and 'Mahayana'. When you receive literature from a Buddhist centre, it will probably state which one is followed. The Theravada doctrine prevails in South-east Asia, including Sri Lanka, Burma, Thailand, Kampuchea and Laos. Mahayana doctrine predominates further north in China, Tibet, Korea, Japan and Vietnam. There are sects and schools even within these two major divisions so, in a sense, it is similar to Christianity in having many different groups and divisions around the world. Yet all spring from a single spiritual inspiration.

Much of the current interest in the West in Buddhism is due to its being non-exclusive and non-dogmatic. To be a Buddhist does not mean you have to wear strange robes or adopt Eastern customs or reject the cultural background of the West. Buddhism is often called 'a way of harmony', for the Buddha's teaching offers a set of tools to find inner peace and harmony by working with your own feelings and experience of life. By learning to look closely and honestly at your thoughts, emotions and physical feelings, you come to a new perspective for understanding your frustrations and discontent. Then, you can start to deal effectively with them. From such insights you may develop a joyful, kind and thoughtful attitude to others and to yourself. This is supposed to lead onwards to a state of love and peace. This inner examination and insight is a direct method of transforming consciousness and is termed meditation.

WHAT IS MEDITATION?

Meditation is a stillness of body and a stillness of mind. There are many different meditation techniques to help you attain this state of being. They range from Insight or Vipassana Meditation practice, from the Buddhist tradition, to Christian meditation such as that set out by the monk Dom John Main (1926–82), which now enjoys a worldwide following among Christians.

Meditation begins by relaxing the body into a state of stillness, then the mind into inner silence. Many of the techniques that achieve this start with a deliberate breathing pattern. (It is claimed that the breath is a bridge from the known to the unknown.) Most forms of meditation start with a breathing pattern. Such an approach is widely employed to marshal the body and mind and is used as well in yoga and the oriental practices of T'ai Ch'i and Shiatsu.

A single word or a phrase, sometimes called a 'mantra', is often used to help the regularity of your breathing. For example, in John Main's approach to meditation, the word 'Maranatha' is repeated in a slow and rhythmical fashion. This word means ' Come, Lord' in Aramaic, the language Jesus himself spoke, and is used by both St Paul and St John to conclude their writings.

Many people, even Christians, believe meditation is some strange state in which they will somehow lose control of themselves. Nothing could be further from the truth, for the aim of meditation is not concerned with thinking but with being. In such a state of consciousness, you are at peace – a peace which would not exist if you felt insecure. Millions of men and women of all faiths, and those of none, have found in meditation a method of reaching through deep, inner silence to an experience of self that leads to a more loving response to life.

THE NEW AGE APPROACH

It is easier to describe the New Age movement than to define it, for it is a collection of all manner of ideas and practices aimed at personal growth. What is included at New Age centres ranges from past-life therapy, environmental concern, telepathy, healing and animism, to the incorporation of elements from Eastern religions. For many New Age followers it is simply a way forward to self-discovery, self-help and the realisation of personal growth. Many dismiss New Age thinking as crazy, even threatening. Yet the majority of the New Age ideas, techniques and approaches are quite sensible and spring from well-established traditions of healing and self-discovery.

The New Age is a diffuse cult which embraces a wide range of thinking and includes the work of prominent scientists whose discoveries – particularly in such disciplines as subatomic physics, psychology, parapsychology and geology – bring a new validity to the ancient teachings of Eastern spiritual traditions. The New Age movement has no established dogma or leaders and is very much a phenomenon of our time. Some Christians may wish to make certain before attending a New Age centre that the course or ideas put forward are not in conflict with their religious beliefs. New Age places do offer an approach to self-growth that is helpful to many people who do not want to enter an established way as offered by, say, Buddhism or Christianity. The aspect of New Age that appeals to most people is the great emphasis placed on a holistic approach, treating mind, body and spirit as inseparable. This approach is hardly new, as it is part of all the major faiths, and it is probably fair to say that the New Age draws on some of the most ancient healing traditions in the world.

The criterion for including New Age places of retreat in this guide has been that their approach is holistic, genuinely interested in helping people, fairly wide in scope and includes traditional spirituality of long standing, for example that of the North American Indians. New Age centres do not share a common central basis of belief like established religious places, so you will find each New Age place different from the other. However, lecturers and workshop leaders who are authorities in particular fields – such as North American Indian spirituality, colour therapy, healing through sound – tend to be invited back regularly to particular centres. Most centres have very active workshop programmes and will be happy to provide details. You may also find there is much talking and discussion. If you want silence then ask if that is a feature of the programme before you book.

HOW THE GUIDE IS ORGANISED

The guide is divided into six sections: England, Wales, Scotland, Northern Ireland, the Republic of Ireland and France.

Those sections covering Great Britain and Ireland are then sub-divided according to geographical region of the country. For example, South-east England. In that region you will find the county and after it the name of the city, town or village where the retreat centre is located. Maps at the end of the guide will help you.

After the name, address and telephone number of the retreat centre, the guide specifies the tradition to which it attaches. In the majority of cases, a short description will follow which tells you something about the place. After that, the following information is given. When it is open and to whom. The number and kinds of rooms. What facilities are on offer and if any spiritual help is provided. Where you can and cannot go in the house, monastery or grounds. What kind of meals are served and whether or not vegetarians and special diets can be catered for. What special activities are available. What the situation is like: is it in the countryside, in a village; is it quiet or noisy? How long you may stay. Finally, how to book, what the charges are and how to get there. Many places can send you a brochure or a programme of their activities and courses and, if they have one, it will be indicated in the guide.

For France, the listing is by department and then by city, town or village. By each department name you will find its number, so you should not have any trouble finding the place, whatever map of France you are using.

Please remember to write rather than telephone and always enclose a stamped, self-addressed envelope for your reply.

London

The Buddhapadipa Temple
14 Calonne Road
Wimbledon
London SW19 7NR   Telephone: 081-946 1357

Buddhist

On offer are three forms of study and meditation retreat. Classes are held at weekends and on two weekdays. They cover a variety of subjects, from walking and sitting meditation, Buddhist study for beginners, Abhidhamma study, to a Buddhist school for children. Non-residential meditation retreats are held on one Saturday each month, and residential ones are held three times a year, usually of four days' duration.

Open: *All year. Receives men, women, young people, children.*
Rooms: *The temple has no facilities for guests but arrangements are made for retreatants elsewhere.*
Facilities: *Shrine room, study room.*
Spiritual Help: *One-day retreats, personal talks, meditation, directed study.*
Guests Admitted to: *Temple.*
Meals: *Ask when you enquire about a specific course or retreat.*
Special Activities: *Send for leaflet.*
Situation: *Quiet, in town.*
Maximum Stay: *For duration of study/meditation period, class or course.*
Bookings: *By letter.*
Charges: *On application.*
Access: *London Underground and bus (regular service).*

Campion House
112 Thornbury Road
Isleworth
London TW7 4NN   Telephone: 081-560 1924

Roman Catholic

Campion House is situated in spacious grounds just outside London. It is a college for Roman Catholic men who have late vocations to the priesthood or who do not have the necessary academic background to enter a major seminary. It is usually possible to arrange a private retreat, and the organised programme of retreats includes one for younger people from 20 years old to their early 30s. Most of the retreats last for six days but can be shorter or longer depending on circumstances as they are all individually guided ones.

Open: *All year except August, Easter and Christmas holidays. Receives men, women, young people and groups.*
Rooms: *30 singles and 4 doubles.*
Facilities: *Conferences, garden, guest lounge and pay phone.*

Spiritual Help: *Personal talks, group sharing and meditation.*
Guests Admitted to: *Chapel.*
Meals: *Everyone eats together and there are DIY facilities. Traditional food with provision for vegetarian and special diets.*
Special Activities: *Varied programme of events, including retreats and workshops. Send for brochure.*
Situation: *Close to Central London and Heathrow Airport with a large park and nearby banks and shops. They claim it is 'pitched between Heaven and Charing Cross'.*
Maximum Stay: *10 days.*
Bookings: *By letter.*
Charges: *On application, but residential retreats are £15 per day waged, £7 unwaged.*
Access: *London Underground or by car.*

Christian Meditation Centre
29 Campden Hill
London W8 7DX   Telephone: 071-937 0014

Roman Catholic – Interdenominational

The Centre is a focal point for the development of Christian meditation in the United Kingdom. It employs a method of meditation that is inspired by the work of Dom John Main (1926-82), who first learned to meditate while serving in Malaya. As a Benedictine monk, he later founded the Priory of Montreal, which has become a worldwide centre for the development of Christian meditation. While the Centre is an excellent place at which to learn a form of prayer that goes back to the desert fathers of the fourth century AD, many groups that meet throughout the country use Main techniques and the Centre can probably tell you which is the closest one to you. There are no special requirements for beginners and you will be helped to feel relaxed and comfortable when you first learn this very popular form of meditation.

Open: *All year except Christmas and Easter. Receives men, women, young people and non-retreatants.*
Rooms: *4 singles.*
Facilities: *Garden, library, guest lounge, TV and guest telephone. There are a lot of stairs in the house, which can be a problem for the elderly and the disabled.*
Spiritual Help: *Personal talks, meditation. Tapes of Dom John Main's teaching available, in addition to a video on meditation.*
Guests Admitted to: *Unrestricted access to all areas, including shrine room, and to meditation work of the community.*
Meals: *Everyone eats together. Traditional food, with provision for vegetarian and special diets.*
Special Activities: *Meditation as a community three times a day, preceded by the Divine Office, and guests can join in. There are also teaching groups*

on Mondays at 8.00 p.m. and Wednesdays at noon and 8.00 p.m.
Situation: *In the city.*
Maximum Stay: *7 days, with some exceptions.*
Bookings: *By telephone or letter.*
Charges: *£20 per person per day and £120 per week.*
Access: *High St Kensington Underground (Circle, District Lines). Buses: Nos. 9, 10, 27, 28, 33, 49, 52, 52A. Car: not recommended as parking difficult.*

Community of the Resurrection of Our Lord
St Peter's Bourne
40 Oakleigh Park South
London N20 9JN   Telephone: 081-445 5585

Anglican

A nice warm old-fashioned house, situated in a pleasant part of north London. One of the sisters is available on request for individually guided retreats, and the Community tries to create an atmosphere that allows guests to get some physical rest and really feel that they have escaped from the cares of ordinary daily life.

Open: *All year except August. Receives men, women, young people, groups and non-retreatants.*
Rooms: *5 singles, 4 doubles.*
Facilities: *Conferences, chapel, garden, library, guest lounge, TV and guest telephone.*
Spiritual Help: *Personal talks, group sharing.*
Guests Admitted to: *Chapel and work of the community.*
Meals: *Everyone eats together. Traditional food, with provision for vegetarians.*
Special Activities: *Quiet evening open to anyone on third Tuesday of the month except in August. One planned retreat in July.*
Situation: *Quiet, in North London, green-belt countryside within easy reach.*
Maximum Stay: *Two weeks.*
Bookings: *By telephone or letter.*
Charges: *Negotiable.*
Access: *London Underground to Totteridge, BR to Oakleigh Park.*

Damascus House Retreat & Conference Centre
The Ridgeway
Mill Hill
London NW7 1HH   Telephone: 081-959 8971

Roman Catholic – Ecumenical

The Vincentian Fathers, the Daughters of the Charity Sisters and a lay retreat team are the forces that operate this very large centre. In spite of the size and potential number of guests, there is a warm and friendly atmosphere. Retreats for those seeking personal growth, for one-parent families, and for recovering alcoholics and their families are part of the Damascus House attempt to open a way forward for those who may need special help.

Open: *All year except for a few days over Christmas. Receives all.*
Rooms: *50 singles, 12 doubles; annexe with 12 singles, 8 doubles.*
Facilities: *Disabled (but no ramp or lift), conferences, 2 chapels, garden, library, guest lounge, TV and pay phone. Children are welcome, but please enquire first; no pets.*
Spiritual Help: *Personal talks by arrangement, group sharing, meditation, and directed study as part of the Mill Hill Institute pastoral studies. Individually directed retreats and special retreat programmes for the disadvantaged. The facilities are open to self-help groups.*
Guests Admitted to: *Unrestricted access.*
Meals: *Everyone eats together. There is an outside catering firm so a wide choice of dishes is on offer and provision can be made for both vegetarians and special diets.*
Special Activities: *Extensive planned programme – tries to provide seminars for personal growth, parish work and counselling. Send for brochure.*
Situation: *North suburbs of London, only one hour from centre but on edge of green belt, so countryside is immediately to hand, with sheep and goats grazing on the adjacent Totteridge Common.*
Maximum Stay: *Usually a week but special arrangements can be made.*
Bookings: *By telephone or letter.*
Charges: *Retreats £21 per person per 24 hours, conferences £28 per 24 hours. Special arrangements are possible, so please ask.*
Access: *Mill Hill Underground, Bus No. 240 from Edgware and Golders Green Underground stations.*

Eagle's Wing Centre for Contemporary Shamanism
58 Westbere Road
London NW2 3RU   Telephone: 071-435 8174

North American Indian Spirituality – New Age

A shaman is a 'master of ecstasy', in touch with the realm of experience or reality that exists outside the limited, narrow state of our normal waking consciousness. He is also a healer, visionary, artist, and someone who can change consciousness to bring about a greater state of wholeness. Native Americans say that we are all dreamers and that there is both a collective dream of all humanity and a personal one. Chanting, drumming, dancing, instruction in the use of the medicine wheel, ceremony and celebration are all part of the Centre's teaching. While there is only day-time accommodation at the Centre, there are a number of interesting day courses and workshops which explore these traditions of spirituality.

Open: *According to programme. Receives men and women.*
Rooms: *Day accommodation only.*
Special Activities: *Send for brochure.*
Bookings: *By telephone or letter.*
Charges: *See brochure.*
Access: *London Underground and local bus.*

Ealing Abbey
Charlbury Grove
Ealing
London W5 2DY   Telephone: 081-998 2158

Roman Catholic – Inter-faith

The monks serve a large parish and there are schools attached to the Abbey, so this is a busy place, well and truly integrated into the world at large. Yet guests are welcome to share in the liturgy and community prayer, which help sustain all the various activities of the Abbey. The retreat programme is an exciting one. It includes a 'monastic experience' weekend, reflections on justice and peace, and a study of Eastern and Western approaches to mysticism. Individually guided retreats lasting a weekend, a few days or a full eight days are available, as well as preached retreats.

Open: *All year except last 2 weeks of July and the whole of August. Both men and women are received in the retreat house but no women are permitted in the monastery.*
Rooms: *6 singles, 3 doubles.*
Facilities: *Chapel, garden, library, lounge.*
Spiritual Help: *Personal talks, private and directed retreats, spiritual guidance.*
Guests Admitted to: *Liturgy and community prayer.*
Meals: *Meals eaten in the guest house and sometimes in the refectory (for men only). Traditional food.*
Special Activities: *Planned programme of events and regular retreats. Send for brochure.*
Situation: *Quiet but in the middle of busy Ealing.*
Maximum Stay: *By arrangement.*
Bookings: *By letter.*

Charges: *Private retreats £16 per day.*
Access: *BR: Ealing Broadway station 1 mile away. Bus: No. E2 from Ealing Broadway station to Greenford, alight at Marchwood Crescent.*

The London Buddhist Centre
51 Roman Road
London E2 0HU   Telephone: 081-981 1225

Buddhist

The Friends of the Western Buddhist Order strive to put Buddhism's essential teachings into practice in the West, and the London Buddhist Centre is part of that worldwide movement. The purpose of the Centre is to teach meditation and other Buddhist practices and to provide information.

Open: *All year. Receives everyone, but is non-residential.*
Facilities: *Shrine room, information service.*
Spiritual Help: *The Centre is open for personal meditation and for enquiries about Buddhism. The atmosphere is helpful and friendly.*
Access: *London Underground Bethnal Green. Buses: Nos. 253 and 8.*

London Buddhist Vihara
5 Heathfield Gardens
Chiswick
London W4 4JU   Telephone: 081-995 9493

Buddhist

There are six monks resident at the Theravada Buddhism Centre and the Vihara is open every day from 9.00 a.m. to 9.00 p.m. Evening classes explore a wide range of subjects: Bhavana (meditation) instruction and practice, Beginner's Buddhism, Dhamma study, Buddhist psychology, the Sinhala language and Pali, which is the language of the Buddhist Canon. A Buddhist discussion group meets twice a month in an informal atmosphere. There are monthly retreats and a children's Sunday school. In conjunction with London University, there is a two-year curriculum giving students an intensive insight into Buddhism. The Vihara also caters for the needs of expatriate Buddhists from Asia – mainly Sri Lanka.

Open: *All year except August. Receives everyone.*
Rooms: *Only for monks at this time, due to lack of space.*
Facilities: *Conferences, shrine room, garden, excellent library, sitting area for guests, pay phone, bookstall, lecture hall.*
Children welcomed.
Spiritual Help: *One-day retreats, personal talks, meditation and directed study.*

Guests Admitted to: *Everywhere except monks' rooms. Private meditation room and shrine room.*
Meals: *Traditional Sri Lankan food – monks eat separately, everyone else together. Vegetarians are catered for to the extent that vegetables are served separately.*
Special Activities: *See programme.*
Situation: *Quiet in the house.*
Maximum Stay: *One day.*
Bookings: *By telephone or letter.*
Charges: *By donation, but only if inclined. Charges made for university courses.*
Access: *London Underground or bus.*

Marie Reparatrice Retreat Centre
115 Ridgway
Wimbledon
London SW19 4RB   Telephone: 081-946 1088

Roman Catholic

A resident team of sisters, whose main purpose is retreat work and whose spirituality is Ignatian, run this purpose-built centre. They are available for counselling and spiritual help and offer a small but very interesting annual programme of retreats and events. These bear such headings as 'I see His face in every flower' referring to Sioux Indian spirituality – how it is in tune with the Scriptures and reveals the invisible God through aspects of creation and through contemplative prayer.

Open: *All year except first 2 weeks July. Receives men, women and groups for retreat only.*
Rooms: *29 singles, including a limited number of ground-floor rooms. Bring towels and soap.*
Facilities: *Conferences, garden, library, guest lounge, pay phone, Bibles in each guest room.*
Spiritual Help: *Personal talks, group sharing, meditation and directed study retreats.*
Guests Admitted to: *Chapel and all retreat-house facilities, but not to community quarters.*
Meals: *Taken in the retreat house. Traditional food with provision for vegetarian and special diets.*
Special Activities: *Planned programme of events. Send for brochure.*
Situation: *This is a modern, purpose-built centre situated in town, but it is very quiet in the house and close to Wimbledon Common and parks.*
Maximum Stay: *8 days.*
Bookings: *Telephone enquiries, confirmation by letter.*
Charges: *£18. 50 per night.*

Access: *BR to Wimbledon from Waterloo. Underground District Line for Wimbledon. Bus No. 200 or taxi from BR station. See brochure for car route.*

The National Retreat Centre
24 South Audley Street
London S1Y 5DL   Telephone: 071-493 3534

Ecumenical

The National Retreat Centre, in the middle of Mayfair, is a resource centre for those involved in retreat work. In addition it co-ordinates training opportunities, promotes the work of retreat houses, and serves to encourage the exploration of the different expressions of Christian spirituality. The organisation comprises three groups. Anglican in origin, the Association for Promoting Retreats has been established for over 70 years and produces an annual journal, *Vision,* which lists retreats and programmes, and articles relating to them. The National Retreat Movement, essentially Roman Catholic, and the Methodist Retreat Group are the other two constituents. There is also a regional Retreats Promotion Centre in York at the church of St Martin le Grand.

Open: *As information centre only. Day events, such as 'open door' retreat workshops and talks, are sometimes held; help is offered to people seeking a spiritual director, and the Centre tries to respond to questions on all aspects of retreats.*
Access: *Buses: Nos. 10, 16, 26, 36, 73, 135, 137. London Underground: Bond Street or Green Park.*

Priory of Christ the King
Bramley Road
London N14 4HE   Telephone: 081-440 7769
                                                          081-441 4719

Roman Catholic but open to all

The Priory provides a relaxing atmosphere where guests can come for a little 'space' among a small group of Benedictine monks whose main work is pastoral care. The guest house is in its own garden, adjacent to the church where the monks conduct the Divine Office and Mass three times a day. They are able to converse with guests in French, Italian, German, Dutch and Spanish. There is a special ministry for the sick, available to anyone, in which a group comes and ministers three times a week, offering prayer and the laying on of hands. The Prior, Dom Benedict Heron, OSB, has written a clear and informative book, *Praying for Healing: The Challenge,* which explores the subject of Christian healing. It is full of practical wisdom and gives examples of testimonies to the healing power of prayer.

Open: *All year. Receives men, women, young people under supervision, families and children, groups and non-retreatants.*
Rooms: *5 singles, 1 double and a hermitage.*
Facilities: *Disabled, conferences for up to 30 day-visitors, garden, nearby park, library, guest lounge and guest telephone.*
Spiritual Help: *Personal talks, group sharing, meditation (teachings of Dom Main), directed study. An Ecumenical Charismatic Prayer Group meets in the church once a week.*
Guests Admitted to: *Chapel, choir, and may help in the garden or with light household duties in the guest house. Guests are not usually admitted to the monastery enclosure.*
Meals: *Self-catering. Enquire about what is provided and what you need to bring yourself.*
Special Activities: *There are activities available but everything is optional. All guests are free to come and go as they please.*
Situation: *On the edge of a North London suburb, with walks near by and opposite a large country park in the green belt. Usually quiet but can be rather busy, especially in summer.*
Maximum Stay: *Two weeks.*
Bookings: *By letter.*
Charges: *£15 per person per day. £5 for a 'quiet day' retreat.*
Access: *Piccadilly Line to Oakwood. Bus No. 307 Barnet/Enfield stops outside church. Car route A110.*

Royal Foundation of St Katherine
2 Butchers Row
London E14 8DS   Telephone: 071-790 3540

Anglican

The St Katherine community of men and women serves people living in the area through teaching, spiritual ministry and social work. The retreat and conference programmes are wide-ranging and interesting. For example, there is a two-day session on Zen Christian Practice, seeking to discover a way which can strengthen personal spiritual practice and at the same time help to unite two major spiritual traditions of East and West. There are weekends of music-making and drawing, and a workshop based on the notion that our gifts and qualities are reflections of the divine image, especially as understood in Sufism.

Open: *All year except July. Receives men, women, young people, groups and non-retreatants.*
Rooms: *20 singles, 5 doubles.*
Facilities: *Conferences, garden, library, guest lounge and pay phone.*
Spiritual Help: *Personal talks, group sharing, meditation and directed study.*
Guests Admitted to: *Chapel.*

Meals: *Everyone eats together. Traditional food, with provision for vegetarian and special diets.*
Special Activities: *Planned programme of events. Send for brochure.*
Situation: *In the city.*
Maximum Stay: *According to length of retreat.*
Bookings: *By letter.*
Charges: *According to the brochure.*
Access: *London Underground: Docklands Line. Buses: Nos. 5, 15, 40 from Central London.*

St Peter's Community
522 Lordship Lane
Dulwich
London SE26 8LD   Telephone: 081-693 6885

Interdenominational

The Church of England, Roman Catholic monks and lay people of both traditions combined to create an unusual venture at St Peter's. Three Benedictine monks from Worth Abbey shared their life with an Anglican priest and with laymen who were invited to come as residents for a period as part of their Christian formation. In time others, including women and married people, came to support the venture. Now the monks have returned to Worth Abbey and the wider group that makes up St Peter's is taking over to continue as an ecumenical lay community. The aim is to maintain the Benedictine spirit with respect to prayer, community and hospitality. This seems a stimulating and exciting challenge and should help St Peter's to continue to provide a good place for day retreats

Open: *All year except Christmas/New Year and September. Receives men, women and groups for day retreats only.*
Rooms: *No over-night facilities.*
Facilities: *Conferences and garden.*
Spiritual Help: *Personal talks and group sharing.*
Guests Admitted to: *Chapel, choir and work of the community.*
Meals: *Everyone eats together, vegetarians catered for.*
Special Activities: *Although much is bound to change, the current summer programme gave an opportunity to any young person to share in the life of the community for a week. There were 3 full-week programmes enabling participants to take a full part in the monastic life, in addition to helping adults who have learning difficulties and some physical handicaps, accompanying wheelchair-bound people on sightseeing trips, and assisting in outings for local children.*
Situation: *In the city, with a quiet garden, large wood and playing-fields behind.*
Maximum Stay: *Day-time only.*
Bookings: *By letter or telephone.*

Charges: *£6 per person for a day retreat.*
Access: *BR: Forest Hill. Bus: London buses pass the door. Car: South Circular Road near Horniman Museum.*

St Saviour's Priory
18 Queensbridge Road
London E2 8NS   Telephone: 071-739 9976

Anglican

There are no conducted retreats and no group facilities, but a great many people find this a good place for a private retreat.

Open: *Most of the year. Receives mainly women who are recommended to the Priory.*
Rooms: *5 singles, 2 doubles.*
Facilities: *Chapel, garden, lounge, TV.*
Spiritual Help: *No conducted retreats available.*
Guests Admitted to: *Chapel, garden.*
Meals: *Traditional; DIY available.*
Special Activities: *None.*
Situation: *A purpose-built house in London.*
Maximum Stay: *By arrangement.*
Bookings: *By letter.*
Charges: *Please enquire.*
Access: *By London bus – enquire when booking accepted.*

Tyburn Convent
8 Hyde Park Place
Bayswater Road
London W2 2LJ   Telephone: 071-723 7262

Roman Catholic

Just opposite Hyde Park, the Convent is right in the heart of London. Amid the busy outside world the sisters preside over the perpetual exposition of the Blessed Sacrament – the chapel is open all day and retreat guests may go there at night. Near by was Tyburn's place of execution, which operated from 1196 to 1783 following the dissolution of the monasteries. Over a hundred officially recognised martyrs died there for their faith and the Convent's Martyrs' Altar is a replica of the Tyburn tree, erected in honour of the memory of its victims.

Open: *All year. Receives men occasionally; women who wish to make a private retreat; groups for day retreats.*

Rooms: *4 singles. Guests are expected to be in by 8.30 p.m., when the Convent is locked.*
Facilities: *Chapel, small garden, library.*
Spiritual Help: *Retreatants are left to spend their time as they wish. If anyone feels the need, they can arrange to talk with a sister.*
Guests Admitted to: *Chapel – a sister is available 3 times a day or by appointment to give individuals or groups a guided tour of the Martyrs Crypt.*
Meals: *Everyone eats together in the guest house. Traditional food, with provision for vegetarian and special diets (within reason).*
Special Activities: *The perpetual exposition of the Blessed Sacrament in the chapel which is open to the public from 6.15 a.m. to 8.40 p.m.; the full sung Divine Office; the Shrine of the Martyrs.*
Situation: *In the city but quiet – Hyde Park is across the road.*
Maximum Stay: *10 days.*
Bookings: *By letter or telephone.*
Charges: *£20 per person per night, or by arrangement.*
Access: *London Underground to Marble Arch. Central London buses. Parking not easy.*

'Prayer is a matter of being more aware, of being more ready still to lift up one's heart' – Dom Edmund Jones

South and South East

Ascot

Society of the Holy Trinity
Ascot Priory
Ascot
Berks. SL5 8RT   Telephone: 0344 882067

Anglican

Open: *All year. Receives men, women, young people, groups and non-retreatants.*
Rooms: *8 singles, 2 doubles.*
Facilities: *Garden, park, guest lounge and pay phone.*
Spiritual Help: *Personal talks and meditation.*
Guests Admitted to: *Chapel.*
Meals: *Very plain, with provision for vegetarian and special diets.*
Special Activities: *No special activities.*
Situation: *Very quiet, in the countryside.*
Maximum Stay: *Unlimited.*
Bookings: *By letter.*
Charges: *By arrangement.*
Access: *Rail and bus both possible. Send for detailed instructions.*

Kintbury

St Cassian's Centre
Kintbury
Berks. RG15 OSR   Telephone: 0488 58267

Roman Catholic – Ecumenical

The De La Salle Brothers run this centre for young people, from sixth-formers to university students, as well as young working people – any young person searching for spiritual growth will be welcomed. Thousands come here to participate in the various sessions, so you need to book about a year in advance. Meals are wholefood and the place is surrounded by gardens, fields and woods.

Open: *Most of year, possibly closed in September. Receives young people only.*
Rooms: *5 singles, 31 doubles.*
Facilities: *Conferences, camping, garden, guest lounges and pay phone.*
Spiritual Help: *Personal talks, group sharing and meditation.*
Guests Admitted to: *Unrestricted access everywhere.*
Meals: *Everyone eats together. Wholefood, with provision for vegetarian and special diets.*
Special Activities: *There is a planned programme of events.*

Situation: *Very quiet, in the countryside.*
Maximum Stay: *Unrestricted.*
Bookings: *By letter.*
Charges: *£35 per head. Monday/Thursday or Thursday/Sunday.*
Access: *BR: Kintbury. Car: via A4.*

'Let all guests that come be received like Christ' – St Benedict

Maidenhead

Burnham Abbey
Lake End Road
Taplow
Maidenhead
Berks. SL6 OPW   Telephone: 0628 604080

Anglican

A contemplative, enclosed community. Guests are left to themselves and
need to be prepared for silence and solitude. The food is plain and only the
midday meal is prepared for you – breakfast and supper you make yourself.

Open: *All year except Lent. Receives men and women, young people over
20, and non-retreatants.*
Rooms: *3 or 4 singles.*
Facilities: *Chapel, guest telephone.*
Spiritual Help: *Daily offices in the chapel. Limited time for personal talks.*
Guests Admitted to: *Chapel.*
Meals: *Traditional, very plain food. Guests eat in their own room and there
are DIY facilities for drinks, breakfast and supper.*
Special Activities: *Quiet and rest in private retreat. The chapel is available
most of the day.*
Situation: *Very quiet, though near Heathrow – aircraft can be noisy.*
Maximum Stay: *1 week.*
Bookings: *By letter. References or recommendations required for first-time
visitors.*
Charges: *£9 per person per night with a reduction for OAPs and students.*
Access: *BR: Burnham. Buses: Heathrow, Victoria and Reading. Car: via
M4.*

Newbury

Cold Ash Centre
The Ridge
Cold Ash
Newbury
Berks. RG16 9HU   Telephone: 0635 65353

Roman Catholic

The planned programme of retreats here is short but good, offering both preached and directed retreats, Christian meditation and a Franciscan retreat. There are pleasant rooms and fine views.

Open: *All year except August. Receives men, women, groups and non-retreatants.*
Rooms: *31 singles, 2 doubles.*
Facilities: *Limited disabled (including handrails and a lift), conferences, chapel, library, guest lounge, direct-dialling telephone.*
Spiritual Help: *Personal talks, group sharing, meditation and directed study. Retreats organised for individuals. Groups book for their own needs.*
Guests Admitted to: *Unrestricted access.*
Meals: *Everyone eats together. Traditional food, with provision for vegetarian and special diets.*
Special Activities: *Planned programme of events. Send for leaflet.*
Situation: *Very quiet, in the countryside.*
Maximum Stay: *Unrestricted.*
Bookings: *By telephone or letter. Deposit required.*
Charges: *Send for details.*
Access: *BR: Thatcham. Bus: Newbury or Reading. Car: Centre is 4 miles from Newbury.*

Newbury

Elmore Abbey
Church Lane
Speen
Newbury
Berks. RG13 1SA   Telephone: 0635 33080

Anglican

Open: *All year except over Christmas. Receives men, non-resident women and non-retreatants.*
Rooms: *5 singles, 4-bed dormitory.*
Facilities: *Garden, library, car park.*

Spiritual Help: *Personal talks, meditation, spiritual counsel, personal assistance with retreat if requested.*
Guests Admitted to: *Chapel and occasionally work of the community.*
Meals: *Everyone eats together. Traditional food, with provision for veg-*
Special Activities: *No planned programme of events.*
Situation: *Very quiet, in the village and countryside. Next to the parish church where the community go for Eucharist on Sundays and major feast days. Guests usually join the community as parishioners.*
Maximum Stay: *1 week.*
Bookings: *By letter.*
Charges: *On application.*
Access: *By rail (to Newbury) or car.*

Newbury

The Order of the Cross
Snelsmore House
nr. Newbury
Berks. RG16 9BG   Telephone: 0635 41266

Christian

The Order holds events at the house in order to further its ideals, which are to attain by mutual helpfulness the realisation of the Christ-life, to proclaim the unity of all living creatures, and to return to a peaceful and pure way of living. All members are vegetarian or vegan. There are no guest facilities but non-members can attend the programme, sometimes in the form of a retreat. Send for details which explain what the Order is about.

Open: *All year. Receives men and women as members.*
Rooms: *Singles and doubles are available.*
Facilities: *See programme.*
Spiritual Help: *To reinterpret the Christian teachings, showing them to be mystical, related both to the planet and to the soul in its journey.*
Guests Admitted to: *Event and house.*
Meals: *Vegetarian and vegan.*
Special Activities: *Planned programme of events. Send for information.*
Situation: *Outskirts of the town.*
Maximum Stay: *For the duration of the event only.*
Bookings: *By telephone or write to: The Trustee, The Order of the Cross, 10 De Vere Gardens, Kensington, London W8 5AE.*
Charges: *See leaflets.*
Access: *By rail (to Newbury) or car.*

Reading

Douai Abbey
Upper Woolhampton
Reading
Berks. RG7 5TH   Telephone: 0734 713163

Roman Catholic

One of the most famous monastery names – a place for men to make a private retreat in an atmosphere of community prayer.   There is a retreat house for both men and women, but here you must cater for yourself. A traditional monastic place in the countryside and yet not far from London, Reading or Oxford.

Open: *All year except Christmas and religious men only in July. Receives men, women, young people, groups, families and non-retreatants.*
Rooms: *12 singles for men and mixed accommodation for 21 in a separate house. Camping possible.*
Facilities: *Conferences, chapel, garden, park, library for male guests, guest lounge and guest telephone for out-going phone calls only.   Children welcome.*
Spiritual Help: *Personal talks, possible group sharing, meditation and directed study.*
Guests Admitted to: *Chapel, and possibly work of the community.*
Meals: *Male guests eat together. Traditional food, with some provision for vegetarians. Self-catering for everyone else.*
Special Activities: *Various events. Send for brochure.*
Situation: *Quiet and in the countryside.*
Maximum Stay: *By arrangement.*
Bookings: *By letter or telephone.*
Charges: *£3. 50 per night per person.*
Access: *BR: Midgham $1^1/_2$ miles away. Bus: No. 102 Newbury/Reading. Car: via M4, Exit 1.*

Windsor

Convent of St John Baptist
Hatch Lane
Windsor
Berks. SL4 3QR   Telephone: 0753 850618

Anglican

The atmosphere is warm and homely here, and you may join the sisters in the convent chapel. They will provide individually directed retreats and personal talks. In addition there is a pleasant garden in which to walk.

Open: *All year, with some exceptions. Receives men, women, young people, groups and non-retreatants.*
Rooms: *21 singles.*
Facilities: *Conferences, garden, library, guest lounge, TV and pay phone. Children welcomed when part of a school group.*
Spiritual Help: *Personal talks, group sharing, meditation, individually directed retreats. Leaders available for quiet days and retreats.*
Guests Admitted to: *Chapel.*
Meals: *Taken in retreatants' dining room. Wholefood home-cooking, with provision for vegetarian and special diets. DIY for tea and coffee.*
Special Activities: *'Drop-in Day', planned programme of events. Send for brochure.*
Situation: *Quiet, on the edge of the town. Large garden, separate chapel for retreat use. Groups also welcome to join in community worship.*
Maximum Stay: *2 weeks.*
Bookings: *By letter or telephone.*
Charges: *£15 per person per 24 hours.*
Access: *BR: Windsor. Buses: Windsor. Car: via M4, Exit 6.*

BUCKINGHAMSHIRE

Bourne End

Ramakrishna Order
Unity House
Blind Lane
Bourne End
Bucks. SL8 5LG   Telephone: 06285 26464

Hindu – Inter-faith

Although Hindu temples are to be found in many towns, and although there exist Hindu societies with monastic elements, this is apparently the only Hindu monastery in Britain. Founded by Swami Bhavyananda in 1969, it offers excellent facilities for private retreatants, whether of the Hindu tradition or belonging to other faiths. A long weekend retreat over the May bank holiday and a week's retreat in July, plus Sunday talks open to everyone, constitute the more formal programme. Otherwise you will find silence and privacy in which to be still. There are special facilities offered to women and the library is a good one, encompassing mostly books on Indian spirituality but including Christian texts too.

Open: *All year. Receives men and women.*
Rooms: *Main house contains 5 singles, 3 doubles; there is a bungalow for women.*
Facilities: *Disabled women, shrine room, garden and large grounds, guest*

lounge, women's guest lounge, library, bookstall, kitchenette, DIY for drinks.
Spiritual Help: *Personal talks, Sunday lectures, 2 formal retreat times.*
Guests Admitted to: *Most areas including shrine room, work of community.*
Meals: *Taken together – vegetarian food.*
Situation: *Very quiet, set in 10 acres of grounds in the countryside.*
Maximum Stay: *By arrangement.*
Charges: *By donation, but suggested minimum charge is £5 per day.*
Access: *BR: Paddington to Bourne End. Car: via M40, Exit 3, then A4094; or M4, Exit 7, then A4094.*

Most of the trouble in the world is caused by people wanting to be important' – T.S.Eliot

---

HAMPSHIRE

Alton

The Abbey of Our Lady and St John
Alton
Hants. GU34 4AP   Telephone: 0420 62145

Anglican

Open: *All year except for Christmas week. Receives men, women, young people and groups.*
Rooms: *26 singles and 3 twin-bedded rooms.*
Facilities: *Conferences, garden, guest lounge and pay phone. Children welcome, if accompanied by adults.*
Spiritual Help: *Personal talks, group sharing, meditation and directed study, spiritual direction.*
Guests Admitted to: *Chapel.*
Meals: *Everyone eats together in refectory. Traditional food, with provision for vegetarians.*
Special Activities: *None.*
Situation: *In the countryside, where the Abbey provides an opportunity for freedom from every-day pressures in a setting where quiet and reflection lead to worship and prayer at both the daily community Mass and at the Divine Office, celebrated in the monastery church.*
Maximum Stay: *1 week.*
Bookings: *By letter or telephone.*
Charges: *£12. 50 per person per night.*
Access: *BR: Alton, then No. 208 bus. Car: Abbey is off A339.*

Basingstoke

Malshanger Estate
Newfound
Basingstoke
Hants.   Telephone: 071-223 6188
                                                            (for enquiries)
Anglican – Ecumenical

Do not call or write to the estate, as it is used by several church groups in
London (such as Holy Trinity, Brompton, and All Souls, Langham Place) for
group events and for 'Land-Mark Retreats', and you must apply through them
(see address below).
Malshanger itself is a large country house in a private estate of over 3,000
acres, with wonderful walks and the use of private squash-courts. The retreats
are very much of a renewal and inspirational nature, looking to transformation
by the Holy Spirit. A lot of younger adults attend them.

Open: *For retreatants – men, women, young people.*
Rooms: *Singles and doubles are available.*
Facilities: *Bring Bible, notebook, sheets, towel and soap.*
Spiritual Help: *Group sharing, talks.*
Guests Admitted to: *Most facilities.*
Meals: *Depends on event.*
Special Activities: *Planned programme of events. Send for brochure.*
Situation: *Quiet, in the countryside.*
Maximum Stay: *For duration of event only.*
Bookings: *Please contact St Mark's Church, Battersea Rise, London SW11
1EJ in the first instance.*
Charges: *See programme.*
Access: *BR: Basingstoke. Car: via A34, then B3400.*

Fareham

Park Place Pastoral Centre
Wickham
Fareham
Hants. PO17 5HA   Telephone: 0329 833043

Roman Catholic

There is lots of room here, including a dormitory, camping site and even a
hostel for young people. All of it is situated in some 18 acres of grounds,
overlooking open countryside. The Centre is fairly heavily booked by parish
groups, but it is a good place for a family to go on retreat.

Open: *All year except August. Receives men, women, young people,*

families, groups, religious, non-retreatants.
Rooms: *32 singles, 13 doubles, dormitory, hostel, camping site.*
Facilities: *Disabled, conferences, garden, park, guest lounge, TV and pay phone. Children welcomed.*
Spiritual Help: *Personal talks, group sharing, meditation.*
Guests Admitted to: *Chapel, quiet areas.*
Meals: *Everyone eats together. Traditional food, with provision for vegetarian and special diets. Self-catering in hostel.*
Special Activities: *Planned programme of events. Send for brochure.*
Situation: *Very quiet, in the village and countryside.*
Maximum Stay: *5 days.*
Bookings: *By letter.*
Charges: *£20 per person per day.*
Access: *BR: Fareham. Buses: from Southampton, Winchester, then Fareham No. 69. Car: via M3 and A333.*

Farnborough

St Michael's Abbey
Farnborough
Hants. GU14 7NQ   Telephone: 0252 546105

Roman Catholic

Open: *All year except 24 December to 6 January. Open during July and August for foreign students only. Receives men, women, young people, groups and non-retreatants.*
Rooms: *9 singles, 1 double.*
Facilities: *Small conferences, garden, park, guest lounge and pay phone.*
Spiritual Help: *Personal talks, group sharing.*
Guests Admitted to: *Chapel, outdoor work of the community if wished.*
Meals: *Traditional, healthy food taken in the guest house, vegetarians catered for.*
Special Activities: *None. Guest house being refurbished and guest house chapel being completed.*
Situation: *Quiet, but in town.*
Maximum Stay: *2 weeks.*
Bookings: *By letter.*
Charges: *By donation.*
Access: *Easily accessible by public transport. BR: Five minutes walk from Farnborough station. Car: to Farnborough.*

Old Alresford

Old Alresford Place
Old Alresford
Hants. SO24 9DH   Telephone: 0962 732518

Anglican

A Georgian 'pile' set in extensive grounds in Old Alresford – the birthplace of the Mothers' Union. Run as a diocesan retreat, conference and training centre, the whole place is tastefully decorated and furnished, the library and meeting rooms light and airy. The team who run the house provide good food and are happy to help with any queries. All the bedrooms are warm and each has a wash basin. One room has been set up for use by a disabled person.

Open: *Most of the year. Receives men, women, young people, families, groups, non-retreatants.*
Rooms: *25 singles, 11 doubles.*
Facilities: *Some provision for the disabled, conferences, camping, garden, library, guest lounge and pay phone. Children welcomed.*
Spiritual Help: *Personal talks and meditation.*
Guests Admitted to: *Unrestricted access to all areas, including chapel.*
Meals: *Everyone eats together. Traditional (some wholefood), with provision for vegetarian and special diets.*
Special Activities: *Planned programme of events – send for brochure. Clergy in-service training and lay training courses available.*
Situation: *Very quiet, in the village and countryside.*
Maximum Stay: *4 weeks, subject to availability.*
Bookings: *By telephone or letter.*
Charges: *£19 per person per day.*
Access: *BR: Alton or Winchester. Bus: from Alton. Car: via A31, then B3046.*

Portsmouth

Catherington House
Five Heads Road
Catherington
Horndean
Portsmouth
Hants. PO8 9NJ   Telephone: 0705 593251

Anglican

This old red-brick house has provided the stage for half a century of retreat work and caters mainly for parish and diocesan groups, but individuals can be accommodated from time to time when space allows. The house is set in three acres of grounds, with a lovely garden. Healing conferences and weekend holidays are on offer.

Open: *All year. Receives men, women, families with children, and groups.*
Rooms: *9 singles, 9 twin-bedded rooms.*
Facilities: *Conferences, garden, library, guest lounge and pay phone.*
Guests Admitted to: *Unrestricted access everywhere.*
Meals: *Everyone eats together. Food is 'English', home-cooked (low fat, low sugar, high fibre), with provision for vegetarian and special diets.*
Special Activities: *Planned programme of events. Send for the brochure.*
Situation: *In the village, fairly quiet.*
Maximum Stay: *6 days.*
Bookings: *By telephone or letter.*
Charges: *See brochure.*
Access: *BR: Havant. Bus: from Portsmouth. Car: House is off A3.*

KENT

Maidstone

Aylesford Monastery
Aylesford
Maidstone
Kent ME20 7BX   Telephone: 0622 717272

Roman Catholic – Ecumenical

The Carmelite Friars say that hope is a source of joy and that joy is a source of strength. At Aylesford Monastery they offer an open door to everyone seeking spiritual renewal. The Marian Shrine is a special feature.

Open: *All year except Christmas. Receives men, women, young people, families, groups, religious and non-retreatants.*
Rooms: *23 singles, 37 doubles, plus dormitories.*
Facilities: *Disabled, conferences, extensive park and grounds for walking, pottery, bookshop. Children welcome.*
Spiritual Help: *Personal talks, group sharing (during retreats), meditation and prayer, directed study.*
Guests Admitted to: *Chapel.*
Meals: *Guests eat together. Traditional food, with provision for vegetarian and special diets. DIY for tea and coffee.*
Special Activities: *See brochure for programme. Pilgrimages May to October.*
Situation: *Mostly quiet, set in the village.*
Maximum Stay: *2 weeks.*
Bookings: *Letter preferred but telephone calls accepted.*

Charges: *As per brochure.*
Access: *BR: Aylesford 1 mile away. Bus: No. 155 from Maidstone East.*

Ramsgate

St Augustine's Abbey
Ramsgate
Kent CT11 9PA

Roman Catholic

The guest house was once the home of Pugin and he built the Abbey church. Men are welcomed into the monastic ambience and to share the life of quiet and prayer here – but the community does do parochial work and run a school, which is not on site. You will be expected at Mass and for the Evening Office and Compline.

Open: *All year except Christmas. Receives men only.*
Rooms: *6 singles.*
Facilities: *Garden and library.*
Spiritual Help: *Personal talks.*
Guests Admitted to: *Chapel, with restricted access to some parts of Abbey.*
Meals: *Everyone eats together, food is traditional.*
Special Activities: *None.*
Situation: *Quiet.*
Maximum Stay: *2 weeks.*
Bookings: *By letter.*
Charges: *Guests contribute as they are able.*
Access: *BR: Ramsgate. Bus: from Ramsgate. Car: via A253.*

Sevenoaks

Stacklands Retreat House
West Kingsdown
Sevenoaks
Kent TN15 6AN   Telephone: 0474 852247

Anglican

The first purpose-built retreat house in England, Stacklands is concerned now with training retreat conductors, but there is a programme of retreats, and individually directed ones are available. It is a quiet place with many acres of grounds in which to wander in order to enhance the atmosphere of solitude and silence.

Open: *All year except Holy Week and Christmas. Receives men, women,*

young people and groups.
Rooms: *20 singles.*
Facilities: *Some disabled, garden, library, guest lounge, direct-dialling telephone.*
Spiritual Help: *Personal talks, meditation, directed study, preached addresses and individual interviews.*
Guests Admitted to: *Unrestricted access.*
Meals: *Everyone eats together. Traditional food, with provision for vegetarian and special diets. Optional self-catering for day visitors only.*
Special Activities: *Planned programme of events, training of retreat conductors according to Ignation methods.*
Situation: *Quiet and in the countryside.*
Maximum Stay: *As arranged.*
Bookings: *By letter or telephone.*
Charges: *Moderate – upon application.*
Access: *BR: from Victoria to Swanley. Bus: not available. Car: via A20.*

Westgate on Sea

St Gabriel's Retreat & Conference Centre
Elm Grove
Westgate on Sea
Kent CT8 8LB   Telephone: 0843 32033

Anglican

Open: *All year except Christmas, Easter and end of August. Receives men, women, young people, groups, families and non-retreatants.*
Rooms: *12 singles, 7 doubles, 2 three-bedded rooms.*
Facilities: *Conferences, garden, library, guest lounge, TV and pay phone. Children welcome.*
Spiritual Help: *Though the Centre mostly attracts self-organised groups, private retreats are available by arrangement, as are quiet days.*
Guests Admitted to: *Chapel.*
Meals: *Everyone eats together. Wholefood, with provision for vegetarian and special diets.*
Special Activities: *Planned programme of events. Send for brochure.*
Situation: *Quiet, at the seaside.*
Maximum Stay: *By arrangement.*
Bookings: *Contact the Warden by letter or telephone.*
Charges: *Send for details.*
Access: *BR: Westgate on Sea. Car: via A28. Ask for detailed directions.*

West Wickham

Emmaus Retreat and Conference Centre
Layhams Road
West Wickham
Kent BR4 9HH   Telephone: 081-777 2000

Roman Catholic

Run by a religious community and a lay team, this rather large centre manages
to be very homely and offers good-sized, well-equipped rooms. There are
two chapels – one grand and one more modest. Good walks can be taken in
the nearby woods. There is a small flat for silent private retreats. The Centre
is a popular place for organisations to hold annual retreats and meetings.

Open: *All year except over Christmas period. Receives men, women, young
people, families, groups, religious and non-retreatants.*
Rooms: *11 singles, 29 doubles.*
Facilities: *Disabled, conferences, 2 chapels, garden, 2 libraries, guest
lounge, bookstall, shop, small flat, pay phone. Children welcome.*
Spiritual Help: *Spiritual direction, individually directed retreats, days of
prayer and quiet. Personal talks are also available.*
Guests Admitted to: *Chapel, shrine room and all retreat-house facilities.*
Meals: *Everyone eats together. A combination of traditional meals and
wholefood, with provision for vegetarian/vegan and special diets.*
Special Activities: *Planned programme of events. Send for brochure.*
Situation: *Very quiet, on the edge of the countryside – good walks.*
Maximum Stay: *Unlimited.*
Bookings: *By telephone or letter.*
Charges: *Send for sheet indicating proposed offerings.*
Access: *BR: Hayes, Bromley South or East Croydon. Bus: No. 119. Car:
Centre is near A232.*

MIDDLESEX

Harrow on the Hill

St Mary's Vicarage Annexe
Church Hill
Harrow on the Hill
Middlesex HA1 3HL   Telephone: 081-422 8409

Anglican

The annexe at St Mary's Vicarage is a self-contained wing which has been
converted to comfortably accommodate small groups and individual

retreatants. It is self-catering and the bedrooms are arranged like small dormitories with bunk-beds. Not a suitable site or place for the disabled. Most groups bring a leader but personal consultation is available as required.

Open: *All year. Receives men, women, young people, families, groups and non-retreatants.*
Rooms: *Double rooms and dormitories.*
Facilities: *Small conferences, garden, library, TV and pay phone. Children welcomed.*
Spiritual Help: *Personal talks if required. This is a good place for individuals or small groups to use for study, discussion and prayer.*
Guests Admitted to: *Unrestricted access to all areas and to chapel in church next door.*
Meals: *Self-catering.*
Special Activities: *Send for brochure.*
Situation: *In an area of character amidst the vast suburban sprawl of West London. Next door is the 900-year-old Church of St Mary, while beyond the churchyard stretch woods and open fields.*
Maximum Stay: *Negotiable.*
Bookings: *By letter or telephone.*
Charges: *Send for details.*
Access: *By London Underground, bus or car.*

Pinner

The Grail
Waxwell Farm House
125 Waxwell Lane
Pinner
Middlesex HA5 3ER   Telephone: 081-866 0505

Roman Catholic – Ecumenical

Just 25 minutes from Baker Street Underground station, the centre stands in some 10 acres of grounds. It offers small cedar-wood chalets set in the woods, where you can experience 'poustinia', which in Russian means 'a place apart'. Here you may live in silence, reflection and prayer like a hermit. Some food is supplied for you to prepare yourself, while some meals are brought to you ready-made. There is an extensive programme of events and courses, one of which is a family week, which provides a good opportunity for adults to be together and the children to be cared for – not exactly a retreat but at least a good start in that direction. The centre is run by a Catholic lay community of women, and everyone of whatever faith, or of none, is welcomed.

Open: *Most of the year. Receives men, women, young people, families, groups and non-retreatants.*
Rooms: *5 singles, 15 doubles (or singles), hermitage chalets.*

Facilities: *Conferences, large garden, library, guest lounge and pay phone. Children welcome during family week. Pets allowed.*
Spiritual Help: *Personal talks, prayer groups twice a week, assistance with meditation, some counselling on an informal basis, with a view to long-term spiritual support.*
Guests Admitted to: *Chapel and work of the community.*
Meals: *Everyone eats together. Traditional food, with provision for vegetarian and special diets. Self-catering available.*
Special Activities: *Planned programme of events. Send for brochure.*
Situation: *Quiet.*
Maximum Stay: *Unlimited.*
Bookings: *By letter or telephone.*
Charges: *Send for details as there are various charges.*
Access: *London Underground from Baker Street to Pinner.*
Bus: from Harrow.

SURREY

Godalming

The Company of Christ the King
Tuesley Manor
Godalming
Surrey GU7 1UD   Telephone: 04868 7281

Roman Catholic

Guests are received at the Quarry, a largish house. It is claimed that the Roman Catholic charismatic movement started here in 1969, and the atmosphere is contemplative and ecumenical in the broadest sense. Psychotherapy and rebirthing are part of the spiritual help on offer.

Open: *All year. Receives men, women, young people, families, groups, religious and non-retreatants.*
Rooms: *4 singles, 3 doubles, hermitage and caravan.*
Facilities: *Small conferences, garden, guest lounge, pay phone.*
Spiritual Help: *Personal talks, psychotherapy and rebirthing.*
Guests Admitted to: *Unrestricted access to all areas, including chapel.*
Meals: *Self-catering only.*
Special Activities: *No planned programme of events.*
Situation: *Very quiet, in the countryside.*
Maximum Stay: *10 days.*
Bookings: *By letter or telephone.*
Charges: *£10 per person per night.*
Access: *By car.*

Godalming

Ladywell Retreat Centre
Ladywell Convent
Ashstead Lane
Godalming
Surrey GU7 1ST   Telephone: 04868 23764

Roman Catholic

Guests who only want a holiday or to rest, and are not prepared to make an effort to use the contemplative environment to seek peace through prayer, should try another place. Personal talks, directed study retreats and assistance in meditation are available to help each person along this path, combined with the community's notable spirit of hospitality.

Open: *All year except August. Receives men, women, young people, families, parish groups, religious and clergy.*
Rooms: *27 singles and 2 doubles. Accommodation for day groups of up to 100.*
Facilities: *Disabled – with lifts to bedrooms and a loop system for the hard of hearing – conferences, garden, park, library, guest lounge and direct-dialling pay phone.*
Spiritual Help: *Personal talks, meditation, directed retreats.*
Guests Admitted to: *Chapel, choir and work of the community.*
Meals: *Guests eat together. Freshly cooked traditional food, with provision for vegetarian and special diets.*
Special Activities: *No planned programme of events.*
Situation: *Quiet, in the countryside, with spacious grounds and gardens.*
Maximum Stay: *1 month.*
Bookings: *By telephone, but confirm by letter.*
Charges: *£18 per person per day (residential).*
Access: *By rail or car.*

Hindhead

Cenacle Retreat House
Headley Road
Grayshott
Hindhead
Surrey GU26 6DN   Telephone: 042 873 4412

Roman Catholic

Cenacle means 'upper chamber' and refers to the room where the Last Supper was held. The sisters belong to an international congregation ministering to men and women of all faiths. There is an extensive retreat programme, including courses and both directed and private retreats. A holistic physician forms part of the team and is available for counselling and for advice on stress problems and nutrition.

Open: *Nearly all year. Receives men, women, young people, families and groups.*
Rooms: *16 singles, 11 doubles.*
Facilities: *Conferences, large gardens, library and pay phone.*
Spiritual Help: *Adult faith education, spiritual direction and a range of retreats and workshops aimed at personal and spiritual development. Personal talks, group sharing, meditation.*
Guests Admitted to: *Chapel, prayer room, sitting rooms.*
Meals: *Everyone eats together. Traditional food, with provision for vegetarians and DIY for tea and coffee.*
Special Activities: *Planned programme. Send for brochure.*
Situation: *Very quiet, less than a mile from the village. Within easy walking distance are some beautiful National Trust properties.*
Maximum Stay: *By negotiation.*
Bookings: *By letter or telephone.*
Charges: *See brochure, as fees range from £4 per person for a day retreat with a packed lunch to 8-day retreats costing £168.*
Access: *BR: from Waterloo to Haslemere. Bus: No. 268 from Hindhead and Haslemere will stop on request. Car: via A3 to B3002.*

Richmond

St Michael's Convent
Ham Common
Richmond
Surrey TW10 7JH   Telephone: 071-940 8711

Anglican

St Michael's Convent is a smart place on Ham Common in Richmond, with the park near by for walks and a large garden in which to sit. The community has a special interest in the idea of prayer and the clown, running 'clown' workshops as part of its activity programme, which also includes sessions on prayer and painting and a 10-day retreat, usually in August, for women 18–30 to live with the community and experience a life of prayer and fellowship.

Open: *Almost all year but closed for two weeks at Easter and six weeks during August and September. Receives men, women, young people, families and occasional groups.*
Rooms: *8 singles, 3 doubles, divided between house, flat and cottage. Camping can be arranged in the garden. Bring your own towel.*
Facilities: *Disabled – loop system for the deaf in chapel and conference areas, lift by request. Conferences, garden, library, guest lounge, TV and guest*

telephone. Children welcomed. No pets.
Spiritual Help: *Personal talks, group sharing, meditation, 8-day retreats, clown workshop, reflexology. 4 daily services and Eucharist to which everyone is welcome.*
Guests Admitted to: *Almost unrestricted access, including chapel, choir. Help always welcomed in the garden.*
Meals: *Everyone eats silently together. Traditional wholefood, with provision for vegetarian and special diets. Self-catering in the flat and cottage.*
Special Activities: *Planned programme of events. Send for brochure.*
Situation: *Quiet, but only 8 miles from Heathrow. Situated in a suburban area near Richmond Park, with access to the Thames.*
Maximum Stay: *By arrangement.*
Bookings: *By letter with s.a.e., please.*
Charges: *£10 per person for 24 hours, or £2.50 for the day; day groups £5 per day per person.*
Access: *By rail, bus or car.*

Woking

St Columba's House
Maybury Hill
Woking
Surrey GU22 8AB   Telephone: 0483 766498

Anglican

Recently resettled from a large convent into smaller but modern premises, the sisters offer a retreat house plus a small guest house with four bedrooms, a sitting room and DIY facilities. A priest and his wife run the retreat house, assisted by the sisters and other staff. St Columba's welcomes men and women of all faiths or none and provides a common ground for ecumenical discussion and prayer.

Open: *All year. Receives men, women, young people, families, groups and non-retreatants. Women religious for holidays and convalescence in convent.*
Rooms: *24 singles and 1 guest room for the disabled in retreat house, plus accommodation in small guest-house.*
Facilities: *Disabled, conferences, garden, library, guest lounge, TV and pay phone. Children welcome.*
Spiritual Help: *Personal talks, group sharing, meditation, individually guided retreats, and counselling.*
Guests Admitted to: *Unrestricted access within retreat area, chapel.*
Meals: *Everyone eats together in the guest house. Traditional food, with provision for vegetarian and special diets. DIY for hot drinks in guest house.*
Special Activities: *Planned programme of events. Send for brochure.*
Situation: *Very quiet, in the countryside. Retreat house is within the grounds of the convent.*

Maximum Stay: *2 weeks.*
Bookings: *By letter or telephone.*
Charges: *£20 per day.*
Access: *BR: from Waterloo station to Woking (1 mile from house). Car: via Maybury Hill off the B382 – avoid entering Woking town. Good map available in brochure.*

SUSSEX (EAST)

Forest Row

Emerson College
Forest Row
East Sussex RH18 5JX   Telephone: 034 282 2238

New Age – Interdenominational

The College is named after the American philosopher Ralph Waldo Emerson, who believed in building a harmonious relationship between nature and the human imagination. The educationalist Rudolph Steiner translated this into practical methods for achieving spiritual development, and Emerson College is one of several establishments which recognise Emerson's work. It is open to all men and women who have the will 'to serve truly human needs and the needs of the earth at this crucial time in history'.

Open: *From Christmas to Epiphany. During the remainder of the year the College offers courses and conferences. Receives men, women and young people.*
Rooms: *8 singles.*
Facilities: *Garden, park, library, guest lounge and telephone. No DIY facilities or TV. Children and pets not permitted.*
Spiritual Help: *Lectures, workshops and study groups.*
Guests Admitted to: *Unrestricted access.*
Meals: *Everyone eats together. Wholefood, with provision for vegetarian and special diets.*
Special Activities: *Planned programme of events. Send for brochure.*
Situation: *Very quiet and in the countryside.*
Maximum Stay: *12–14 days.*
Bookings: *By letter or telephone.*
Charges: *£98 per person per week.*
Access: *BR to East Grinstead and then by taxi. Enquire in letter as to best car route.*

Hastings

Society of the Holy Child
St Michael's
Dunclutha Road
Hastings
East Sussex TN34 2JB   Telephone: 0424 443219

Roman Catholic

Open: *All year except September and early October. Receives men, women and groups for organised retreats.*
Rooms: *8 singles.*
Facilities: *Garden for retreatants and a small library.*
Spiritual Help: *Personal talks, group sharing, meditation. Retreatants are normally expected to observe silence for the sake of other visitors.*
Guests Admitted to: *Unrestricted access within grounds, restricted access to chapel.*
Meals: *Taken in small dining-room; plain food.*
Special Activities: *Planned programme of events. Send for brochure.*
Situation: *Quiet and on the outskirts of town.*
Bookings: *By letter.*
Charges: *See brochure.*
Access: *BR: Hastings. Bus: coach from Victoria station.*
Car: via M25 and A21.

Heathfield

Monastery of the Visitation
Waldron
nr. Heathfield
East Sussex TN21 ORX   Telephone: 04353 2619

Roman Catholic

The sisters are called to be a praying presence in the world and they offer an environment of stillness, prayer and spiritual renewal to those women who wish to share their lives for a time.

Open: *Easter to November. Receives women and girls over 16.*
Rooms: *3 singles.*
Facilities: *Garden, park, library and direct-dialling telephone.*
Spiritual Help: *Personal talks, meditation, daily Mass, daily sharing in the singing of the Divine Office. Resident chaplain available if necessary.*
Guests Admitted to: *Unrestricted access within the enclosure, in addition to chapel, choir and work with community in the garden and kitchen garden.*

Meals: *Everyone eats together. Traditional food, with provision for vegetarian and special diets. Self-catering for hot drinks.*
Special Activities: *No planned programme outside the daily structure and space for prayer.*
Situation: *Very quiet – set in the countryside in 50 acres of parkland, with beautiful views over South Downs.*
Maximum Stay: *10 days, or longer – with permission of the Bishop.*
Bookings: *By letter or telephone.*
Charges: *Terms available on application.*
Access: *By rail and bus to Uckfield, then by taxi to the Monastery.*

Hove

The Only Alternative Left
39 St Aubyn's
Hove
East Sussex BN3 2TH   Telephone: 0273 24739

New Age

A feminist, non-smoking, privately run retreat guest house where women – especially lesbians – can feel safe and accepted. Occasionally there are courses, and on Friday and Saturday evenings a special feature is the 'women's restaurant', which serves delicious vegetarian dishes.

Open: *All year. Receives women, groups and non-retreatants. Not suitable for children under 12.*
Rooms: *Double and twin-bedded rooms are available, plus 1 four-bedded room and a small self-contained flat.*
Facilities: *Small conferences for up to 15 people, garden, guest lounge, TV and pay phone. Meeting rooms and leisure courses available. No wheelchair access to bedrooms. No pets.*
Spiritual Help: *None specifically, but there is a large noticeboard advertising local activities for women.*
Guests Admitted to: *All facilities.*
Meals: *Wholefood, with a special emphasis on vegetarian. Self-catering available.*
Special Activities: *Send for brochure.*
Situation: *Quiet but in the town.*
Maximum Stay: *2 weeks.*
Bookings: *By letter.*
Charges: *From £8 per person per day.*
Access: *BR: to Brighton or Hove. Bus: No. 6 from Brighton station; 10-minute walk from Hove station. Car: via A23.*

Wadhurst

St Benedict's Priory
Beech Hill
Wadhurst
East Sussex TN5 6JS   Telephone: 089 288 2588

Roman Catholic

Open: *All year. Receives men and women.*
Rooms: *3 singles, 2 doubles.*
Facilities: *Garden and library, guest telephone. Not suitable for the disabled as bedrooms are upstairs.*
Spiritual Help: *Personal talks. Guided days of recollection.*
Guests Admitted to: *Chapel.*
Meals: *Lunch together, DIY facilities for other meals, with food provided from stores by the community. Traditional food, with provision for vegetarians.*
Special Activities: *Rest and quiet, enhanced by a good library and beautiful views over the Sussex Downs.*
Situation: *Very quiet, in the countryside with access to good country walks.*
Maximum Stay: *1 week.*
Bookings: *By letter or telephone.*
Charges: *£12 per person per day.*
Access: *BR: to Wadhurst, 1 1/2 miles away from Priory – taxis available at station. No buses. Car: via A21 from London.*

SUSSEX (WEST)

Arundel

Convent of Poor Clares
Crossbush
Arundel
West Sussex BN18 9PJ   Telephone: 0903 88 2536
                                                            0903 88 3125
Roman Catholic

Open: *All year except 1 November to 8 December and over Christmas. Receives women and men with references.*
Rooms: *4 singles, 1 double.*
Facilities: *Caravans, small library, guest lounge, TV and guest telephone.*
Spiritual Help: *Personal talks.*
Guests Admitted to: *Chapel.*
Meals: *House guests only. Traditional food, with provision for vegetarians and special diets. Caravan guests use DIY facilities for meals.*
Special Activities: *Guests mostly enjoy a quiet time or a private retreat, and*

join the sisters at prayer.
Situation: *House is quiet but on a very busy road. Lovely countryside with good walks near by. Few miles from the coast.*
Maximum Stay: *2 weeks.*
Bookings: *By letter.*
Charges: *No set charge but £15 a night per person covers costs.*
Access: *BR: Arundel station 5 minutes away. No easy buses. Car: via A27.*

Bognor Regis

St Joseph's
Albert Road
Bognor Regis
West Sussex PO21 1NJ   Telephone: 0243 864051

Roman Catholic

Open: *All year except for 2 weeks. No closed season. Receives men, women, young people, families and non-retreatants.*
Rooms: *Single rooms available, plus 2 doubles and a hermitage.*
Facilities: *Garden, park, library, guest lounge, TV and pay phone. Children welcomed, pets.*
Spiritual Help: *Chaplain available.*
Guests Admitted to: *Chapel, choir; women admitted to work of community and to the oratory.*
Meals: *Everyone eats together – food is traditional. Self-catering available. No provision for vegetarians.*
Special Activities: *No planned programme of events.*
Situation: *Quiet, in the town close to promenade – countryside within easy access.*
Maximum Stay: *Usually 2 weeks.*
Bookings: *By letter.*
Charges: *By donation.*
Access: *By rail, bus or car.*

Chichester

St Francis House
30 Parchment Street
Chichester
West Sussex PO19 3BX   Telephone: 0243 788345

Interdenominational

All events at St Francis House are ecumenical. It used to be a private house which the Warden, Miss Patricia Holmes, opened to guests seeking tranquillity in a Christian atmosphere. Prayer workshops, meditation, quiet days, and prayer and painting weekends are available. Miss Holmes is an Open Door and an Ignation directed-retreat leader.

Open: *All year. Receives women on individually guided retreats and as non-retreatants.*
Rooms: *2 singles.*
Facilities: *Garden, library, guest lounge.*
Spiritual Help: *Personal talks, meditation, guided study and help in spiritual direction.*
Guests Admitted to: *Prayer/quiet room.*
Meals: *Eaten in the dining-room. Traditional food, with provision for vegetarian and special diets. Self-catering if required.*
Special Activities: *Small, quiet retreat house giving opportunity for a rest, for 'space' or for directed retreat. Planned programme of events – send for brochure.*
Situation: *Quiet, in the city.*
Maximum Stay: *6 days.*
Bookings: *By letter.*
Charges: *£15 per person full board, reduction for half-board and self-catering.*
Access: *By rail or car (route map in brochure).*

Crawley

Grace & Compassion Convent
Paddockhurst Road
Turners Hill
Crawley
West Sussex RH10 4GZ   Telephone: 0342 715672

Roman Catholic

Open: *As available. Receives men, women, young people and non-retreatants.*
Rooms: *1 double (or single).*
Facilities: *Small garden. Children and pets may be admitted by special arrangement.*
Spiritual Help: *Basically a quiet place, providing space for reflection.*
Guests Admitted to: *Chapel.*
Meals: *Everyone eats together, or can eat alone if this is preferred. Traditional food, with kettle and toaster for guest use.*
Special Activities: *No structured programme.*
Situation: *In the countryside but rather busy.*
Maximum Stay: *2 weeks.*
Bookings: *By letter or telephone.*
Charges: *By donation.*

Access: *BR to Three Bridges. No bus. Car route from Crawley.*

Crawley

Monastery of the Holy Trinity
Crawley Down
Crawley
West Sussex RH10 4LH   Telephone: 0342 712074

Anglican

Guests are asked to respect the timetable and silence of the monks' daily life. This is not a suitable retreat place for those who are under considerable psychological stress.

Open: *All year. Receives men, women, young people and groups.*
Rooms: *6 singles.*
Facilities: *Park, library, guest lounge and telephone.*
Spiritual Help: *Participation in the Divine Office and group prayer, including the Jesus prayer. Personal talks and directed study.*
Guests Admitted to: *Chapel, grounds of monastery except monastic enclosure, work of the community.*
Meals: *Everyone eats together. Wholefood but no provision for special diets.*
Special Activities: *None.*
Situation: *Quiet, in the midst of woodland, with a small farm.*
Maximum Stay: *1 week.*
Bookings: *By letter or telephone.*
Charges: *£8. 50 per day minimum.*
Access: *BR: to Three Bridges. Bus: to Crawley and change for Crawley Down. Car: via M23, Exit 10.*

Crawley

Worth Abbey
Crawley
West Sussex RH10 4SB   Telephone: 0342 715911

Roman Catholic

Education and pastoral work are the business of this community, and there is a school within the grounds, but the setting is beautiful and quiet can be found.

Open: *All year except 24 December to 6 January and August. Receives men only for the time being.*
Rooms: *5 singles.*
Facilities: *Use of library by arrangement with librarian. Guest pay phone.*

Spiritual Help: *Personal talks.*
Guests Admitted to: *Unrestricted access within the grounds, chapel, choir and educational and pastoral work.*
Meals: *Everyone eats together. Traditional food, with provision for vegetarians. Self-catering kitchenette.*
Special Activities: *Guests are welcome to attend the Monastic Office 4 times daily as well as the Conventual Mass.*
Situation: *In the countryside, with beautiful grounds, but there is a school on the campus.*
Maximum Stay: *Ordinarily 4 nights, 1 week if making a retreat.*
Bookings: *By letter.*
Charges: *No set charge but donations appreciated. For those who wish to give full board, costs are £16 per person per night, £10 for students.*
Access: *BR: from Victoria station to Three Bridges. Car: via M23, Exit 10 to East Grinstead.*

East Grinstead

Neale House Conference Centre
Moat Road
East Grinstead
West Sussex RH19 3LB   Telephone: 0342 312552

Anglican

Neale House offers a centre from which to explore the Sussex countryside and there are plenty of things to do locally. It is usual for groups who have arranged their own special retreat programme to come to stay, but special help on spiritual matters can be arranged for individuals.

Open: *Weekends lasting from Friday supper to Sunday tea-time. Receives men, women, young people, families, groups, and both retreatants and non-retreatants. Closed August and Christmas.*
Rooms: *5 singles, 8 doubles, 3 dormitories providing 13 beds.*
Facilities: *Chapel, conferences, garden, park, guest lounge, TV and pay phone. Children and pets welcomed.*
Spiritual Help: *Guests usually get on with their own programme of activities but can call for help – guidance includes personal talks, group sharing and meditation.*
Guests Admitted to: *Unrestricted access.*
Meals: *Everyone eats together. Traditional wholefood, with provision for vegetarian and special diets if required.*
Special Activities: *Guests usually come in groups, having arranged their own programme.*
Situation: *'Quietish', on edge of town, close to Sussex countryside.*
Maximum Stay: *Weekend only.*
Bookings: *By letter or telephone.*

Charges: *£40 per person per weekend.*
Access: *By rail or car is best.*

East Grinstead

St Margaret's Convent
St John's Road
East Grinstead
West Sussex RH19 3LE   Telephone: 0342 323497

Anglican

The St Margaret's guest house is for those who wish to spend a time of quiet and refreshment in the convent, while the sisters' other facility, St Michael's Retreat House, is reserved for those wishing to make silent retreats – this means what it says, and it is expected that retreatants will maintain silence. The sisters run Neale House, a conference centre near by, which accommodates up to 40 people. A separate brochure is available about this facility.

Open: *All year. Receives men, women, young people occasionally, small groups of clergy, non-retreatants.*
Rooms: *Guest house: 7 singles, 2 doubles. Retreat House: 6 singles.*
Facilities: *Disabled, garden, library, guest lounge, TV in the guest house, pay phone, adjacent park.*
Spiritual Help: *Personal talks.*
Guests Admitted to: *Chapel, work of the community on occasions.*
Meals: *Everyone eats together. Traditional food, with provision for vegetarian and diabetic diets.*
Special Activities: *No planned activities but send for the brochure, which explains about the Society of St Margaret's and describes what is available.*
Situation: *Quiet, in the town.*
Maximum Stay: *Usually 2 weeks.*
Bookings: *By telephone or letter.*
Charges: *By donation.*
Access: *By rail, bus or car.*

Hassocks

Priory of Our Lady
Sayers Common
Hassocks
West Sussex BN6 9HT   Telephone: 0273 832901

Roman Catholic – Inter-faith

'One heart and one soul in God' sums up the way of life of this flourishing

Augustinian monastic community. All men and women of good faith, whether Christian, Buddhist, Hindu or Jew, are welcomed by the sisters at their delightful modern priory set at the end of a drive that is edged with daffodils in the spring. There is a retreat centre in a separate house for guests, and the annual retreat programme ranges from a weekend on 'growth in the spirit' to an ecumenical 'adventure' in painting and prayer.

Open: *All year except mid-August to mid-September. Receives men, women, young people, families, groups and occasionally non-retreatants. Taking children is possible but the facilities are not really very suitable.*
Rooms: *3 singles, 14 doubles, dormitory with 4 beds.*
Facilities: *Limited number of facilities for the disabled, conferences, garden, library, guest lounge, TV and pay phone. Camping can sometimes be arranged. No pets.*
Spiritual Help: *Personal talks.*
Guests Admitted to: *Chapel, choir and community prayers in the church.*
Meals: *Taken in guest house. Traditional food – no provision for special diets.*
Special Activities: *Planned programme of events. Send for brochure.*
Situation: *Quiet and in the countryside.*
Maximum Stay: *2 weeks.*
Bookings: *By letter.*
Charges: *£13 per day for each member of a group, or £14 per day for an individual – plus VAT.*
Access: *By bus, which stops at Sayers Common, or by car.*

Haywards Heath

The Convent of the Holy Rood
Lindfield
Haywards Heath
West Sussex RH16 2RA   Telephone: 04447 2345

Christian

After almost a century of nursing the elderly, this community has moved into a new convent. They have adapted space in a guest house they own in Lindfield to offer quiet days for guests and the facilities for those who want to organise conferences and group retreats. This is a small community of older religious and, while there are limitations on the facilities, the right atmosphere is created for achieving peace and reflection.

Open: *All year. Receives men, women, young people and clergy.*
Rooms: *Single rooms are available.*
Facilities: *Conferences and groups.*
Spiritual Help: *Short-term retreats and quiet days.*
Guests Admitted to: *Unrestricted access within conference and guest areas.*

Meals: *Guests eat together.*
Special Activities: *Small religious and lay-group retreats with one 'quiet day' each in Advent and Lent.*
Situation: *Quiet.*
Maximum Stay: *By arrangement.*
Bookings: *By letter or telephone.*
Charges: *On request.*
Access: *Ask for BR details and bus routes when applying.*

Horsham

Monastery of the Visitation
Partridge Green
Horsham
West Sussex RH13 8EG   Telephone: 0403 710328

Roman Catholic

Here is a straightforward place for the serious retreatant, who will be asked not to leave the enclosure during her period of retreat. The setting is peaceful and not far from London.

Open: *All year round except Holy Week, Easter and 18 December to 18 January. Receives women.*
Rooms: *2 singles.*
Facilities: *Limited, but reading material for study purposes is likely to be available.*
Spiritual Help: *Personal talks, meditation.*
Guests Admitted to: *Chapel, choir and work of the community.*
Meals: *Everyone eats together. Very plain food, with provision for vegetarian and special diets. Self-catering for drinks.*
Special Activities: *No planned programme of events.*
Situation: *Very quiet, in the countryside, a half mile from the village.*
Maximum Stay: *For the agreed period of the retreat.*
Bookings: *Preferably by letter.*
Charges: *£5 per person per day.*
Access: *BR: from Victoria station to Horsham. Buses: Nos. 107 or 137 run every hour from Horsham to Partridge Green.*

Horsham

**St Julian's Community
Coolham
Horsham
West Sussex RH13 8QL**   Telephone: 0403 741220

Interdenominational

Founded almost 50 years ago, St Julian's is a small lay community made up of people who are trying to achieve a happy and fulfilling existence by relating Christ's teaching about love to modern life and thought.   The Community and their guests live together in a small manor-house overlooking a lake and surrounded by fields.

Open: *All year except for special periods which are published in advance. Receives men and women.*
Rooms: *23 singles.*
Facilities: *Chapel, garden with lake surrounded by fields, library, guest lounge. No pets.*
Spiritual Help: *The purpose of the house is to provide a peaceful place for people of whatever religion, denomination or occupation, who want a pause from the pressures of life to read, rest and enjoy the country.*
Guests Admitted to: *Chapel guests are welcome at morning and evening prayers.*
Meals: *Taken in the dining room, no special diets.*
Special Activities: *Occasional talks.*
Situation: *Set in extensive grounds containing a 5-acre lake with wildfowl and swans.*
Maximum Stay: *By arrangement.*
Bookings: *By telephone or letter.*
Charges: *£19 per person per day, £133 per week, reduced rates for clergy, church workers and those on low incomes.*
Access: *BR: Billingshurst station, then by taxi. Car: from Horsham take A24; after 4–5 miles turn right on to A272, signposted Billingshurst. St Julian's is 2 $^1/_2$ miles on the left.*

*'When a man surrenders all desires that come
to the heart and by the grace of God finds the joy of God,
then his soul has indeed found peace'* – the Bhagavad Gita

Ryde

Quarr Abbey
Ryde
Isle of Wight PO33 4ES   Telephone: 0983 882420

Roman Catholic

Open: *Most of year. Receives men.*
Rooms: *10 singles in guest house.*
Facilities: *Disabled, chapel, library, bookstall, guest lounge.*
Spiritual Help: *Mass and Divine Office held daily in Gregorian chant.*
Guests Admitted to: *Chapel, refectory, monastery grounds, and may share in community work.*
Meals: *Everyone eats in refectory. DIY for drinks.*
Special Activities: *No planned programme.*
Situation: *Near sea, farm and countryside, woodlands.*
Maximum Stay: *By arrangement.*
Bookings: *By letter or telephone.*
Charges: *By donation.*
Access: *Ferry to Ryde from Portsmouth.*

Ryde

St Cecilia's Abbey
Ryde
Isle of Wight PO33 1LH   Telephone: 0983 62602

Roman Catholic

Divine Office is sung in Gregorian chant by this Benedictine community of nuns. Many people find great serenity and rest in this peaceful, modal music and in the tranquil rhythm of the liturgy and psalmody. Moreover, the Abbey itself is a very quiet place near the sea.

Open: *All year except Christmas and Holy Week. Receives women and single young people.*
Rooms: *2 singles.*
Facilities: *Small garden; monastery telephone can be used.*
Spiritual Help: *Personal talks. Visitors are free to attend services in their part of the church.*
Guests Admitted to: *Chapel.*
Meals: *Traditional food taken in the guest house.*
Special Activities: *Some years ago, to mark the 15th centenary of St Benedict's birth, a set of slides, with a running commentary on cassette, was made to illustrate the Benedictine monastic life. The slides are still shown occasionally.*

Situation: *Quiet, on the outskirts of a seaside town. Walks in the countryside. Easy access to shopping centre and bus tours of the island.*
Maximum Stay: *1 week provisionally.*
Bookings: *Preferably by letter.*
Charges: *No fixed charge – according to each case.*
Access: *By ferry. Taxi from landing stage if required.*

'In prayer it is better to have a heart without words than words without a heart' – John Bunyan

South West

Bath

The Ammerdown Centre
Radstock
Bath
Avon BA5 5SW   Telephone: 0761 33709

Ecumenical

In principle Ammerdown is more a laity centre than a retreat house but, having said that, they do offer an excellent range of retreat courses and provide people who wish to get away from it all the choice of two 'prayer flats'. Study, personal growth, ecumenical dialogue, and group development are the aims of the courses. The Centre occupies various attractive old buildings in and around the stable-block of Ammerdown House, the private residence of Lord Hylton and his family. Some of the parklands and gardens are open to residents. While predominantly Christian, the governing body represents other religious communities. For example, one of the governors is the well-known Rabbi Lionel Blue. The activities programme reflects this ecumenical base and incorporates, for instance, studies on Julian of Norwich, the early English Christian mystic; icons and the spiritual traditions of the Orthodox Church; and Jewish/Christian Liberation Theology. There is plenty on offer both for the first-time private retreatant and for those who attend religious conferences regularly.

Open: *All year except Easter and Christmas. Receives men, women, young people, groups and non-retreatants.*
Rooms: *32 single, 4 doubles; 2 prayer flats for a maximum of 3 people; peace cottage for young people, with 2 singles and 1 double room.*
Facilities: *Disabled (2 ground-floor rooms with a toilet/bathroom), conferences, garden, park, library, guest lounge, licensed bar, TV and 2 pay phones. No children or pets.*
Spiritual Help: *Personal talks, group sharing and meditation during planned courses, directed study.*
Guests Admitted to: *Chapel, with restricted access to Lord Hylton's gardens and to the swimming pool at particular times.*
Meals: *Eaten together or alone in prayer flats. DIY facilities in flats and cottages. Food is traditional, wholesome and plentiful, with provision for vegetarian and special diets.*
Special Activities: *See brochure. There is a special annexe for day groups.*
Situation: *Very quiet, in the countryside.*
Maximum Stay: *According to course, usually 8 – 10 days maximum.*
Bookings: *By letter or telephone.*
Charges: *Vary according to course.*
Access: *BR: to Bath Spa. Buses: to Radstock. Car: Centre is just off A362.*

Bath

Downside Abbey
Stratton on the Fosse
Bath
Avon BA5 4RH   Telephone: 0761 232295

Roman Catholic

The home of a famous boys' public school, with an abbey church of cathedral proportions. The community welcomes men who wish to share the monastic prayer and quiet, or who may want a peaceful base for a holiday. This is very much a hard-working place with a busy schedule, but the Guestmaster is usually available for a personal talk and to help with spiritual guidance.

Open: *All year except Christmas and mid-July to mid-August. Receives men only and small groups, as well as non- retreatants. Disabled people are welcome, if they can manage the stairs.*
Rooms: *9 singles.*
Facilities: *Abbey church, garden, library (by permission), guest lounge with TV, pay phone.*
Spiritual Help: *Monks give guests help and guidance when they have time; the Guestmaster is more readily available.*
Guests Admitted to: *Chapel, choir by arrangement. Guests are asked not to enter the school area.*
Meals: *Everyone eats together. Traditional food, with provision for vegetarian and special diets. DIY for tea and coffee.*
Special Activities: *No planned programme.*
Situation: *Quiet, near the village, about 12 miles from Bath.*
Maximum Stay: *1 week.*
Bookings: *By letter only, please.*
Charges: *None but donations are welcome.*
Access: *BR: to Bath Spa. Bus: from Bath Spa to Stratton on the Fosse. Car: via A367.*

Bristol

Emmaus House
Clifton Hill
Clifton
Bristol B58 4PD   Telephone: 0272 738056

Roman Catholic

On the hills of Clifton looking out across the Cumberland Basin to green hills, the Sisters of La Retraite continue their 300-year-old Congregation tradition of work in retreats and education and human growth programmes. There is no messing about here - the facilities at Emmaus House are 'state of the art', ranging from video cameras for conferences to a Creation Block that provides resources for creative activities such as painting and pottery, or for relaxation, such as a Jacuzzi. Indeed, modern facilities, combined with a relaxed atmosphere and good food, all help to enhance the retreatant's physical well-being and spiritual growth. The Myers-Briggs courses are on offer, including a basic workshop, together with courses on stress, spiritual life and prayer, leadership and 'type dynamics'. Other workshops reflect a New Age, holistic approach. Subjects include healing and integration of the feminine and masculine; nurturing and healing the body; spirituality for the Third Age; and a holistic-centred journey over a six-day retreat period. Highly recommended.

Open: *All year except immediately after Christmas and Easter. Receives men, women, groups, religious and non-retreatants.*
Rooms: *Singles and doubles are available.*
Facilities: *Disabled (loop-system for deaf in hall); conference facilities include TV, video camera and most necessary equipment; garden, bookshop, Liturgy resource centre, TV, pay phone. Not suitable for children. No pets and no smoking.*
Spiritual Help: *Personal talks, group sharing, meditation, direction for retreats, counselling, spiritual direction.*
Guests Admitted to: *Chapel.*
Meals: *Everyone eats together. Wholefood, with provision for vegetarians but not for special diets.*
Special Activities: *Programme of adult education, personal/ spiritual growth. Send for brochure.*
Situation: *In town. Amount of noise depends on group in house at any given time. Lovely views and pleasant neighbourhood.*
Maximum Stay: *8-day retreat.*
Bookings: *By telephone, but must confirm by letter.*
Charges: *Residential £50, non-residential £40 per person per day; 6-day retreat £133, 8-day retreat £171. Various other prices available on application.*
Access: *BR: to Bristol Temple Meads. Bus: No.8 from station to W. H. Smith in Clifton Down Road. Car: from north take M5, Exit 17, then A4018; from London take M4, Exit 20, then M5, Exit 19, followed by A369.*

Bristol

Omega Order
'The Priory' Winford Manor
Winford
Bristol BS18 8DW   Telephone: 0275 872262

Non-denominational

The Order was founded in 1980, taking its title from the words of Christ – 'I am the Alpha and the Omega, the first and the last.' Guests are welcomed at all times, either to attend courses and retreats, or to find space for rest and reflection and to join the community of lay and religious men and women in the rhythm of a life of prayer. Courses include retreats to enhance insight, through the study of calligraphy, contemplative dance, Christian and Buddhist spirituality, new and scientific concepts of God, and creativity is encouraged through drawing, poetry and working with wax. There are also traditional courses on contemplative prayer and meditation. The Prior, Canon Peter Spink, has written a number of books, and the Order has produced a series of cassettes and offers a correspondence course to help participants develop their own perceptions and insights. In short, Winford Manor offers silence in which to reflect and studies in which to expand and develop consciousness of the spirit. A good location for those who may not want their first retreat to be in a church setting that is overwhelmingly traditional. Indeed here is a place where you will be taken seriously if you ask why God is referred to as masculine – and you will get a considered answer.

Open: *All year. Receives men, women, young people and families.*
Rooms: *6 singles, 8 doubles, cottage with 3 single beds.*
Facilities: *Disabled, garden, park, library, guest lounge, TV and guest pay phone. Children welcomed, pets permitted.*
Spiritual Help: *Personal talks, group sharing, meditation, directed study.*
Guests Admitted to: *Chapel and work of the community.*
Meals: *Everyone eats together. Traditional food, with provision for vegetarian and special diets. DIY facilities in the cottage.*
Special Activities: *Planned programme of events. Send for brochure.*
Situation: *Quiet, near village and countryside. An old manor-house standing in 7 acres of wooded grounds.*
Maximum Stay: *Unlimited.*
Bookings: *By letter.*
Charges: *£20 per person per 24 hours.*
Access: *BR: Bristol Temple Meads station 7 miles away. Buses: Central Bristol Bus Station. Car: via A38 from Bristol to Exeter Road.*

Bristol

St Agnes Retreat House
St Agnes Avenue
Knowle
Bristol BS4 2HH   Telephone: 0272 776806

Anglican

St Agnes is a large Edwardian house set back from a tree-lined road. It is a comfortable and rambling place, with the guest accommodation adjoining the convent area.

Open: *All year apart from mid-July to mid-August. Receives men, women, groups and non-retreatants.*
Rooms: *7 singles, 15 doubles.*
Facilities: *Chapel, conferences, garden, nearby parks, garden ne, shop, library, guest lounge, TV and pay phone. No pets, no facilities for children.*
Spiritual Help: *Personal talks. Conducted quiet days and retreats.*
Guests Admitted to: *Chapel.*
Meals: *Served in the guest house. Traditional food, with provision for vegetarian and special diets.*
Special Activities: *Special programme and planned events. Send for brochure.*
Situation: *Quiet situation in the suburbs.*
Maximum Stay: *1 week.*
Bookings: *By telephone or letter.*
Charges: *£20 per person per 24 hours.*
Access: *BR: Bristol Temple Meads. Bus: from Bristol.*

CORNWALL

Helston

Trelowarren Fellowship
Mawgan in Meneage
Helston
Cornwall TR12 6AD   Telephone: 032622 366

Christian – Interdenominational

Located in an ancient manor-house buried in the heart of the countryside, the Fellowship is open to Christians of all denominations, whether in groups, families or as individuals who want to spend time away from it all. Healing, teaching and renewal conferences are held here, and prayer, counselling and ministry in the power of the Holy Spirit are always available. In addition there are musical concerts and exhibitions of paintings. This is very much a place for those who are already Christians and not for those who feel that the realisation of their spirituality may be obtained through other faiths.

Open: *All year. Receives men, women, young people, families, groups, non-retreatants and Christian religious.*
Rooms: *1 single, 8 doubles, dormitory.*
Facilities: *Conferences, garden, park, library, guest lounge, TV and direct-dialling pay phone. Camping site near by. Children welcomed.*
Spiritual Help: *Personal talks, group sharing, Christian meditation, directed study.*
Guests Admitted to: *Chapel, work of the community.*

Meals: *Everyone eats together. Wholefood, with provision for vegetarian and special diets.*
Special Activities: *Planned programme of events. Send for brochure.*
Situation: *Very quiet, in the countryside.*
Maximum Stay: *2 weeks.*
Bookings: *By letter.*
Charges: *£15 per person per day.*
Access: *Consult the brochure map.*

Truro

'Shalom'
23 Tresawls Avenue
Truro
Cornwall TR1 3LA   Telephone: 0872 41680

Anglican

'Shalom' is a privately owned, large bungalow two miles from the centre of Truro. It is a peaceful base from which to explore locally, with a magnificent cathedral and National Trust gardens near by. For those who find pets a calming influence, 'Shalom' offers two resident cats.

Open: *All year. Receives men, women, young people, families, groups, non-retreatants.*
Rooms: *1 single and 1 double, plus a child's bed.*
Facilities: *Disabled, nearby church, garden, library, guest lounge and TV. Children welcomed. Dogs permitted by arrangement.*
Spiritual Help: *Personal talks, group sharing – meditation and directed study can be arranged. The sick and the elderly are welcome for spiritual healing and the laying on of hands.*
Guests Admitted to: *Unrestricted access.*
Meals: *Everyone eats together. Traditional food, with provision for vegetarian and special diets.*
Special Activities: *No planned programme of events. A peaceful setting is offered for guests to 'come and rest awhile' or to 'find' themselves.*
Situation: *Quiet bungalow $1^1/_2$ miles from Truro, near golf course.*
Maximum Stay: *Unlimited.*
Bookings: *By letter or telephone.*
Charges: *£14 per person per day.*
Access: *By rail or car to Truro.*

Buckfastleigh

Buckfast Abbey
Buckfastleigh
Devon TQ11 OEE   Telephone: 0364 43301

Roman Catholic

Over half a million people come to visit the Abbey, to walk through its
grounds by the River Dart, and to admire the work of these monks whose
history here has been so remarkable. The monastery was founded in 1018.
It experienced centuries of peace, followed by ruin when Henry VIII
dissolved the monasteries and, finally, restoration in 1907, when the monks
returned to rebuild their Abbey. The great church was finished in 1937,
largely restored to its original form, and filled with beautiful artefacts from
the enamelled and bejewelled Stations of the Cross to the glorious marble
mosaic floor of the nave. Down a nearby path, edged with pink cyclamen,
stands the village of hives belonging to the Abbey's famous bees. Apart from
honey, Buckfast is also well known for its herbal tonic-wine and for the
creation of stained-glass windows yet the real work of the monks is to seek
communion with God. A guest at the Abbey should expect food that is plain
and rather stodgy, but a glass of monastery beer helps it go down. The rooms
are simple and comfortable and the community friendly and welcoming. In
the dark shadows of the church the voices of the choir at morning prayer bring
awareness that you have left your ordinary life and are embarking on a new
journey of the spirit.

Open: *All year. Receives men only but there are plans to offer accommoda-
tion for women, so please enquire.*
Rooms: *10 rooms in the monastery, in the form of singles or doubles.*
Facilities: *Church, large garden, river and country walks, library by
permission, bookshop and tearoom.*
Spiritual Help: *Private retreats. Guestmaster is available for help.*
Guests Admitted to: *Choir, community common-room.*
Restricted access to monastic enclosure.
Meals: *Everyone eats together in the refectory. The food is very traditional.*
Special Activities: *No planned programme.*
Situation: *Beautiful location, monastery very quiet but there are a lot of
tourists in grounds and church during the day.*
Maximum Stay: *By arrangement.*
Bookings: *By letter.*
Charges: *According to means.*
Access: *BR: Newton Abbot station 11 miles away. Bus: Devon General No.
188 from Newton Abbot. Coach: National, Exeter – Plymouth. Car: via A38.*

Honiton

The Devon Vihara
Odle Cottage
Upottery
nr. Honiton
Devon EX14 9QE   Telephone: 0404 891251

Buddhist

Down a winding road and up a little hill nestles an ordinary house where the spirit of 'right-mindfulness' lives. Here a small group of mostly young monks have created a place of loving peace. They are in the middle of planting hundreds of trees so that they and others may walk and meditate among natural beauty. When I arrived, the Abbot was in the garden giving spiritual guidance to a middle-aged woman; in another spot two strapping, sun-tanned monks were chopping wood; and in another a 'learner' or novice was preparing food. Soon I was sitting in the sun sipping a glass of tea, enfolded in the happy, positive and companionable atmosphere of this Buddhist Vihara. It is a simple place where you can be silent, meditate in the shrine room, share the common bowl of food, plant a tree – and perhaps discover the power of inner stillness. Highly recommended.

Open: *Closed throughout January and February.*
Rooms: *2 caravans, 2 little hermitage-huts, one in a field and one in the woods.*
Facilities: *Shrine room, very small tape-and-book library, common room, DIY cooking facilities.*
Spiritual Help: *Talks with Abbot, spiritual direction, meditation, guided retreats.*
Guests Admitted to: *Everywhere except monks' area.*
Meals: *Usually people bring food, as everyone eats together. Food almost always vegetarian.*
Special Activities: *Forest and fields used for walking and meditation. Send for brochure of programme.*
Situation: *Buried in the Devon hills, surrounded by fields with views for miles around – delightful spot.*
Maximum Stay: *By arrangement, no limit.*
Bookings: *By letter.*
Charges: *By donation.*
Access: *Car: take A303 towards Honiton, turn at Upottery towards Raw Ridge, turn right at Raw Ridge, follow no-through track to end – about 1 mile.*

Lynton

Lee Abbey
Lynton
North Devon EX35 6JJ   Telephone: 0598 52621

Ecumenical

Lee Abbey is a very large country estate in the Exmoor National Park with facilities that include tennis-courts, a sports hall, and a beach and forest to explore. It is run by a Christian community of about 75 men, women and families. Formal retreats are in the minority among their programmed activities, but there are what are called 'Breakaway' weeks or weekends for those who may wish to benefit from the accommodation and facilities without joining in an organised activity. At such times silence is not to be expected. Peace and quiet can normally be found in one or other of the several public rooms and around the gardens and parks of the estate – but there is no guarantee of this. The Abbey Fellowship includes two other communities: the Lee Abbey International Students' Club, London, and the Aston Cottage Community, Birmingham.

Open: *All year, but closed for 2 months spread over the year, so double-check. Receives men, women, young people (those under 16 to be accompanied by adults), families, groups and non-retreatants.*
Rooms: *20 singles, 7 doubles, 26 twin-bedded rooms, 2 large dormitories.*
Facilities: *Conferences, library, guest lounge, sports hall, tennis, adventure playground and pay phone. Children welcomed.*
Spiritual Help: *Teaching sessions occur each day and there is some opportunity for personal counselling. Retreats form a small part of the organised programme and are best considered as an introduction.*
Guests Admitted to: *Virtually unrestricted access to house and grounds, with the exception of certain living and administration areas used by the community.*
Meals: *Everyone eats together, with provision for vegetarian and certain special diets. Food is balanced and varied.*
Special Activities: *Lee Abbey has an extensive programme of activities, so do send for the brochure and magazine.*
Situation: *The house is set in a 260-acre coastal estate in the Exmoor National Park.*
Maximum Stay: *2 weeks.*
Bookings: *Telephone enquiries, confirmation by letter.*
Charges: *See brochure as these vary.*
Access: *By car is best.*

Lynton

Monastery of Poor Clares
Lynton
Devon EX35 6BX   Telephone: 0598 53373

Roman Catholic

Those who wish to share the quiet, prayer and worship of the Franciscan way
of life will find a warm welcome from the sisters, whose convent in this small
seaside resort is near many beauty spots on the edge of Exmoor. It is an ideal
place for a private retreat or for those who need a very peaceful and modest
base for a holiday.

Open: *All year except for Christmas and Easter. Receives men, women and
religious sisters.*
Rooms: *2-bedded self-contained flatlet; single rooms in monastery for
religious sisters.*
Facilities: *Church, nearby beaches and moor for walking.*
Spiritual Help: *Personal talks by arrangement.*
Guests Admitted to: *Church.*
Meals: *DIY facilities in the flat. Meals served for religious sisters in the
refectory.*
Special Activities: *No planned programme.*
Situation: *A delightful area in which to retreat.*
Maximum Stay: *By arrangement.*
Bookings: *By letter or telephone.*
Charges: *Daily rates very modest for the flat, but enquire about current
prices.*
Access: *Car: via A39. BR and buses to Barnstaple, which is about 18 miles
distant.*

Newton Abbot

Gaia House
Woodland Road
Denbury
nr. Newton Abbot
Devon TQ12 6DY   Telephone: 0803 813188

Buddhist

While those going on personal retreat at Gaia House will need to have
practised Vipassana Meditation for at least six months already, group retreats
are scheduled throughout the year and there is guided meditation for beginners.
Retreatants conduct their stay at Gaia House in silence unless meeting with
the teacher or for group interviews.

Open: *All year. Receives men, women and groups.*
Rooms: *5 singles, 4 doubles, dormitory.*
Facilities: *Meditation room, garden, camping site, library, guest lounge, and pay phone.*
Spiritual Help: *Guided meditation for beginners, work retreats helping meditators to integrate their meditation practice with daily life.*
Guests Admitted to: *Unrestricted access everywhere except kitchen area.*
Meals: *Everyone eats together. Wholefood, with provision for vegetarians.*
Special Activities: *Brochure available.*
Situation: *Quiet, near a village and in the countryside.*
Maximum Stay: *6 months, with permission.*
Bookings: *By letter or telephone.*
Charges: *Through donation, by arrangement.*
Access: *By car is best.*

Totnes

The Barn
Lower Sharpham Barton
Ashprington
Totnes
Devon TQ9 7DX   Telephone: 080423 661

Buddhist – Inter-faith

During your stay here, you will be expected to be fully involved in the daily schedule of activities and to take your turn preparing vegetarian meals for everyone. One evening a week is devoted to discussing personal matters as well as broader issues that relate to the community's life together. You are encouraged to pursue those activities – such as Buddhist-study classes, yoga mornings, and listening to cassettes of Dharma talks – which support a contemplative way of life. The Sharpham North Community is a short walk away across fields and you can participate in their wider range of lectures and events, but you will find only limited opportunity to stray outside the Sharpham Estate because of community commitments there. Considering that the daily schedule includes four to five hours' work on the land and three 45-minute periods of group meditation, this hardly comes as a surprise. If you are reasonably fit, then have a 'go' at this farming retreat community, where you will find the usual warm Buddhist welcome.

Open: *All year. Receives men, women and young people – you do not have to be a Buddhist, but an established background in meditation is necessary.*
Rooms: *6 singles, 1 partitioned room that sleeps 2.*
Facilities: *Garden, library and pay phone. Woodworking equipment is provided.*
Spiritual Help: *Personal talks when a teacher is available, group sharing and meditation. The community offers a supportive environment with regular*

weekly visits from local meditation teachers, who also provide one-to-one meetings.

Guests Admitted to: *Unrestricted access to all areas, including work of the community, which consists of gardening, woodland maintenance, household care and upkeep, cooking, preserving, looking after poultry.*

Meals: *Everyone eats together. Meals consist of vegetarian wholefood.*

Special Activities: *Daily schedule followed 6 days a week. Send for the brochure.*

Situation: *Very quiet and in the countryside. Beautiful location on the Sharpham Estate, on a hillside overlooking the River Dart – no roads visible.*

Maximum Stay: *6 months (minimum is 1 week).*

Bookings: *By letter or telephone, but you will be asked for some personal details, as well as extensive information about your experience of retreat and meditation.*

Charges: *See brochure, as charges range from £4 to £6 per day.*

Access: *By car is best, but enquire if you want to walk from the nearest place served by public transport.*

Totnes

The Dartington Centre
Dartington Hall
Totnes
Devon TQ9 6EL   Telephone: 0803 862271

Non-religious, non-sectarian

The Dartington Hall Trust has been going for 60 years, giving focus and support to a variety of activities connected with education, research, business and the arts. Dartington Hall is part of a busy estate that comprises famous educational colleges in the arts and music, together with tourist attractions such as a cider-press centre and a craft shop. The Centre itself is predominantly a place for conferences, but individuals are welcome to stay. It is perhaps not a place that permits a total escape from ordinary life, but courses on meditation are available. And, indeed, who can say that you will not find the course on lace-making or Indian music to be just the right introduction to a quieter look at what you are doing with your life?

Open: *All year. Receives men, women, young people, families, groups and non-retreatants.*

Rooms: *40 singles, 10 doubles.*

Facilities: *Limited disabled, conferences, garden, library, guest lounge and pay phone.*

Spiritual Help: *Directed study.*

Guests Admitted to: *Most areas of Centre and grounds.*

Meals: *Everyone eats together. Traditional wholefood, with provision for vegetarian and special diets.*

Special Activities: *Planned programme of events. Send for brochure.*
Situation: *Very quiet, in the countryside. Dartington Hall is a medieval manor-house set in a courtyard, with extensive gardens and grounds.*
Maximum Stay: *Unlimited.*
Bookings: *By letter or telephone.*
Charges: *Available on request.*
Access: *By rail or car.*

Totnes

Sharpham North Community
Ashprington
Totnes
Devon TQ9 7UT   Telephone: ~~080423 542/549~~

0803732549

Buddhist – New Age

Sharpham House is a beautiful English Palladian building with views stretching down to the River Dart. It is here that the Sharpham Trust strives to create a new way of life, aiming to achieve a balance between the practical and the spiritual. Occupying part of the house is the Community, which comprises up to nine people from different backgrounds and nationalities who share a common interest in spiritual practice and its application to daily life. Although the approach is Buddhist, it does not adhere to any particular school. The programme is one that combines meditation with talks and recitals. These are broadly based and might range from a talk on the creation of a greener world by Satish Kumar, editor of *Resurgence* magazine and chairman of the Schumacher Society, to a discourse on the art of giving by a teacher of insight meditation from New York or to an evening of Russian music and poetry.

Open: *February to July and September to December. Closed January and August. Receives men, women and young people.*
Rooms: *1 single and 1 double.*
Facilities: *Garden, library, TV and payphone. No smoking permitted in the house.*
Spiritual Help: *Personal talks, meditation, directed study.*
Guests Admitted to: *Shrine room.*
Meals: *Everyone eats together. Meals consist of vegetarian wholefood.*
Special Activities: *2 residential group retreats per year, lasting a weekend each. All guests are expected to participate in the life and work of the community (including approximately 2 hours' gardening and cleaning and 2 hours' meditation daily). Send for the brochure of events.*
Situation: *Very quiet, but a busy and active place.*
Maximum Stay: *3 days.*
Bookings: *By letter; all overnight stays must be booked in advance.*
Charges: *Suggested minimum donation £3 per night.*
Access: *BR to Totnes, then by car or on foot.*

Bridport

Monkton Wyld Court
Charmouth
Bridport
Dorset DT6 6DQ   Telephone: 0297 60342

New Age

Eleven acres of grounds surround this large Victorian rectory that is situated in a secluded valley on the Devon–Dorset border. Monkton is a leading New Age centre for holistic education run by a community of 11 people, including families and children. The emphasis is on encouraging personal and spiritual growth, combined with a firm commitment to 'green' issues and self-sufficiency. There are plenty of courses that reflect this approach. These include a weekend for women to develop their skills in creativity and healing, and instruction in breathing practices, T'ai Ch'i therapy, and transformative arts incorporating contemporary Shamanism.

Open: *All year except Christmas. Receives men, women, young people, families and groups.*
Rooms: *3 doubles, 2 dormitories, 6 rooms each sleeping 3 people.*
Facilities: *For conferences, arts and crafts and pottery. There is also an organic garden, library, guest lounge, meditation room and pay phone. Children welcomed.*
Spiritual Help: *Personal talks, meditation.*
Guests Admitted to: *Work of the community.*
Meals: *Everyone eats together. Wholefood, with provision for vegetarian and special diets.*
Special Activities: *Planned programme of events. Send for brochure.*
Situation: *Very quiet, in the countryside.*
Maximum Stay: *5 days.*
Bookings: *By letter or telephone.*
Charges: *£14 per person per day, midweek; £17.50 per day at weekends.*
Access: *By rail or car (A35).*

Dorchester

Society of St Francis
Hilfield Friary
Hilfield
nr. Dorchester
Dorset DT2 7BE   Telephone: 0300 341345

Anglican

It is up to each guest to decide how best to use his or her time at the Friary, but all are welcome to join the brothers in chapel for prayer. Set in peaceful surroundings, this is a quiet community where you will find space for thinking things through. Many guests have busy and active careers, and find that the Friary is just the place they need for rest and reflection. Hospitality is offered to all, so you may find that the man at prayer next to you could equally well be a successful industrialist or a wayfarer who tramps the road.

Open: *All year, except August. Receives men, women, young people, groups and non-retreatants.*
Rooms: *13 singles.*
Facilities: *Chapel, oratory, choir, library, guest lounge and pay phone. Bring a towel.*
Spiritual Help: *Personal talks and meditation.*
Guests Admitted to: *Chapel, choir and work of the community but not to novices' house, monks' enclosure or Bernard House, unless received there.*
Meals: *Everyone eats together. Traditional food, with provision for vegetarian and special diets, if notification given in advance.*
Special Activities: *No planned programme.*
Situation: *Very quiet, in the countryside; modern guest-house situated on what was once a farm.*
Maximum Stay: *6 days.*
Bookings: *By letter.*
Charges: *By donation – about £10 per day.*
Access: *BR to Dorchester. Guests can be met at the station, but please do make a donation towards such costs.*

Poole

Post Green Pastoral Centre
56 Dorchester Road
Lytchett Minster
Poole
Dorset BH16 6JE   Telephone: 0202 622510

Ecumenical

This is a community made up of people who are committed to live a life of faith combined with a concern for the spiritual healing of both individuals and society. They include married couples, families and single people, all of whom are involved at the Centre. The counselling available can help you to make important choices and decisions, and to grow towards taking full responsibility for your own life in a creative way.

Open: *All year, except Christmas. Receives men, women, young people, families, groups and non-retreatants.*
Rooms: *Both singles and double are available, as well as 2 caravans.*
Facilities: *Conferences, camping, garden, park, library, guest lounge, TV*

and direct-dialling telephone. Spring Bank Holiday camp on farm. Pets allowed.

Spiritual Help: *Personal talks, meditation, directed study, group sharing on residential courses, counselling, spiritual direction and various teaching courses.*

Guests Admitted to: *Chapel, work of the community.*

Meals: *Everyone eats together. Varied well-cooked food, with provision for vegetarian and special diets. Self-catering in the caravans.*

Special Activities: *Planned retreats and courses. Send for brochure.*

Situation: *Quiet open countryside near by. The Centre overlooks Poole Harbour.*

Maximum Stay: *By arrangement, but can vary from 1 night to a year.*

Bookings: *By letter or telephone.*

Charges: *Vary according to course and counselling – see brochure.*

Access: *BR: to Poole. Bus: to Lytchett Minster every hour. Car: via A350 to B3067.*

Wimborne

Gaunts House
Wimborne
Dorset BH21 4JQ   Telephone: 0202 841522

Interdenominational

Open: *All year. Receives men, women, young people, families, groups, religious and non-retreatants.*

Rooms: *40 singles, 50 doubles, dormitories.*

Facilities: *Disabled, conferences, chapel, shrine room, healing room, study centre, theatre, garden, park, camping and caravan site, library, guest lounge, TV and pay phone. Children welcomed.*

Spiritual Help: *Personal talks, group sharing, meditation, directed study, yoga. Study centre has videos, audio tapes, books and information. Healing room is attended by a local practitioner.*

Guests Admitted to: *Unrestricted access to all areas including chapel, shrine room, work of the community.*

Meals: *Everyone eats together. Traditional fare, together with vegetarian wholefood and provision for special diets.*

Special Activities: *Planned programme of events. Send for brochure.*

Situation: *Very quiet, in the countryside, surrounded by miles of parkland. Beautiful country walks.*

Maximum Stay: *Unlimited.*

Bookings: *By letter or telephone.*

Charges: *Send for details as there are various scales of charges.*

Access: *BR to Bournemouth. Take bus or taxi from station.*

Wimborne

The Retreat Centre
Ashton Lodge
Stanbridge
Wimborne
Dorset BH12 4JO   Telephone: 0202 841522

Interdenominational

This is a small retreat-house with a farm, school and a conference centre.
Retreat visitors here can use the Gaunts House sanctuary and study centre,
which is about a mile and a half away.

Open: *All year. Receives men, women, young people, groups and non-
retreatants in the guest cottage.*
Rooms: *18 rooms and a dormitory.*
Facilities: *Disabled (facilities in ground-floor rooms), conferences, chapel,
garden, extensive park-land, camping site, guest lounge, TV and pay phone.
Children welcomed. No pets.*
Spiritual Help: *Personal talks, group sharing, meditation at Gaunts House.*
Guests Admitted to: *Unrestricted access.*
Meals: *Wholefood and traditional. Vegetarians and special diets catered for.*
Special Activities: *Planned programme at Gaunts House which retreat
guests are welcome to attend. Send for brochure.*
Situation: *Quiet, in the countryside.*
Maximum Stay: *Unlimited.*
Bookings: *By letter or telephone.*
Charges: *Send for details.*
Access: *BR: Bournemouth. Car: Centre is 3 miles north of Wimborne
Minster.*

SOMERSET

Castle Cary

St John's Priory
Victoria Road
Castle Cary
Somerset BA7 7DF   Telephone: 0963 50429

Roman Catholic

The guest house at St John's sits behind a little orchard of trees, and the chapel
is small and friendly. Guests are not usually accepted just for overnight visits.
Bring a hot water bottle if you normally use one in winter.

Open: *All year. Receives women.*
Rooms: *6 singles, 1 double (twin-bedded).*
Facilities: *Chapel, garden, guest lounge, TV. No guest phone.*
Spiritual Help: *The sisters do not conduct retreats themselves, but some are available for a 'chat' about prayer and meditation.*
Guests Admitted to: *Chapel, and may join in work of the community in the garden and help with washing-up.*
Meals: *Taken in the guest house. Traditional food for lunch and supper with self-catering for breakfast. No special diets.*
Special Activities: *Everyone is welcome to join the sisters in the celebration of the Eucharist and the Divine Office.*
Situation: *Very quiet, in the countryside.*
Maximum Stay: *3 weeks.*
Bookings: *By letter.*
Charges: *Single room £15 per day, double room £28 per day. A weekly rate is available.*
Access: *BR: Castle Cary. Buses: from Shepton Mallet or Yeovil.*

Glastonbury

Abbey House
Chilkwell Street
Glastonbury
Somerset BA6 8DH   Telephone: 0458 31112

Anglican

This is the Bath and Wells Retreat and Conference House, which is set in 40 acres of beautiful parkland right in the town centre. There is no community here as a lay team manages the place. The great majority of the guests are sponsored by religious and church groups but private retreatants are welcomed and often can be accommodated at short notice if only a small group is in residence at the time. While activities are mostly aimed at group retreats, there are plenty of workshops, talks and events which individuals attend on their own. It is an interesting place and always worth a try.

Open: *All year except late August to mid-September. Usually receives groups. Non-retreatants comprise clergy or those known or recommended to the Centre.*
Rooms: *18 singles and 7 twin-bedded rooms.*
Facilities: *Some visual aids available for conferences.*
Spiritual Help: *Groups bring their own leaders but personal talks can be arranged.*
Guests Admitted to: *Unrestricted access.*
Meals: *Traditional home-cooking and wholefood.*
Special Activities: *Conferences, day meetings and visits from parish parties, while the House is happy to receive individuals for private retreats.*

Situation: *In town, but in a parkland setting.*
Maximum Stay: *14 days.*
Bookings: *By letter or telephone.*
Charges: *£17.50 per person per day. Group rates as advertised.*
Access: *BR: nearest railway station is Castle Cary (15 miles). Bus: Badgerline No. 376 travels hourly at 5 minutes to the hour from Bristol coach station; National Express coach runs daily from London Victoria.*

Glastonbury

Denton Realisation Healing Centre
Laurel Lane
Queen Camel
Glastonbury
Somerset BA22 7NU   Telephone: 0935 850266

New Age

The Centre is a charitable trust run by a team of six experienced counsellors and healers living and working together as a family unit. It is set within its own grounds near the River Cam and open countryside. The ancient spiritual centres of Glastonbury and Wells are within easy reach.

Open: *All year. Receives men, women, young people, families, groups and non-retreatants.*
Rooms: *5 singles, 4 doubles, dormitories and hermitage.*
Facilities: *Conferences, meditation room, garden, library, guest lounge and pay phone. Children welcome, pets permitted.*
Spiritual Help: *Personal talks, group sharing, meditation, directed study, healing, counselling, spiritual self-development, training and guidance in healing instruction.*
Guests Admitted to: *Unrestricted access to all areas, including meditation room.*
Meals: *Served to individual needs, with wholefood and provision for vegetarian and special diets.*
Special Activities: *This is a 'Self-realisation Centre' with a planned programme, so send for the brochure. The centre arranges individual tuition and training wherever required, together with courses and workshops additional to the scheduled programme.*
Situation: *Very quiet, in the village. Within easy reach of Glastonbury, Wells, Bath, Bristol and Yeovil.*
Maximum Stay: *Unlimited.*
Bookings: *By letter or telephone.*
Charges: *Please enquire.*
Access: *Car: via A303. Collecting service from the nearest BR stations.*

Warminster

St Denys Retreat Centre
2 Church Street
Warminster
Wilts. BA12 8PG   Telephone: 0985 214824

Anglican

This is an attractive house set right on the street, but there is a garden. The community offers individual retreats in the Ignatian tradition as well as 'walk-into-quietness days', where a team of sisters welcome you to a day retreat in the centre. Well organised and friendly.

Open: *All year except part of January. Receives men, women, young people, groups and non-retreatants.*
Rooms: *16 singles, 5 doubles, 1 three-bedded room.*
Facilities: *Disabled, conferences, chapel, garden, library, guest lounge and guest telephone.*
Spiritual Help: *Personal talks, group sharing, meditation.*
Guests Admitted to: *Unrestricted access to all areas, including chapel.*
Meals: *Everyone eats together. Traditional food – vegetarian and special diets can be catered for with advance notification.*
Special Activities: *Planned programme of events. Send for brochure.*
Situation: *Quiet, in the town.*
Maximum Stay: *2 weeks.*
Bookings: *By telephone, but confirm by letter.*
Charges: *£16.50 per person per day.*
Access: *BR: Portsmouth – Cardiff line. Bus: from Salisbury, Bath or Towbridge. Car: via B3414, off A36.*

CHANNEL ISLANDS

Jersey

FCJ Centre of Spirituality
Deloraine Road
St Saviour
Jersey JE2 7NF   Telephone: 0534 26162

Roman Catholic – Ecumenical

The sisters of the Order of the Faithful Companions of Jesus offer individually directed retreats, prayer workshops, parenting programmes, and retreats from daily life.

Open: *All year except July, August, Christmas and Easter. Receives men, women, and young people and groups on a day basis only.*
Rooms: *10 singles.*
Facilities: *Garden and library.*
Spiritual Help: *Personal talks, group sharing, meditation, directed study.*
Guests Admitted to: *Chapel.*
Meals: *Small dining-room for retreatants. Traditional food, with provision for special diets.*
Special Activities: *No planned programme.*
Situation: *Quiet, near to a school.*
Maximum Stay: *According to length of retreat.*
Bookings: *By letter or telephone.*
Charges: *On application.*
Access: *By ferry/air.*

' Try to spread your loving mind and heart to all that they may have peace and happiness in their lives' – Ven. Dhammavijitha Thera

East & East Anglia

Biggleswade

Yoga for Health Foundation
Ickwell Bury
Biggleswade
Bedfordshire SG18 9EF   Telephone: 076 727 271/604

New Age - Non-religious

The Foundation, a charity operating in many parts of the world, is in what must be the last unspoiled bit of this commuter-belt county. A 17th-century manor and farm, it is surrounded by parkland, has fine gardens, and a fishing lake left over from the Middle Ages when an abbey occupied the site. Inside the house all is different and a B&B atmosphere prevails, but the food is excellent with much that is home-produced. There are nursing staff and the place is well equipped for the disabled. Yoga training, reflexology and Swedish massage are available. You do need to become a member before you can stay here but the fee is only £10 for the year. All this may make it sound like a clinic, but it is far more a place where people share and grow in strength together. The health benefits of regular yoga practice, particularly for those suffering from stress, are well established.

Open: *All year except over Christmas. Receives men, women, young people, families, groups.*
Rooms: *3 singles, 7 doubles, plus accommodation for another 13 people.*
Facilities: *Excellent for disabled, gardens, park, library to be opened soon, guest lounge and pay phone. Camping and caravans permitted at festival time. Guide dogs only.*
Spiritual Help: *Yoga technique training.*
Guests Admitted to: *Unrestricted access.*
Meals: *Everyone eats together. Vegetarian wholefood; vegans pay £1. 50 a day extra for special meals.*
Special Activities: *Send for programme of events, which includes a 10-day festival specifically for families.*
Situation: *Peaceful, in countryside – setting is hard to fault.*
Maximum Stay: *Three months.*
Bookings: *By telephone or letter.*
Charges: *About £210 per person per week, £60 per weekend. Ask what is included in these charges when you enquire about booking.*
Access: *BR: to Biggleswade then by taxi. Buses: coach to Bedford. Local bus runs twice a day. Car: via A1 to Biggleswade.*

'It is sad not to be loved,
but it is much sadder not to be able to love' – Miguel de Unamuno

Turvey

Monastery of Christ Our Saviour
Abbey Mews
Turvey
Bedfordshire MK43 8DH   Telephone: 023 064 211

Roman Catholic

The monks' guest house has been converted from a stone barn. There are lots of books to read, easy chairs in every room and a guest kitchen. If you are on a private retreat, you will be left in peace to get on with it. As it is a small community, help in the garden is usually welcomed. This is one of two Benedictine communities at Turvey who worship in common and work in close co-operation. The village has a lot of traffic, but the guest house and gardens are quiet.

Open: *All year except first 2 weeks of September and January. Receives men, women, young people, families, groups and non-retreatants.*
Rooms: *4 singles, 1 double.*
Facilities: *Small meetings, garden, library, guest lounge and pay phone. Children welcomed.*
Spiritual Help: *Participation in the liturgy.*
Guests Admitted to: *Chapel, choir, garden.*
Meals: *Taken in the guest house. Traditional food with self-catering available.*
Special Activities: *Planned programme of events. Send for the brochure.*
Situation: *Very quiet, in the village.*
Maximum Stay: *To be agreed according to each particular case.*
Bookings: *By letter or telephone.*
Charges: *Guests are asked to make an offering.*
Access: *BR: to Bedford, then by local bus. Car: via M1, Exit 14 to Olney.*

Turvey

Priory of Our Lady of Peace
Turvey Abbey
Turvey
Bedfordshire MK43 8DE   Telephone: 023 064 432

Roman Catholic

Although the Abbey is next to a busy road, the sisters have created an oasis of peace in this picturesque stone village by the River Ouse. The modern guest house is warm and the bedrooms are well-appointed and light. There is a Japanese-style garden in which to sit, while the grounds offer good walks through a park and beyond to open fields. Guests do not have to join the daily offices of prayer but the beautifully sung liturgy helps immeasurably in the quietening of mind and body and in the opening of the heart. The meals are among the best available in any religious house, consisting mainly of wholefood, with home-baked bread, fresh fruit and delicious puddings. The programme of events is very popular. Highly recommended.

Open: *All year, with exceptions. Receives women, young people, families, groups, non-retreatants.*
Rooms: *16 singles, doubles available.*
Facilities: *Disabled, small conferences, garden, library, guest lounge and pay phone. Children welcomed. No pets.*
Spiritual Help: *Guests are welcome to join in the Divine Office and are provided with books. From time to time introductory talks are given to help people participate more deeply. Daily Mass is also open to all.*
Guests Admitted to: *Chapel, occasionally work of the community.*
Meals: *Meals are taken in the guest house. Wholefood – with advance notice, provision can be made for vegetarian and special diets. Self-catering available.*
Special Activities: *Planned programme of events. Send for brochure.*
Situation: *In the village and countryside.*
Maximum Stay: *2 weeks, with some exceptions.*
Bookings: *Preferably by letter.*
Charges: *By donation – a suggested £16 per person per day, full board, £8 per day if self-catering.*
Access: *BR: to Bedford and Turvey. Car: via A428.*

CAMBRIDGESHIRE

Cambridge

**Sisters of the Adoration
17 Glisson Road
Cambridge CB1 2HA**   Telephone: 0223 352432

Roman Catholic

The Sisters of the Adoration are a very small contemplative community and have only one single room available for women guests. There may be no limit here to the warmth of their welcome – but lots of letters can mean too much work for too few hands. So try to decide why you want to make a retreat here before enquiring, and remember to send an s.a.e. This kind of small community is often best suited to those who have already been on retreat elsewhere and may be now considering a religious vocation.

Open: *All year except Holy Week and Christmas. Receives women on retreat only.*

Rooms: *1 single.*
Facilities: *Library, the sisters' quiet lounge.*
Spiritual Help: *Personal talks and sometimes group sharing. The special mission of the sisters is 'Eucharistic Adoration', in the sense of acquired knowledge, appreciation and meditation. Mass is held in the nearby parish church.*
Guests Admitted to: *Chapel.*
Meals: *Everyone eats together or in guest house. Traditional food.*
Special Activities: *No planned programme of events.*
Situation: *Rather busy, in the city.*
Maximum Stay: *8 days.*
Bookings: *By letter.*
Charges: *£10 per person per day.*
Access: By rail to Cambridge. Local buses are available.

'Our hearts are made for thee, O God,
and will not rest 'til they rest in thee' – St Augustine

Ely

Bishop Woodford House
Barton Road
Ely
Cambs. CB7 4DX   Telephone: 0353 663039

Anglican – Interdenominational

Open: *All year. Receives men, women, young people, families, groups and non-retreatants.*
Rooms: *3 singles, 1 twin-bedded room.*
Facilities: *Limited for disabled, conferences, chapel, garden, nearby park, library, guest lounge, TV and guest telephone. Children welcome.*
Spiritual Help: *Personal talks, group sharing, meditation, directed study, with ministers and counsellors available as required.*
Guests Admitted to: *Unrestricted access everywhere.*
Meals: *Everyone eats in the dining room. Traditional food, with provision for vegetarian and special diets.*
Special Activities: *Some planned events – brochure available.*
Situation: *Quiet and on the outskirts of the city.*
Maximum Stay: *Unlimited.*
Bookings: *By telephone or letter.*
Charges: *£24.50, plus VAT, per person, with 35% discount for retreatants.*
Access: *By rail, bus or car to Ely.*

Huntingdon

St Francis House
Hemingford Grey
Huntingdon
Cambs. PE18 9BJ   Telephone: 0480 62185

Anglican but accepts all denominations

Renovated about five years ago, St Francis House is designed for retreatants, and the aim is to maintain a peaceful atmosphere at all times. Although the house is in the village, there is a large garden and you can walk beside the nearby river and through the meadows.

Open: *All year.*
Rooms: *17 singles, 3 twin-bedded rooms.*
Facilities: *Disabled, garden, guest lounge, library.*
Spiritual Help: *Peaceful atmosphere at all times.*
Guests Admitted to: *Unrestricted access.*
Meals: *Everyone eats together – traditional food.*
Special Activities: *Send for current retreat list.*
Situation: *Quiet, and in a picturesque village.*
Maximum Stay: *See current retreat list.*
Bookings: *By letter or telephone.*
Charges: *Available on application.*
Access: *Car: via A604.*

Peterborough

Society of the Precious Blood
St Pega's Hermitage
Peakirk
Peterborough
Cambs. PE6 7NP   Telephone: 0733 252219

Anglican

This is a small, enclosed community of nuns. It is best suited for a private, mostly silent retreat, bearing in mind that in such a place you will find a great degree of stillness and will be left on your own.

Open: *All year. Receives men, women and young people.*
Rooms: *2 singles.*
Facilities: *Small garden.*
Spiritual Help: *Some personal talks.*
Guests Admitted to: *Chapel.*
Meals: *Very plain food served in the rooms. DIY for tea and coffee.*

Special Activities: *No planned programme of events.*
Situation: *In the village. On an RAF flight path, but not unduly noisy. Adjoining the Peakirk Wildfowl Wetlands Trust.*
Maximum Stay: *1 week.*
Bookings: *By letter*
Charges: *On application.*
Access: *BR: Peterborough station is 7 miles away. Bus: runs 3 times daily (not Sunday) to Flinton – 2 miles away. Car: via A15.*

---

*'There are two ways to go about getting enough – one is to continue to accumulate more and more.
The other is to desire less' – G. K. Chesterton*

ESSEX

Chelmsford

Brentwood Diocesan Pastoral Centre
Newhall
Boreham
Chelmsford
Essex CM3 3HT   Telephone: 0245 467588

Roman Catholic – Ecumenical

Open: *Most of the year, but closed in August. Receives men, women and young people – mainly non-residential.*
Rooms: *7–10 singles, 4 doubles.*
Facilities: *Conferences, camping, garden, park, library, guest lounge, TV and pay phone.*
Spiritual Help: *Individual spiritual direction and counselling.*
Guests Admitted to: *Access to mainly non-residential areas, but consideration is being given to developing school facilities for residential use during the holidays.*
Meals: *Traditional, with provision for special diets.*
Special Activities: *Those staying can share in the common prayer of the community. There is an extensive programme of events, so send for brochure.*
Situation: *Quiet, in the countryside.*
Maximum Stay: *2 weeks.*
Bookings: *By letter if possible.*
Charges: *For full board and lodging, according to the programme.*
Access: *BR and coaches to Chelmsford, local buses.*

Chelmsford

House of Retreat
The Street
Pleshey
Chelmsford
Essex CM3 1HA   Telephone: 0245 37251

Anglican

The House of Retreat is mostly used by parish groups; individuals are welcome when there is room. A good range of weekend courses are available, ranging from an introduction to the John Main method of meditation, to instruction about how to breathe and use the body most effectively when you have embarked on the journey of prayer.

Open: *Most of the year. Receives men, women, young people, groups and religious.*
Rooms: *21 singles, 1 double; ground-floor bedroom for the disabled; cottage in the grounds.*
Facilities: *Garden, library, guest lounge and pay phone.*
Spiritual Help: *Personal talks, occasional group sharing, meditation, directed study. The retreats here cater for widely differing spiritual needs.*
Guests Admitted to: *Unrestricted access.*
Meals: *Everyone eats together. Traditional food, with provision for vegetarian and special diets by prior arrangement. Self-catering in the cottage.*
Special Activities: *Quiet days, children's days, course for spiritual directors – send for the leaflet.*
Situation: *Quiet, in historic Essex village in countryside.*
Maximum Stay: *Unspecified.*
Bookings: *By telephone or letter.*
Charges: *£17 per person per 24 hours.*
Access: *BR/bus: to Chelmsford. Car: via M11.*

Ingatestone

Family Ministry of West Ham Central Mission
Bodley House
Stock Road
Stock
nr. Ingatestone
Essex CM4 9DH   Telephone: 0277 840668

Baptist

This is a modern bungalow in a quiet garden, catering for day retreats and group meetings. Bodley House works with local churches and it is worth writing to ask what courses or day retreats are planned.

Open: *All year. Receives men and women.*
Rooms: *For day conferences only.*
Facilities: *Disabled, garden, lounge.*
Spiritual Help: *None.*
Guests Admitted to: *Most of the centre, grounds.*
Meals: *DIY.*
Special Activities: *Special courses on pastoral guidance.*
Situation: *Quiet, in countryside.*
Maximum Stay: *For the day.*
Bookings: *Apply to secretary.*
Charges: *By donation.*
Access: *BR: Billericay. Buses: Nos. 152, 153 to Stock. Car: via B1007.*

HERTFORDSHIRE

Barnet

Poor Clare Monastery
102 Galley Lane
Arkley
Barnet
Herts. EN5 4AN   Telephone: 081 449 8815

Roman Catholic

The sisters live an enclosed, contemplative life, and the Monastery is open to people only on recommendation. Retreatants prepare their own meals in the guest house and, although guests are only rarely received, plenty of people apply to stay. Before you decide to ask, however, establish why you want to stay with this community rather than somewhere else.

Open: *All year. Receives men and women.*
Rooms: *Single rooms available in the guest house.*
Facilities: *Guest house rooms, chapel.*
Spiritual Help: *None.*
Guests Admitted to: *Chapel.*
Meals: *Self-catering in the guest house.*
Special Activities: *No planned programme.*
Situation: *Quiet.*
Maximum Stay: *By arrangement.*
Bookings: *By letter.*
Charges: *By donation.*
Access: *Bus/Car: to Barnet.*

Hemel Hempstead

Amaravati Buddhist Centre
Great Gaddesden
Hemel Hempstead
Herts. HP1 3BZ   Telephone: 044 284 2455

Buddhist

This is a residence for Buddhist monks and nuns of the Theravada tradition, but people of any or of no formal religious affiliation are welcomed. Retreats are held in separate facilities away from the often busy life of the Armarvati community. Accommodation is basic in the dormitories, so bring a warm sleeping-bag, a blanket for use during meditation, and a towel and soap. Pack heavy socks or slippers too, as no shoes are worn indoors. There is a full calendar of events, talks and retreats, so have a look at the programme. It is possible to stay with the monastic community for a time, but you must participate fully in the daily routine of meditation, meals and work.

Open: *March to December inclusive. Receives men, women, young people, sometimes families and groups, non-retreatants.*
Rooms: *Dormitories, but the sexes are separated.*
Facilities: *Park and library, pay phone.*
Spiritual Help: *Personal talks, formal and informal talks on the theory and practice of meditation and the spiritual life.*
Guests Admitted to: *Shrine room, work of the community, all daily routine.*
Meals: *Everyone eats together; rice-based Asian food.*
Special Activities: *Festivals, retreats, workshops. Send for brochure.*
Situation: *Quiet.*
Maximum Stay: *1 week, which can be extended at the discretion of the Guestmaster.*
Bookings: *By letter.*
Charges: *By donation and contributions to the cost of food.*
Access: *By car is easiest.*

Royston

Christian Meditation Centre
St Mary's Park
Melbourn Road
Royston
Herts. SG8 7DB   Telephone: 0763 246110

Roman Catholic

The John Main Trust runs this centre based on his teachings about meditation and prayer. All are welcome who seek guidance through the Gospels. Even if you don't want to learn about the Main approach, you can still come for a private retreat with the small community that runs the place.

Open: *All year. Receives men, women, young people and groups.*
Rooms: *8 singles, 2 doubles.*
Facilities: *Day retreats only for the disabled, plus conference facilities, garden, small library, guest lounge, TV and guest telephone. Pets permitted.*
Spiritual Help: *Personal talks, group sharing, meditation, counselling and listening service, directed study. Conferences related to Dom Main teaching. Mass is celebrated daily in the convent immediately adjacent to centre.*
Guests Admitted to: *Unrestricted access.*
Meals: *Everyone eats together. Traditional food, with provision for vegetarian and special diets.*
Special Activities: *None – this is a quiet place to be with oneself and God. Everyone is expected to join in periods of meditation, morning and evening.*
Situation: *Very quiet but in the town. Large and pleasant heath near by.*
Maximum Stay: *Flexible.*
Bookings: *By telephone or letter.*
Charges: *£20 per person per night. £5 to £10 per day retreat.*
Access: *Easy access by rail and bus.*

St Albans

Verulam House
Verulam Road
St Albans
Herts. AL3 4DH   Telephone: 0727 53991

Anglican

Near St Albans Cathedral, this is a small Diocesan centre which is run for group retreats. Sometimes it is possible for individual retreatants to stay here, and various open events are being planned.

Open: *All year except August. Receives everyone.*
Rooms: *15 singles, 9 twin-bedded rooms.*
Facilities: *Conferences, garden, library, guest lounge and pay phone.*
Spiritual Help: *Personal talks.*
Guests Admitted to: *Unrestricted access to all areas, including chapel.*
Meals: *Everyone eats together. Varied food, with provision for vegetarian and special diets.*
Special Activities: *No planned programme of events.*
Situation: *Quiet, in the city, near St Albans Cathedral.*
Maximum Stay: *Not specified.*
Bookings: *By letter or telephone.*
Charges: *Various – please ask.*
Access: *By rail, bus or car to St Albans.*

Dereham

The Old Bakery
Hindolveston
Dereham
Norfolk NR20 5DF   Telephone: 0263 861325

Anglican – open to all

A modest programme of retreats is offered here in the private home of the Reverend and Mrs Percy Gandon, and guests are welcomed as part of the family. The Old Bakery is a restored 18th-century house, with the added benefits of a games room, sun lounge and chapel. It is a member of the Churches Council for Health and Healing.

Open: *All year. Receives men, women, young people, families, groups and non-retreatants.*
Rooms: *3 singles, 5 doubles. Bring your own towels and bed linen.*
Facilities: *Conferences, chapel, garden, small library, guest lounge, TV and pay phone. Children welcomed.*
Spiritual Help: *Personal talks, group sharing, meditation, directed study, healing ministry, counselling.*
Guests Admitted to: *Unrestricted access.*
Meals: *Everyone eats together. Traditional and wholefood, with provision for vegetarian and special diets.*
Special Activities: *Planned programme of events including special weekends. Send for brochure.*
Situation: *Quiet and in the village.*
Maximum Stay: *Usually 1 week.*
Bookings: *By letter or telephone.*
Charges: *£32 per person per week, £16 per day.*
Access: *BR: nearest main-line station (Norwich, King's Lynn) about 25 miles away. Bus: to Fakenham, 8 miles away, but guests can be met. Car: via A148 – map available with booking confirmation.*

King's Lynn

Massingham St Mary
Little Massingham
nr. King's Lynn
Norfolk PE32 2JU   Telephone: 0485 520245

Roman Catholic

Massingham St Mary is an informal and homely place, even if it is a large country-house. The facilities are simple and basic but provide all you probably need. Arrangements can be made for individually directed retreats and for spiritual direction.

Open: *All year except Christmas, Easter and throughout September. Receives men, women, young people, families, groups. Non-retreatants taken, if room available, for quiet time but not for a holiday.*
Rooms: *22 singles, 8 doubles, plus a bungalow for 8 and a self-contained hermitage for 2–3. Bring soap and towels.*
Facilities: *Limited for disabled, conferences, garden, library, guest lounge, TV and pay phone. Children welcomed.*
Spiritual Help: *Personal talks, group sharing, meditation, directed study, spiritual direction and non-professional counselling. Ignatian-trained guidance.*
Guests Admitted to: *Unrestricted access to all areas, including chapels, choir.*
Meals: *Everyone eats together in the guest house. Traditional food, with provision for vegetarian and special diets. Self-catering in the bungalow and hermitage.*
Special Activities: *Planned programme of events. Send for the brochure.*
Situation: *Quiet, in the countryside.*
Maximum Stay: *According to length of programme event, or by personal arrangement.*
Bookings: *By letter.*
Charges: *Programme fees in brochure. Retreats £18 per person per night or what you can afford, if there is a problem.*
Access: *By rail or car.*

Norwich

All Hallows House
Rouen Road
Norwich
Norfolk NR1 1QT   Telephone: 0603 624738

Anglican but open to all denominations

Though it is on a busy street, beset with traffic noise, All Hallows House has a peaceful atmosphere inside. St Julian's Church is next door and contains a chapel that is built on the site of the cell of the 14th-century mystic Julian of Norwich. Her *Revelations of Divine Love* is one of the classic English Christian works and is easily obtained at all good bookshops.

Open: *All year apart from Christmas. Receives men, women, small groups and families occasionally, as well as non-retreatants.*
Rooms: *4 singles, 3 doubles.*
Facilities: *Chapel, garden, small library, guest lounge, TV, guest telephone. Children welcome, but it is not always possible to accommodate them. No pets.*

Spiritual Help: *Personal talks as necessary.*
Guests Admitted to: *Chapel and fairly free access everywhere.*
Meals: *Everyone eats together. Food is traditional, healthy without being cranky. Vegetarian and special diets on request. DIY for tea and coffee.*
Special Activities: *No special activities or events.*
Situation: *In the town, but despite the busy location, there seems to be a peace within.*
Maximum Stay: *14 days.*
Bookings: *Telephone in the first instance and confirm by letter.*
Charges: *By donations of between £5 and £10 per person per night.*
Access: *By rail, bus or car to Norwich. Good map is available on request.*

Norwich

Bowthorpe Community Trust
1 St Michael's Cottages
Bowthorpe Hall Road
Bowthorpe
Norwich
Norfolk NR5 9AA   Telephone: 0603 746380

Interdenominational

The Trust offers short-stay accommodation set up through the combined sponsorship of Anglican, Baptist, Methodist, Quaker, Roman Catholic and United Reform churches. Near by is a woodcraft workshop for the disadvantaged. A small sitting room, a library and devotional books and a prayer and study room with all meals provided make this one of the more cosy places to stay. The Walsingham shrines are only an hour's drive away.

Open: *All year. Receives men, women and non-retreatants.*
Rooms: *1 single and 1 double.*
Facilities: *Garden, small library, private prayer and study rooms, TV.*
Spiritual Help: *Personal talks, prayer counselling. The adjoining Worship Centre is available for private prayer and study.*
Guests Admitted to: *Most areas.*
Meals: *Everyone eats together. Traditional food with provision for vegetarians. No special diets.*
Special Activities: *No planned events but information brochure available.*
Situation: *Quiet, next to countryside.*
Maximum Stay: *3 weeks.*
Bookings: *By letter or telephone.*
Charges: *£40 per person per week, £8 per day, £6 B&B.*
Access: *BR: from Norwich to Thorpe. Car: via A47.*

Norwich

Padmaloka Buddhist Retreat Centre for Men
Lesingham House
Surlingham
Norwich
Norfolk NR14 7AL   Telephone: 05088 310

Buddhist

A Buddhist retreat centre for men only, run by the Western Buddhist Order.
Here, no time is wasted in getting you into stillness and simplicity, and the
study of what some claim to be the fastest growing spiritual tradition in the
West. In addition to meditation and other related classes, you can discover
how to make spiritual practice work in your career through talks by men who
have achieved it. They may be managing directors of successful companies
or even medical school lecturers – but all have developed what Buddhists
term, 'Right Livelihood'. Bring a sleeping-bag, towel, soap, and old clothes and
shoes for the work periods that everyone does during the day. For meditation
wear loose clothes. Vegetarian food and vegans can be catered for. A happy,
peaceful and justly famous place.

Open: *All year. Receives men only.*
Rooms: *Dormitories – bring your own towel and sleeping-bag.*
Facilities: *Disabled, garden, library, guest lounge and guest telephone.*
Spiritual Help: *Personal talks, group sharing, meditation and directed
study.*
Guests Admitted to: *Unrestricted access.*
Meals: *Everyone eats together. Vegetarian wholefood. Vegan and special
diets catered for by prior arrangement.*
Special Activities: *Planned programme. Send for brochure.*
Situation: *Very quiet, in a village and close to countryside.*
Maximum Stay: *Unlimited.*
Bookings: *By letter.*
Charges: *£18 per person per night. There are concessions, so please
enquire.*
Access: *By rail to Norwich then by taxi or bus. Bus to Surlingham village
drops you at the gate.*

Swaffham

Pickenham Resource Centre
Brecklands Green
North Pickenham
Swaffham
Norfolk PE37 8LG   Telephone: 0760 440427

Interdenominational

The Centre is part of the Pickenham Trust which also runs an activities camp and a book publishing enterprise. It is designed to cater for a great many people. Facilities range from a young people's camp to a piano and an organ, and even an outdoor relief map of the Holy Land. In many respects it is like a holiday place and, therefore, is perhaps best suited to the non-retreatant who wants a short break or to those who are attending the Centre as members of a group.

Open: *March to December. Receives men, women, young people, families, groups, non-retreatants.*
Rooms: *There are 67 beds, including singles, doubles, dormitories, plus an activities camp.*
Facilities: *Conferences, garden, bookshop, guest lounge, TV and pay phone. Children welcomed. Hoping soon to offer provision for the disabled, so please enquire.*
Spiritual Help: *See the programme on offer.*
Guests Admitted to: *Unrestricted access.*
Meals: *Everyone eats together. Traditional home-cooking, with provision for vegetarian and special diets. Self-catering possible at certain times of the year.*
Special Activities: *No planned programme of events.*
Situation: *Very quiet, in the countryside.*
Maximum Stay: *Unlimited.*
Bookings: *By letter or telephone.*
Charges: *Send for tariff.*
Access: *BR: to Downham Market, 11 miles away. Buses: to Swaffham from London, Norwich, King's Lynn, Peterborough.*

Walsingham

Hospice of Our Lady
Walsingham
Norfolk NR22 6BW   Telephone: 0328 820239

Anglican

Walsingham Shrine is a place of ancient Christian pilgrimage and the Hospice is a famous and comfortable pilgrimage centre. This means that you will not find facilities for silence or for spiritual guidance. To go on a pilgrimage to a holy place is a long-established religious practice of most major world faiths. It can, and ought to be, regarded as a kind of retreat, especially as the pilgrim hopes for a deepening of personal spirituality. Before starting out, read about the history of Walsingham so that you may understand what has drawn Christians there over the centuries. This should put meaning into what might otherwise simply be a visit to another 'monument'. The Hospice, with its gardens and modern rooms, is a pleasant place to stay and from which to visit either the local Anglican shrine or the Roman Catholic one a mile away. Both continue to attract thousands of people every year.

Open: *All year except mid-December to the end of January. Receives men, women, young people, families, groups and non-retreatants.*
Rooms: *200 places divided between single, double and three-bedded rooms.*
Facilities: *Disabled, conferences, garden, guest lounge, TV and pay phone. Children welcome.*
Spiritual Help: *No facilities for silence, and no on-site spiritual guidance.*
Guests Admitted to: *Unrestricted access.*
Meals: *Everyone eats together. Traditional food, with provision for vegetarians.*
Special Activities: *Each weekend there is a programme organised by the parish groups attending. This includes Stations of the Cross, Procession and Benediction.*
Situation: *Rather busy in the village, near countryside.*
Maximum Stay: *12 days, including only 1 weekend.*
Bookings: *By letter.*
Charges: *Send for details.*
Access: *By car is best.*

SUFFOLK

Bungay

All Hallows House
Ditchingham
Bungay
Suffolk NR35 2DZ   Telephone: 0986-892840

Anglican

Open: *All year except Christmas. Receives men, women, families, small groups and non-retreatants.*
Rooms: *3 singles, 2 doubles.*
Facilities: *Chapel, large garden, guest lounge, TV and guest telephone. Children welcome.*

Spiritual Help: *The Chaplain, when available, is willing to talk to visitors and occasionally to direct personal retreats.*
Guests Admitted to: *Convent grounds, the garden and chapel.*
Meals: *Meals taken in guest house. Very plain food, with vegetarian meals and self-catering available. Tea and coffee facilities in every room.*
Special Activities: *None.*
Situation: *Very quiet and in the countryside. The house is very comfortable and homely, and guests are encouraged to help with washing-up.*
Maximum Stay: *2 weeks.*
Bookings: *By letter or telephone.*
Charges: *By donation – costs about £8 per person per day, full board.*
Access: *By car is best.*

Bungay

St Michael's House
All Hallows Convent
Ditchingham
Bungay
Suffolk NR35 2DT   Telephone: 0986 892749

Anglican

There is a peaceful, happy atmosphere here, and group retreatants often return on an individual basis. Open retreats of various kinds are held, bearing such titles as Beginners, Way of Life, Julian and Healing, while Advent and summer courses are available for groups of up to 25.

Open: *All year except Easter, Christmas and All Saints' Week. Receives men, women, young people, families, groups and non-retreatants.*
Rooms: *17 singles, 4 doubles.*
Facilities: *Conferences, chapel, garden, library, guest lounge, pay phone. Children welcome.*
Spiritual Help: *Personal talks, group sharing, meditation.*
Guests Admitted to: *Convent chapel and gardens.*
Meals: *Everyone eats in St Michael's House. Traditional food, with provision for vegetarian and special diets. The food is prepared by professional caterers.*
Special Activities: *Planned programme of events. Send for brochure.*
Situation: *Very quiet.*
Maximum Stay: *2 weeks.*
Bookings: *By telephone but confirm by letter.*
Charges: *By donation – £12.50 per person per day.*
Access: *Car: via B1332 from Norwich to Bungay.*

Bury St Edmonds

Water Hall Retreat Centre
Great Ashfield
Bury St Edmonds
Suffolk IP31 3HP   Telephone: 081-981 1225
                                                               for enquiries
Buddhist

Water Hall is run by the London Buddhist Centre specifically for introductory
retreats. These are in the form of introductory weekend retreats for adults
wishing to learn meditation as well as attending more advanced classes.
Classes are taken by full-time practising Buddhists who are members of the
Western Buddhist Order. There are also courses about Buddhism, where you
can learn who the Buddha was, what he taught and what relevance his
teaching has for us in the West today. The telephone number above is for the
London Centre, who will deal with your enquiry.

Open: *During organised group retreats. Receives men, women, groups and
religious only.*
Rooms: *Accommodation for 20 adults in double rooms, dormitories and a
caravan.*
Facilities: *Disabled, conferences, camping, garden, guest lounge and pay
phone.*
Spiritual Help: *Personal talks, group sharing, meditation and directed
study.*
Guests Admitted to: *Unrestricted access everywhere, including shrine
room and work of the community.*
Meals: *Everyone eats together. Vegetarian wholefood, with provision for
special diets.*
Special Activities: *There is a special programme of planned events – see
brochure. Water Hall is available (particularly during the week, from
Monday to Friday) for use by groups sympathetic to Buddhism.*
Situation: *Very quiet, in the village and countryside. No passing traffic.*
Maximum Stay: *10 days.*
Bookings: *By letter or telephone.*
Charges: *See brochure as charges depend on course.*
Access: *By rail to Bury St Edmonds, or by car.*

---

*'We can never know God
until we first know clearly our own soul' – Julian of Norwich*

Newmarket

The Old Stable House
3 Sussex Lodge
Fordham Road
Newmarket
Suffolk CB8 7AF   Telephone: 0638 667190

Roman Catholic – Inter-faith

Very close to Newmarket Heath with lots of good walks, this former stable offers a warm, comfortable environment with as much freedom as possible for individuals and groups to work on their personal and spiritual development. The atmosphere is informal and homelike. The focus of the workshops is holistic, promoting the integration of spiritual, physical, psychological and intellectual elements, and helping to release the mysticism, creativity and wisdom inherent in the individual. Open to all who are committed to healing, growth and the desire to increase their spiritual awareness.

Open: *All year. Receives men, women, groups of young people for day events only, families, religious and non-retreatants.*
Rooms: *4 singles, 3 doubles.*
Facilities: *Disabled, small conferences, camping, garden, guest lounge and pay phone. Children welcomed, pets permitted within reason.*
Spiritual Help: *Retreats and workshops designed to meet the needs of individual groups, in addition to group sharing, spiritual direction and counselling.*
Guests Admitted to: *Unrestricted access.*
Meals: *Self-catering for individual guests. Provision for vegetarians.*
Special Activities: *Planned programme of events. Send for brochure.*
Situation: *Quiet, with a small woodland area and paddock. 12 miles from Cambridge.*
Maximum Stay: *1 week, negotiable.*
Bookings: *By letter or telephone.*
Charges: *Send for leaflet.*
Access: *BR: Newmarket station 5 minutes away. Local buses. Car: via A45.*

'A pure heart create for me, O God,
put a steadfast spirit within me' – Psalm 50

Central England

Ashram Community House
23–25 Grantham Road
Sparkbrook
Birmingham B11 1LU   Telephone: 021-773 7061

Christian – Non-denominational

This is a radical Christian community set in one of the poorest inner-city
districts. It actively participates in a multi-cultural neighbourhood that is
composed primarily of people from Pakistan. The community comprises
some who live at the Ashram and many others who join on special projects
which involve them in a wider community network. The Ashram works to
foster relationships between Christians and Muslims. Most weekends see a
number of guests in the house who want to find out more about this kind of
Christian life which seeks to translate faith into radical action, responding to
the challenge set by the gospel.

Open: *All year except 27 December to 2 January.*
Rooms: *More like impromptu sleeping arrangements than rooms, but all are
singles.*
Facilities: *Chapel, lounge and reading material.*
Spiritual Help: *Group and personal talks.*
Guests Admitted to: *Everywhere except the business offices, and may
participate in work projects of the community.*
Meals: *Everyone eats together. Provision for vegetarians.*
Special Activities: *There is a lot going on here, so you can probably join one
or other of the current projects.*
Situation: *Busy, right in the middle of an urban area.*
Maximum Stay: *By arrangement.*
Bookings: *By letter, giving some details about yourself.*
Charges: *Depends on what you want to do at the Ashram, but no one is turned
away simply because they have no money.*
Access: *BR or bus to Birmingham, then local bus. If you are arriving by car,
ask about parking.*

Vipassana Trust
107 Handsworth Wood Road
Handsworth Wood
Birmingham B20 2PH   Telephone: 021-554 1153

Buddhist – Inter-faith

Vipassana means 'to see things as they really are'. It is a way of self-
purification by self-observation and is one of India's most ancient meditation
techniques. The Trust offers a 10-day course in it, to which you must give all
your efforts, observing the rules of the house and taking your study seriously.
There are also courses available for Punjabi and Hindi speakers. The Trust

is located in a suburb of Birmingham in a Victorian house with a nice garden. The food is ascetic but sufficient. There are local practising groups in London, Bedfordshire, Bristol, Liverpool, Suffolk, Sussex, Devon and Wales.

Open: *All year. Receives men, women and young people.*
Rooms: *6 dormitories containing 6 beds each.*
Facilities: *Library, garden, pay phone. Good central-heating.*
Spiritual Help: *Meditation and directed study.*
Guests Admitted to: *Almost anywhere.*
Meals: *Vegetarian only. Plain and simple fare. No special diets.*
Special Activities: *Send for information.*
Situation: *Quiet, in city. Large garden.*
Maximum Stay: *10 days.*
Bookings: *By telephone or letter.*
Charges: *By donation.*
Access: *By rail, coach or car to Birmingham.*

DERBYSHIRE

Belper

Convent of St Lawrence
Field Lane
Belper
Derby DE5 1DD   Telephone: 0773 822585

Anglican

Open: *All year. Receives men, women, groups and non-retreatants.*
Rooms: *10 singles, 5 doubles.*
Facilities: *Conferences, guest lounge, TV and pay phone.*
Spiritual Help: *Personal talks if requested.*
Guests Admitted to: *Chapel.*
Meals: *Mostly taken together. Very plain food, with provision for vegetarians. DIY facilities.*
Special Activities: *No planned programme of events.*
Situation: *Very quiet, in a small town.*
Maximum Stay: *1 week.*
Bookings: *By telephone and confirm by letter.*
Charges: *Enquire when booking.*
Access: *BR: to Belper, then a 5-minute walk. Bus: from Derby to Belper. Car: via A6.*

Morley

Morley Retreat House
Church Lane
Morley
Derby DE7 6DE   Telephone: 0332 831293

Interdenominational

Modern accommodation has been built for guests next to the old Morley
Rectory. There is a good programme of retreat and house events, ranging
from quiet days to a weekend devoted to silent prayer called, appropriately,
'Listening to God'. There is also a Taizé weekend to give you a taste of the
spirituality and music of that popular and famous French community. While
many of the retreat houses in this book say that they accept young people,
what they usually mean is people who are in their 20s. At Morley teenagers
will be welcomed to weekend retreats designed especially for them.

Open: *All year. Receives men, women, young people, families and groups.*
Rooms: *24 singles, 5 doubles. Bring soap and towels.*
Facilities: *Very limited for disabled, conferences, garden, library, guest
lounge, TV and pay phone. Children welcomed, pets sometimes.*
Spiritual Help: *Depends on retreat programme so please enquire when
booking.*
Guests Admitted to: *Unrestricted access.*
Meals: *Everyone eats together. Traditional food, with provision for veg-
etarian and special diets.*
Special Activities: *Planned programme of events. Send for brochure.*
Situation: *Very quiet, in the countryside, with a walled garden and 14th-
century parish church, set in the midst of 5 acres of grounds.*
Maximum Stay: *Unlimited.*
Bookings: *By telephone or letter.*
Charges: *£19 per person for 24 hours.*
Access: *BR: to Derby, but there are no local bus services. Car: via M1, Exit
25, followed by A52, A61 and A608.*

Coleford

Christchurch Retreat House
The Old Vicarage
Christchurch
nr. Coleford
Glos. GL16 7NS   Telephone: 0594 35330

Anglican – Ecumenical

This is a place to read and pray in comfort, and where you will be well looked after by Reverend John Grover and his wife, who run the Retreat House without outside help. The philosophy here is one of help and listening, in the hope that all who need calm and counsel will return to their ordinary daily life refreshed and encouraged. Guided retreats include one for those who have never been on a retreat before.

Open: *All year except Christmas. Receives men, women, young people (not children), groups, religious and non-retreatants.*
Rooms: *2 singles, 4 doubles.*
Facilities: *Conferences, garden, library, guest lounge.*
Spiritual Help: *Personal talks, group sharing, meditation, directed study, guided retreats, quiet days, prayer groups.*
Guests Admitted to: *Unrestricted access to all areas, including chapel and croquet lawn.*
Meals: *Everyone eats together; traditional food.*
Special Activities: *Planned programme of events. Send for brochure.*
Situation: *Quiet, in the Forest of Dean/Wye Valley.*
Maximum Stay: *5 days.*
Bookings: *By letter or telephone.*
Charges: *£18 per person per day; ask for other rates.*
Access: *BR: to Gloucester, 20 miles away. Bus: from Gloucester. Car: via A40 and B4228.*

Cranham

Prinknash Abbey
Cranham
Gloucester CL4 8EX   Telephone: 0452 813592
                                Grange: 0452 8124455
Roman Catholic

St Peter's Grange is now the guest house of the monks. It is an old and distinguished place and was used as the monastery until a new Abbey was completed in 1972. The new monastery is rather like a fort, sitting proudly on its hill, and it is hard not to think that the guests at the Grange have the better deal – but inside the monastery all is warm, comfortable, and purpose-built.

Single-men retreatants may be received there in separate guest accommodation, while all others, including women and groups, stay at the Grange. Over time the community has offered hospitality to many people, but it is now in the process of making major changes to guest accommodation and you should enquire what is available. All guests may attend the daily round of services, and there is usually work to do if you feel you want to contribute in that way. Try not to telephone when booking, as letters are preferred. Please write for the latest details of what is available which will include information on all aspects of making a retreat at the monastery or guest house.

Stroud

More Hall Convent
Randwick
Stroud
Glos. GL6 6EP   Telephone: 0453 764486

Roman Catholic

Open: *All year. Receives men, women, young people, small families and non-retreatants.*
Rooms: *3 bed-sitting rooms.*
Facilities: *Garden, library, TV, guest telephone and pay phone. Children welcome.*
Spiritual Help: *Personal talks.*
Guests Admitted to: *Chapel and the work of the community.*
Meals: *Taken in the guest house. Traditional food, with provision for vegetarians. DIY facilities.*
Special Activities: *No special activities.*
Situation: *Quiet and in the countryside.*
Maximum Stay: *Usually 2 weeks.*
Bookings: *By letter.*
Charges: *No fixed charge.*
Access: *BR: to Stroud then by bus. Enquire for car-route directions at time of booking.*

Stroud

St Michael's House of Prayer
Whitbourne Cottage
The Pitch
Brownshill
Stroud
Glos. GL6 8AJ   Telephone: 0453 885584

Roman Catholic – Interdenominational

Two Roman Catholic sisters run their small home as a house of prayer, where guests of all denominations are welcome to share the prayer rhythm of their lives. Silence is expected after night prayer until lunch the next day, and guests must observe this silence rule. So if you are one of those who must always find some reason to chat, don't bother to come here. For those who do go, warmth, wholesome food, nearby walks and – best of all – participation in the Divine Office, sung daily in the house, are all waiting. If you are a non-retreatant looking for a cheap holiday, try somewhere else.

Open: *All year. Receives men, women, young people over 17 and non-retreatants if they want a quiet, prayerful time and keep the silence.*
Rooms: *2 singles, 1 double.*
Facilities: *Small garden, library in guest lounge, no guest telephone.*
Spiritual Help: *No counselling or direct guidance but informal conversation at the evening meal and as occasion dictates.*
Guests Admitted to: *Chapel.*
Meals: *Everyone eats together in the dining room. Largely health food, often vegetarian, always good and interesting. DIY for tea and coffee.*
Special Activities: *No planned programme of events. Divine Office is sung daily in the house. There is daily Mass in the church opposite the house. Details of other Christian services in the locality are available.*
Situation: *Quiet, in the countryside, edge of village.*
Maximum Stay: *10 days. 3–4 days recommended for first visit.*
Bookings: *By telephone and confirm by letter.*
Charges: *£10 per person per night. Minimum stay 2 nights.*
Access: *BR and bus to Stroud, then by taxi.*

HEREFORD and WORCESTER

Hereford

Belmont Abbey
Hereford HR2 9RZ   Telephone: 0432 277475

Roman Catholic

Open: *All year except Christmas/New Year and 'Low' Week. Receives men, women, young people, families, groups and non-retreatants.*
Rooms: *8 singles, 1 double; dormitories available in school holidays.*
Facilities: *Conferences, park, small library, TV and pay phone. Disabled people and children considered.*
Spiritual Help: *Personal talks, group sharing, meditation, confession and counselling. Many visitors come specifically for the choral monastic offices.*
Guests Admitted to: *Chapel; only clergy permitted in choir, only male retreatants admitted to monastic enclosure.*
Meals: *Eaten in guest house. Traditional food, with provision for vegetarians.*

Special Activities: *Planned programme of events. Send for the brochure.*
Situation: *Quiet, and in the countryside but incorporating an active boys'
school. Close to beautiful countryside, River Wye, Welsh mountains, golf
course and school sports facilities.*
Maximum Stay: *9 days.*
Bookings: *By letter.*
Charges: *Send for details.*
Access: *Hereford is easily reached by rail, bus or car.*

Pershore

Holland House
Retreat and Conference Centre
Cropthorne
Pershore
Worcs. WR10 3NB   Telephone: 0386 860330

Anglican – Interdenominational

Holland House is an Anglican foundation set up to help people who are trying
to relate their prayer life more closely to the world around them. It is a big
old 17th-century place, with lots of thatch and gardens laid out by Lutyens.
There is a new chapel and a modern conference and bedroom wing. The
house is close to the village church, and although not far from busy roads, it
is quiet.

Open: *All year except Christmas. Receives men, women, young people,
families, groups and non-retreatants.*
Rooms: *18 singles, 6 doubles.*
Facilities: *Conferences, garden, library, guest lounge and pay phone.
Children welcome.*
Spiritual Help: *All possible help is given to guests to make best use of their
stay.*
Guests Admitted to: *Almost unrestricted access.*
Meals: *Traditional. No special diets.*
Special Activities: *Planned programme of events. Send for the brochure.*
Situation: *Quiet, in the village and countryside.*
Maximum Stay: *Unlimited.*
Bookings: *By letter.*
Charges: *Send for details.*
Access: *BR: to Evesham, $3^1/_2$ miles away. Buses: from Evesham. Car: via
M5, Exit 7, then A44.*

Shrawley

Society of St Francis
Glasshampton
Shrawley
Worcs. WR6 6TQ   Telephone: 0299 896345

Anglican

Open: *All year except for 1 week in August. Receives men and male non-retreatants.*
Rooms: *5 singles.*
Facilities: *Garden, library, guest lounge and direct-dialling telephone.*
Spiritual Help: *Personal talks, taking part in the worship of the brothers. There are 4 offices a day and a daily Eucharist.*
Guests Admitted to: *Chapel.*
Meals: *Everyone eats together or in the guest house. Very plain, traditional food, with provision for vegetarians.*
Special Activities: *No planned programme of events.*
Situation: *Quiet and peaceful, in the countryside.*
Maximum Stay: *1 week.*
Bookings: *By letter.*
Charges: *£7 per person per day.*
Access: *By bus or car (not rail).*

Worcester

St Mary's House
Stanbrook Abbey
Callow End
Worcester
Worcs. WR2 4TD   Telephone: 0905 830307

Roman Catholic

St Mary's is the guest house of Stanbrook Abbey, one of the best- known Benedictine communities in Britain, with a national reputation for literary, musical and artistic work. Its influence can be seen and heard in the liturgical arrangements of many other monastic communities. This is perhaps one of the most classic Christian places for making a private retreat, and it would be wasting a great spiritual opportunity to go there simply for a holiday.

Open: *All year except 2 weeks at Christmas and during annual community retreat. Receives men, women, young people and a restricted number of groups.*
Rooms: *10 singles, 4 doubles.*
Facilities: *Disabled, conferences, guest-house chapel, garden, library,*

guest lounge and pay phone.
Spiritual Help: *Personal talks.*
Guests Admitted to: *Extern chapel in monastery.*
Meals: *Eaten in the guest house. Traditional food, with provision for vegetarian and special diets. DIY for cold drinks and breakfast.*
Special Activities: *No planned programme of events, but send for brochure describing the facilities.*
Situation: *Quiet and in the village.*
Maximum Stay: *2 weeks.*
Bookings: *Preferably by letter.*
Charges: *£15 per person per day. Other rates available on request.*
Access: *BR: to Worcester Shrub Hill or Foregate Street, then by taxi. Buses are very infrequent. Car: via M5, Exit 8, then take Malvern Road.*

LEICESTERSHIRE

Coalville

Mount St Bernard Abbey
Coalville
Leics. LE6 3UL   Telephone: 0530 32298/32022

Roman Catholic

Built of local stone, the buildings are simple, not over-ornate, and in keeping with the Cistercian traditions. In the fine and very large granite church, Latin Mass is sung once a month and the vernacular Mass daily. Rooms are clean, comfortable, look out on to a courtyard, and have good new beds. Although the rooms are heated, pyjamas are a good idea. There is a small library of general spiritual texts in the main corridor of the guest house, with more specific texts for study available from the Chapter House. The Abbey has a large working pottery, as well as carpentry and printing shops. Meals are very traditional and contain lots of vegetables as these are raised by the monks. Located in the middle of the famous Quorn Hunt country, the Abbey offers good walking over hill, pasture and moor. But be warned that this monastery is a very popular place and you may find it hard to get accommodation.

Open: *All year. Receives men, women, young people, families sometimes, groups, retreatants.*
Rooms: *13 singles, 2 doubles.*
Facilities: *Garden, park, library, guest lounge and telephone. Children only permitted by arrangement.*
Spiritual Help: *Personal talks, meditation, directed study if required.*
Guests Admitted to: *Chapel, choir, work of the community, but not monastic enclosure.*
Meals: *Taken in refectory. Traditional, plain food – ample, if not*

imaginatively prepared.
Special Activities: *No planned programme.*
Situation: *150-acre estate in hills of Charnwood Forest, with commanding views of Soar river-valley.*
Maximum Stay: *By arrangement.*
Bookings: *By letter.*
Charges: *By donation.*
Access: *BR: to Loughborough, then by taxi. Car: via M1, Exit 23.*

'Compassion is aroused when we realise we are One with all life'
– Throssel Hole Buddhist Priory

East Norton

Launde Abbey
East Norton
Leics. LE7 9XB   Telephone: 057286 254

Anglican

This is a huge red-brick house built by Thomas Cromwell in 1540 on the site of an early Augustinian priory. It retains today the comfort and charm of a distinguished private country-mansion, with a cheerful drawing room fire, a panelled dining-room and games room. A beautiful chapel, still intact from the 15th century, is the jewel of Launde Abbey. You might be given a room in either the house, a small annexe or in the refurbished Georgian stable-block, which overlooks a large pond.

Open: *All year except August and over Christmas. Receives men, women, young people, families, groups and non-retreatants.*
Rooms: *15 singles, 20 doubles, a hermitage and 2 caravans.*
Facilities: *Disabled, camping, chapel, garden, park, library, guest lounge, TV and pay phone. Children welcomed, some pets permitted.*
Spiritual Help: *Personal talks.*
Guests Admitted to: *Almost everywhere.*
Meals: *Everyone eats together. Traditional food, with provision for vegetarian and special diets.*
Special Activities: *Planned programme of events. Send for the brochure.*
Situation: *Very quiet, in the countryside.*
Maximum Stay: *1 week.*
Bookings: *By letter or telephone.*
Charges: *£20 per person per 24 hours.*
Access: *BR: to Oakham, 6 miles away. Bus: No. 147 to Leicester. Car: via A47 from Leicester.*

Theddingworth

Hothorpe Hall
Theddingworth
Leics. LE17 6QX   Telephone: 0858 880257

Interdenominational

Hothorpe Hall is more a conference than a retreat centre, but having said that, individuals are welcomed as well as groups. Much effort has recently gone into improving the comfort of the rooms and many now boast en-suite facilities. There is also a new 200-seat conference room. The garden runs to 12 acres, so there is plenty of space and quiet for doing some walking meditation. With many recreational facilities available on site, it is a good place in which to take a holiday amid fellow Christians – and children should enjoy it too.

Open: *All year. Receives men, women, young people, families, groups, religious and non-retreatants.*
Rooms: *45 rooms comprising some singles but mainly doubled.*
Facilities: *Disabled, conferences, recreation, chapel, garden, park, library, guest lounge, TV and pay phone. Children welcome.*
Spiritual help: *Personal talks. Staff are happy to listen, but there is no ordained person on site.*
Guests Admitted to: *Unrestricted access to all areas, including some work of the Hall.*
Meals: *Everyone eats together. Traditional food, with provision for vegetarian and special diets.*
Special Activities: *Planned programme – send for brochure.*
Situation: *Very quiet, close to the village and in the countryside.*
Maximum Stay: *Unlimited.*
Bookings: *By letter or telephone.*
Charges: *Send for details.*
Access: *to Market Harborough, 5 miles away.*

Ecton

Peterborough Diocesan Retreat House
Ecton House
Church Way
Ecton
Northants NN6 OQE   Telephone: 0604 406442

Anglican

This is a late-17th-century rectory set in a charming village between Northampton and Wellingborough. It is a warm, comfortable place with a family
atmosphere.

Open: *All year except 2 weeks at Christmas, 2 weeks at Easter and
throughout August. Receives men, women, young people, groups and non-
retreatants.*
Rooms: *26 singles.*
Facilities: *Conferences, chapel, garden, library, guest lounge, TV and pay
phone. Children permitted by arrangement.*
Spiritual Help: *Personal talks can be arranged.*
Guests Admitted to: *Unrestricted access to all areas, including chapel.*
Meals: *Everyone eats together. Traditional food, with provision for veg-
etarian and special diets.*
Special Activities: *No planned programme of events.*
Situation: *Quiet, in the village and countryside.*
Maximum Stay: *Unlimited.*
Bookings: *By letter or telephone.*
Charges: *Send for price list.*
Access: *BR: to Northampton. Local buses: Nos. 45, 46. Car: to North-
ampton via A4500.*

OXFORDSHIRE

Burford

Priory of Our Lady
Burford
Oxon. OX8 4SQ   Telephone: 099382 3141/3605

Anglican

Pretty Burford, with its stone houses, antique shops, tourists and air of new
money and material success, is also the home of a twin community of
Benedictine monks and nuns. Community members are able to give guests
individual attention and informal spiritual guidance. Soon the Old Rectory

retreat house, which accommodates 16 people, will be reopened. Otherwise guest rooms are in the Priory. Disabled people have the benefit of that rare monastic facility – an electric lift to the first-floor accommodation, which includes a bathroom for the disabled.

Open: *All year except Christmas, Easter and the first 2 weeks of October. Receives men, women, young people, families, groups and non-retreatants.*
Rooms: *3 singles and 1 double in the Priory, and accommodation in the retreat house.*
Facilities: *Some for the disabled, small conferences and English-language teaching; chapel, gardens, woodland, park, library, guest lounge and pay phone. Children welcome in the retreat house.*
Spiritual Help: *Personal talks, group sharing, meditation, directed study. Individually guided retreats, non-resident groups.*
Guests Admitted to: *Chapel, choir and some work of the community.*
Meals: *Everyone eats together or in the guest house, depending on numbers. Traditional food, with provision for vegetarians and diabetics. DIY facilities.*
Special Activities: *Enquire about events, but there is no brochure for the present.*
Situation: *Quiet, in the village – splendid views of Windrush Valley.*
Maximum Stay: *By negotiation.*
Bookings: *By letter with deposit.*
Charges: *No fixed charge except for individually guided retreats.*
Access: *BR: Charlebury station is 8 miles away or travel to Oxford and take a bus. Buses: from Oxford/Cheltenham.*

Charney Bassett

Charney Manor
Charney Bassett
nr. Wantage
Oxon. OX12 OEJ   Telephone: 0235 868206

Religious Society of Friends (Quakers)

The Manor is a Grade 1 listed house. There are just two Friends living here, so there is not really a resident community as such, but a warm welcome awaits all guests none the less. Quaker workshop meetings are held every Wednesday evening.

Open: *All year. Receives men, women, young people, families, groups and non-retreatants.*
Rooms: *Main house for group bookings only – 10 singles, 10 twin-bedded rooms in addition to folding beds. Self-catering cottage; barn can be used for overflow, with camping-style accommodation.*
Facilities: *Conferences, garden, library, guest lounge, TV, guest telephone and pay phone. Children welcomed. Pets permitted by arrangement, but not*

in public areas of the house.
Spiritual Help: *Depending on nature of group's programme at any time.*
Guests Admitted to: *Unrestricted access everywhere.*
Meals: *Everyone eats together. Traditional and wholefood –vegetarian and special diets can be catered for with advance notice.*
Special Activities: *Planned programme of retreats. Send for brochure.*
Situation: *Very quiet, in the countryside, on edge of village. Nearest shop $3^1/_2$ miles.*
Maximum Stay: *1 week but negotiable.*
Bookings: *By telephone or letter.*
Charges: *See brochure.*
Access: *BR: to Didcot station, 11 miles away, then by taxi. Bus: runs from Southmoor, 3 miles away.*

Faringdon

St Mary's Priory
Fernham
Faringdon
Oxon. SN7 7PP   Telephone: 0367 240133

Roman Catholic

Plans are in the pipeline to build a small guest house with four double rooms, DIY facilities and a lounge, so in time men as well as families and groups may be able to stay with the sisters. Meanwhile guests have to be accommodated within the Priory, so only religious sisters may be received and younger women who would like to share the contemplative life for a short time.

Open: *All year except first fortnight of August. Receives religious sisters and younger women considering a religious vocation.*
Rooms: *2 singles.*
Facilities: *Garden, park, library.*
Spiritual Help: *Personal talks.*
Guests Admitted to: *Chapel, choir sometimes, work of the community.*
Meals: *Everyone eats together. Traditional food, with provision for vegetarian and special diets. Self-catering available.*
Special Activities: *None.*
Situation: *Very quiet, in the Vale of the White Horse, with unbroken views over Downs. Nearest shops 3 miles away.*
Maximum Stay: *By arrangement.*
Bookings: *By letter.*
Charges: *By donation.*
Access: *BR: to Oxford or Swindon. Bus: No. 66 from Oxford/Swindon. Car: via A420 – take turning signposted to Fernham and White Horse Hill.*

Freeland

**St Mary's Convent
Freeland
Oxon. OX7 2AJ**   Telephone: 0993 881225

Anglican

The Anglican Franciscan sisters live a traditional enclosed life of prayer, but all guests are able to share in their worship.   For non-retreatants the surrounding area is full of interest: Blenheim Palace, Woodstock, Combe, Stanton Harcourt and glorious Oxford itself are all at hand.   A few open retreats are held each year and there are conducted retreats for members of the Third Order of the Society of St Francis.   This is a popular place and guests make bookings up to a year in advance.

Open: *All year with occasional closed periods, usually mid-August. Receives men, women, young people, families, small groups and non-retreatants.*
Rooms: *11 singles of which 3 can be used as doubles.*
Facilities: *Chapel, guest-house oratory, garden, library, guest lounge and guest telephone. Children welcomed. Blind guests may bring guide dogs. Parish church near by.*
Spiritual Help: *Personal talks.*
Guests Admitted to: *Chapel, and encouraged to help in guest house and garden.*
Meals: *In the guest house. Mainly traditional food, with provision for vegetarians, if advance notice given. DIY for tea and coffee.*
Special Activities: *2 or 3 open retreats a year.*
Situation: *Quiet, in a village and surrounded by countryside.*
Maximum Stay: *10 days.*
Bookings: *By letter, or telephone between 6.00 and 7.00 p.m. only.*
Charges: *By donation.*
Access: *BR: to Oxford or Witney. Bus: No. 11 Oxford/Witney. Car: via A40.*

Oxford

**Carmelite Centre of Prayer and Retreats
nr. Youlbury
Boars Hill
Oxford OX1 5HB**   Telephone: 0865 730183

Roman Catholic

Boars Hill is an ideal location for this centre run by the Teresian Discalced Carmel Friars. The Centre, where a lot of new building has been going on so that it may offer even better facilities, stands in its own 17 acres of woodland. It aims to provide courses on prayer and spirituality, special attention being given to the teaching on prayer of the great Carmelite writers, such as St Teresa of Avila, St John of the Cross and St Teresa of Lisieux. Sometimes arrangements can be made for individuals who desire to experience a hermitage retreat. This will be discussed with you – but it is unlikely that a person with a busy lifestyle, going on a retreat for the first time, is really a suitable candidate for such a period of silent contemplation. There is an annual 'vocation' weekend open to all young men interested in the religious life and the Carmelites in particular.

Open: *All year except Christmas and New Year. Receives men, women, young people, families and groups.*
Rooms: *15 singles, 14 twin-bedded rooms.*
Facilities: *Chapel, garden, park, guest lounge with pay phone, book service.*
Spiritual Help: *Personal talks, meditation and directed study.*
Guests Admitted to: *Chapel.*
Meals: *Meals taken in the guest house, which also has DIY facilities. Traditional food, with provision for vegetarian and special diets.*
Special Activities: *Programme includes planned retreats. Send for brochure.*
Situation: *Very quiet, in the countryside.*
Maximum Stay: *10 days.*
Bookings: *By telephone but confirm by letter with a deposit.*
Charges: *£18.50 per person per day.*
Access: *BR: to Oxford (5 miles away), then by taxi. Car: via A34 – send for a map as route is a little complicated.*

Oxford

The Cherwell Centre
16 Norman Gardens
Oxford OX2 6QB   Telephone: 0865 52106

Roman Catholic

Open: *All year except August and over Christmas and Easter. Receives men, women, young people, groups and non-retreatants.*
Rooms: *10 singles, 10 doubles.*
Facilities: *Limited for disabled, conferences, garden, nearby park, guest lounge, TV and pay phone.*
Spiritual Help: *Spiritual direction and individually guided retreats on request. Many different groups use the residential and non-residential conference and retreat facilities.*
Guests Admitted to: *Chapel.*
Meals: *Everyone eats together. Good variety of food, with provison for vegetarian and special diets.*
Special Activities: *No special programme.*
Situation: *In the city – quiet, but rather busy during conferences.*
Maximum stay: *2 weeks*

Bookings: *By letter or telephone.*
Charges: *On request.*
Access: *BR: to Oxford. Buses: enquire at Oxford bus station. Car: any route to Oxford.*

Sutton Courtenay

The Abbey Community
The Abbey
Sutton Courtenay
nr. Abingdon
Oxon. OX14 4AF

Telephone: 0235 847401

Inter-faith

The aim of the community is to discover the universal truth of Christ within the particular issues of our own day, and it is engaged in projects ranging from the dynamics of unemployment to the complementary relationship of men and women working in the ministry. The programme of events is designed to encourage personal, social and ecological transformation. There are many courses on offer at the Abbey, including the study of inner sound; non-violence and the social order; Buddhists and Christians in social action; art and consciousness; spirituality and ecology; intuitive massage; and Shiatsu.

Open: *All visits by arrangement. Receives men, women, young people, groups – especially midweek. Gandhians welcomed.*
Rooms: *4 singles, 5 doubles, dormitories and camping for organised groups.*
Facilities: *Very limited for disabled, conferences, camping, park, library with Gandhi archive, craft centre, dining room, pay phone. Children welcomed if accompanied by adults. No pets.*
Spiritual Help: *None offered to individual guests, only given to groups at conferences.*
Guests Admitted to: *Meditation room.*
Meals: *All food is vegetarian, wholefood and organic where possible. Vegans can be accommodated by arrangement. Self-catering facilities.*
Special Activities: *Courses on crafts and sculpture. 'Green' lectures. Gandhi school of non-violence may be offered.*
Situation: *Surrounded by 4 acres of wooded grounds, the Abbey is archaeologically important because of the underlying Roman and Saxon remains. Location is quiet, in a village.*
Maximum Stay: *1 week.*
Bookings: *By letter.*
Charges: *£15 per day for a single room, full board.*
Access: *BR: to Didcot Parkway, 3 miles away. Bus: No. 32 from Oxford runs every half an hour. Car: via A34.*

Ellesmere

The Grange
Ellesmere
Shropshire SY12 9DE   Telephone: 0691 623495

Interfaith – New Age

Rooted in Christianity but open to all faiths, the Grange offers both traditional meditation study and a New Age approach, reflected in a range of courses from stress management to sacred dance. For older women there is a weekend to reflect, reassess and search for new personal potential within the security of a small group. Those who delight in nature may find on offer a course on how to link their concern for the environment with a life of prayer.

Open: *March to October inclusive. Receives men, women, young people, families, groups – non-retreatants only permitted during non-retreat periods.*
Rooms: *4 singles, 9 doubles, 2 three-bedded rooms. Most rooms have en-suite and tea/coffee-making facilities.*
Facilities: *Disabled, conferences, garden, pasture and woodland, small library, guest lounge, TV if required, guest telephone. Children welcome with parents or guardians. Pets possible.*
Spiritual Help: *Personal talks, meditation, yoga tuition, reflex therapy.*
Guests Admitted to: *Reasonably unrestricted access.*
Meals: *Everyone eats together. Wholefood (mainly vegetarian), with provision for special diets.*
Special Activities: *The aim of the courses is to promote international understanding and to explore the potential of women for healing and peace-making, especially in the second half of life.*
Situation: *Quiet, near a small town.*
Maximum Stay: *Unlimited.*
Bookings: *By letter or telephone.*
Charges: *Send for details. Bed and board may be earned by 4–5 hours' gardening a day.*
Access: *BR: to Shrewsbury, 17 miles away. Infrequent buses. Car: via A528 from Ellesmere.*

Shrewsbury

Hawkstone Hall
Weston
Shrewsbury
Shropshire SY4 5LG   Telephone: 063 084 242

Roman Catholic

Hawkstone Hall is a great pile of a country-house, whose rooms contain fine plasterwork and much decoration. There is a comfortable modern wing more suited to the scale of a personal retreat; but no less than five guest lounges should give you an idea of what to expect. If you are disabled, then forget it as there are stairs and more stairs. This is basically a centre for men and women who have been in the service of the Church for a long time and need a period of renewal, but individuals and groups are welcomed at other times.

Open: *All year. Receives men, women, young people, non-retreatants. Families and groups are received when no courses are in progress.*
Rooms: *64 singles, 1 double.*
Facilities: *Conferences, chapel, garden, park, library, guest lounges, TV and pay phone. Children welcome.*
Spiritual Help: *Groups attending between courses should bring their own chaplain.*
Guests Admitted to: *Reasonably unrestricted to all areas, including chapel, choir.*
Meals: *Everyone eats together. Traditional food, with provision for vegetarian and special diets.*
Special Activities: *Courses only.*
Situation: *Very quiet, in the countryside.*
Maximum Stay: *By arrangement.*
Bookings: *By letter.*
Charges: *By arrangement.*
Access: *There are no buses and BR stations are distant. Transport can be arranged on request, so do enquire. Car: via A41 from Whitchurch turning on to the A442.*

Whitchurch

Taraloka Buddhist Retreat Centre for Women
Cornhill Farm
Bettisfield
nr. Whitchurch
Shropshire SY12 2LV   Telephone: 094875 646

Buddhist

Situated peacefully on the plains of the Welsh borderlands, this Buddhist women's community has been going for over five years and acts as a focal point for women throughout the world from various walks of life. It provides inspiration, relaxation and affords a glimpse of new spiritual and personal vistas for all who come. The retreat centre is separate from the community house, but many of the facilities are shared, as well as meals. Workshops include meditation, music and movement, yoga, newcomers' meditation and a massage weekend. Teachers are well qualified both in Buddhist teaching and in their specialist subject, such as music.

Open: *Specific programme of retreats for women – no other guests received.*
Rooms: *Dormitories, each sleeping 22 women.*
Facilities: *Caravans accommodating 2–3.*
Spiritual Help: *Meditation and study. The programme teaches Buddhist meditation and study within the context of the Friends of the Western Buddhist order. Introductory events are also offered in addition to those only open to the more experienced.*
Guests Admitted to: *Shrine room.*
Meals: *Everyone eats together; all meals are vegetarian or vegan. Special diets catered for.*
Special Activities: *Planned events – see brochure.*
Situation: *Very quiet, in the countryside with beautiful country walks – near the Shropshire Union Canal.*
Maximum Stay: *By arrangement.*
Bookings: *By letter.*
Charges: *By arrangement.*
Access: *Map and details are provided with booking confirmation.*

STAFFORDSHIRE

Stone

Lichfield Diocesan Retreat & Conference Centre
Shallowford House
Norton Bridge
Stone
Staffs. ST16 ONZ   Telephone: 0785 760233

Anglican

Open: *All year. Receives men, women, families, groups and non-retreatants.*
Rooms: *15 singles, 10 doubles.*
Facilities: *Disabled, conferences, chapel, large garden, library, guest lounge, TV and pay phone. Children welcomed if accompanied by adults.*
Spiritual Help: *None outside programme events.*
Guests Admitted to: *Unrestricted access except to part of the grounds.*
Meals: *Everyone eats together. Traditional cooking, with provision for vegetarian and special diets if advanced warning given. Self-catering in the kitchen for drinks.*
Special Activities: *Planned programme of events. Send for brochure.*
Situation: *Quiet and in the countryside.*
Maximum Stay: *Friday to Sunday, or Monday to Friday.*
Bookings: *By letter or telephone.*
Charges: *Available on application.*
Access: *BR: to Norton Bridge. No buses.*

Leamington Spa

Offa House
Offchurch
Leamington Spa
War. CV33 9AS   Telephone: 0926 423309

Anglican

The Coventry Diocesan Retreat House and Conference Centre is situated in
an old Georgian vicarage, with a large garden. The house has been organised
in such a way that all visitors are helped to feel that this is their own 'special'
place, and the staff try to be as non-intrusive as possible.

Open: *All year. Receives men, women, young people, families, groups and*
non-retreatants.
Rooms: *16 singles, 8 doubles.*
Facilities: *Disabled, conferences, chapel, garden, library, bookstall, guest*
lounge, TV and pay phone. Children welcomed.
Spiritual Help: *Personal talks and the opportunity to join in events offered*
by other groups.
Guests Admitted to: *Chapel.*
Meals: *Everyone eats together. Meals are traditional, with a bias towards*
wholefood and provision for vegetarian and special diets.
Special Activities: *Planned programme of events. Send for brochure.*
Situation: *Quiet, in the village and countryside.*
Maximum Stay: *Unlimited.*
Bookings: *By letter or telephone.*
Charges: *£6 per person per night for guests applying individually.*
Access: *Rail, bus, car and airport links are all excellent.*

Solihull

Monastery of Poor Clares
Baddesley Clinton
Knowle
Solihull
War. B93 0DE

Roman Catholic

Open: *All year – all are welcome.*
Rooms: *4 singles, plus rooms with bunk beds.*
Facilities: *Camping, garden and guest lounge. Children welcome.*
Spiritual Help: *Some personal talks can be arranged.*
Guests Admitted to: *Chapel, choir, seating for guests outside enclosed*
area.

Meals: *Self-catering only. Bread and milk can be provided.*
Special Activities: *No planned programme, but there is an atmosphere of peace and simplicity.*
Situation: *Very quiet, in the village and countryside.*
Maximum Stay: *1 week.*
Bookings: *By letter and giving references.*
Charges: *No fixed charge, but a donation to cover basic costs would be appreciated.*
Access: *Enquire when you write.*

' To rejoice at another person's joy is like being in heaven'
– Meister Eckhart

Northern England

Chester

Chester Diocesan Retreat House
11 Abbey Square
Chester
Cheshire CH1 2HU   Telephone: 0244 321801

Anglican

The sisters lead retreats and quiet days when asked. In addition there are
individually guided retreats and Myers-Briggs workshops.

Open: *Most of the year apart from the beginning of August. Receives men,*
women, groups and non-retreatants.
Rooms: *25 singles, 2 doubles.*
Facilities: *Garden, library, guest lounge and guest telephone.*
Spiritual Help: *Personal talks, meditation and directed study as required.*
Guests Admitted to: *Unrestricted access except to the sisters' quarters.*
Meals: *Everyone eats together. Traditional food – vegetarians are catered*
for and there is limited provision for special diets (by arrangement).
Special Activities: *Planned programme of events, with open retreats held*
about once a month.
Situation: *In the city square, by the cathedral.*
Maximum Stay: *1 week.*
Bookings: *By telephone but confirm by letter.*
Charges: *£16 per person per 24 hours.*
Access: *By rail, bus or car to Chester.*

Crewe

Oblate Retreat Centre
Wistaston Hall
89 Broughton Lane
Crewe
Cheshire CW2 8JS   Telephone: 0270 68653

Roman Catholic – Ecumenical

This is a 200-year old country-house, set in four acres of peaceful countryside.
Much effort goes into making guests feel comfortable, and cared for, and there
is professional catering for meals.

Open: *All year except August. Receives men, women, young people,*
families, groups and non-retreatants.
Rooms: *22 twin-bedded rooms.*
Facilities: *Disabled, conferences, large garden, library, guest lounge, TV*
and pay phone. Children welcomed.

Spiritual Help: *Personal talks, group sharing, meditation, directed study.*
Guests Admitted to: *Unrestricted access to all areas, including chapel.*
Meals: *Everyone eats together. Traditional wholefood, with provision for vegetarian and special diets.*
Special Activities: *Planned programme of events. Send for brochure.*
Situation: *Very quiet, in the village and countryside.*
Maximum Stay: *By arrangement.*
Bookings: *By letter or telephone.*
Charges: *Send for details.*
Access: *BR: to Crewe, then 5 minutes by taxi to Centre. Car: via M6.*

Malpas

St Joseph's Retreat & Conference Centre
Tilston Road
Malpas
Cheshire SY14 7DD   Telephone: 0948 860416

Roman Catholic

Open: *All year. Receives men, women, groups and non-retreatants.*
Rooms: *Singles and doubles are available.*
Facilities: *Conferences, garden, library, guest lounge, TV and pay phone.*
Spiritual Help: *Personal talks, group sharing, meditation and directed study.*
Guests Admitted to: *Chapel*
Meals: *Taken in the dining room. Traditional food, with provision for vegetarian and special diets.*
Special Activities: *Send for details.*
Situation: *Very quiet.*
Maximum Stay: *By arrangement.*
Bookings: *By letter or telephone.*
Charges: *Tariff on request.*
Access: *By car is best.*

Ambleside

Carlisle Diocesan Retreat & Conference Centre
Rydal Hall
Ambleside
Cumbria LA22 9LX   Telephone: 05394 32050

Anglican – Ecumenical

There is a relaxed atmosphere in this big Georgian house set in the heart of
the Lake District, in a 30-acre estate with waterfalls and formal gardens. It
is mainly used by groups, but individuals are welcomed and there is no
pressure to join in any activities that may be taking place.

Open: *All year except December. Receives men, women, young people,
families, groups and non-retreatants.*
Rooms: *10 single, 15 twin-bedded, plus a dormitory with bunks for 36, and
camping facilities for youth groups.*
Facilities: *Disabled, chair lift, conferences, garden, library, guest lounge,
TV and pay phone. Children welcome.*
Spiritual Help: *Personal talks, meditation and an opportunity to share the
community life (worship, gardening, etc.).*
Guests Admitted to: *Unrestricted access to all areas, including chapel,
work of the community.*
Meals: *Everyone eats together. Traditional food, with provision for veg-
etarian and special diets. Self-catering facilities in youth centre.*
Special Activities: *Planned programme of events. Send for the brochure.*
Situation: *Quiet, in the village and countryside.*
Maximum Stay: *2 weeks.*
Bookings: *By letter or telephone.*
Charges: *£21.85 per person per 24 hours, full board.*
Access: *BR: to Windermere. Bus: Ambleside. Car: via M6, Exit 40 from
north, Exit 36 from south, then A591.*

Penrith

The Fellowship of Healing
Lattendales
Penrith
Cumbria CA11 OUE   Telephone: 085 33 229

Quaker

The Fellowship is run in accordance with the principles of the Society of
Friends (Quakers) but is open to all, irrespective of religious beliefs. The
house is situated on the edge of Lakeland National Park, with easy access to
the Lake District, Scotland and the North Pennines.

Open: *April to October, and to groups for winter weekends. Receives men, women, groups and non-retreatants.*
Rooms: *5 singles, 5 doubles, plus a self-catering flat.*
Facilities: *Conferences, garden, guest lounge and pay phone. No pets.*
Spiritual Help: *Personal talks, group sharing, meditation.*
Guests Admitted to: *Unrestricted access.*
Meals: *Taken in the guest house. Traditional food, with provision for vegetarian and special diets. Self-catering in the flat.*
Special Activities: *Planned programme of events. Send for brochure.*
Situation: *Quiet, in the village and countryside.*
Maximum Stay: *3 weeks.*
Bookings: *By letter or telephone.*
Charges: *Available on application.*
Access: *By rail, bus or car. See brochure.*

DURHAM

Durham

St Joseph's House of Prayer
Burn Hall
Durham DH1 3SR   Telephone: 091 378 2207

Roman Catholic

Silence is observed throughout the day except at evening meal. Attractive grounds around the house make for quiet walks, relaxation and reflection. Near by there are woodlands and a little river.

Open: *All year except August and Christmas season. Receives men, women, young people.*
Rooms: *8 singles.*
Facilities: *Chapel, garden, park, library, direct-dialling pay phone.*
Spiritual Help: *Personal talks, meditation.*
Guests Admitted to: *Unrestricted access.*
Meals: *Everyone eats together. Traditional wholefood, with provision for vegetarian and special diets.*
Special Activities: *Bible-sharing daily, prayer of the Church in common. Holy hour once a week. Daily Mass with singing and full liturgy. Send for the brochure.*
Situation: *Very quiet, prayerful atmosphere at all times. Silence observed throughout the day except evening meal. Quiet music at mealtimes.*
Maximum Stay: *By arrangement.*
Bookings: *By letter or telephone.*
Charges: *£15 per person per day for directed retreats, £13 for non-directed ones.*

Access: *Durham station 3 miles away. Excellent bus service. Car: via A167, south of Durham.*

HUMBERSIDE

Great Driffield

Lamplugh House
Thwing
Great Driffield
Humberside YO25 ODY   Telephone: 026 287 282

Interdenominational

Lamplugh House is a centre for spiritual renewal set in the countryside not far from the Yorkshire coastal resorts. The programme ranges from a seminar day for the clergy, parish-group weekends, and 'relax-and-unwind' breaks to a special week's holiday for the over-60s.

Open: *All year except Christmas. Receives men, women, young people, families, groups and non-retreatants.*
Rooms: *3 singles, 16 doubles, plus a dormitory.*
Facilities: *Conferences, garden, guest lounge and pay phone. Children welcomed.*
Spiritual Help: *Personal talks, group sharing.*
Guests Admitted to: *Unrestricted access.*
Meals: *Everyone eats together. Traditional food, with provision for vegetarian and special diets.*
Special Activities: *Planned programme of events. Send for the brochure.*
Situation: *Very quiet and in the countryside.*
Maximum Stay: *Unlimited.*
Bookings: *By telephone or letter.*
Charges: *Send for leaflet.*
Access: *BR to Great Driffield, or by car.*

Pocklington

Madhyamaka Buddhist Centre
Kilnwick Percy Hall
Pocklington
Humberside YO4 2UF   Telephone: 0759 304832

Buddhist

The Centre is located in a very large country mansion. Its aim is to preserve and promote the teachings and traditions of Tibetan Buddhism. There are group discussions, weekend and day courses throughout the year, plus a nine-day summer school.

Open: *All year. Receives men, women, young people, families, groups and non-retreatants.*
Rooms: *4 singles, 4 doubles, plus dormitories.*
Facilities: *Shrine room, camping, garden, library and pay phone. Children welcomed.*
Spiritual Help: *Personal talks, meditation, directed study.*
Guests Admitted to: *Unrestricted access. Guests may use shrine room and share the work of the community.*
Meals: *Everyone eats together and there are DIY facilities. The food is vegetarian.*
Special Activities: *There is a special programme. Send for brochure.*
Situation: *In the countryside.*
Maximum Stay: *Unlimited.*
Bookings: *By letter or telephone.*
Charges: *See the brochure.*
Access: *Please ask for directions when you are booking.*

LANCASHIRE

Blackburn

Whalley Abbey
Blackburn Diocesan Conference & Retreat Centre
Whalley
Blackburn
Lancs. BB6 9SS   Telephone: 0254 822268

Anglican

Here is a great old former Cistercian abbey, steeped in history, which attracts many visitors every year. The programme of events includes holidays for walking and for senior citizens, a craft fair, and an open retreat on calligraphy and prayer. A place perhaps more for an active retreat than a meditative one.

Open: *All year except Christmas and New Year. Receives men, women, young people, groups and non-retreatants.*
Rooms: *19 bedrooms, sleeping 40 in total.*
Facilities: *Disabled, chair lift, conferences, garden, library, guest lounge, TV and pay phone. Children welcome.*
Spiritual Help: *Personal talks, group sharing, meditation, directed retreats and resident chaplain.*
Guests Admitted to: *Unrestricted access to all areas, including chapel.*

Meals: *Everyone eats together. Traditional food, with provision for vegetarian and special diets on request.*
Special Activities: *Walking and painting holidays. Send for the brochure.*
Situation: *Quiet and peaceful environment, with beautiful tranquil gardens.*
Maximum Stay: *By arrangement.*
Bookings: *By letter.*
Charges: *Various – ask for tariff.*
Access: *BR: to Blackburn. Bus: to Whalley. Car: via A59 to Whalley.*

Blackpool

Sisters of Marie Reparatrice
183 Newton Drive
Blackpool
Lancs. FY3 8NU   Telephone: 0253 31549

Roman Catholic

Open: *All year except Christmas and New Year. Receives men, women, groups and non-retreatants.*
Rooms: *8 singles.*
Facilities: *Conferences, garden, guest lounge, TV and pay phone.*
Spiritual Help: *Personal talks, meditation, directed retreats – especially Ignation.*
Guests Admitted to: *Chapel, choir, work of the community.*
Meals: *Taken in the guest house. Traditional food, with provision for vegetarian and special diets by prior arrangement.*
Special Activities: *No planned programme of events.*
Situation: *Quiet, near shops, a park and the sea.*
Maximum Stay: *2 weeks.*
Bookings: *By letter.*
Charges: *£15 per person per day, £17 including directed retreat.*
Access: *BR: to Blackpool North, then by taxi. Bus: No. 10. Car: to Blackpool.*

Carnforth

Monastery of Our Lady of Hyning
Warton
Carnforth
Lancs. LA5 9SE   Telephone: 0526 732684

Roman Catholic – Ecumenical/Inter-faith

Particularly suitable for private retreats, the Monastery is set in private grounds. In some rooms cheerful fires greet you in winter, while there is a peaceful and welcoming atmosphere everywhere. A barn has been converted into a church where guests may join the sisters in their daily schedule of prayer.

Open: *All year except for mid-July to late August. Receives men, women, young people from 6th form upwards, groups and non-retreatants.*
Rooms: *20 rooms, some single – 35 beds in all.*
Facilities: *Disabled, loop system for the deaf in the chapel and dining-room, conference room, garden, pasture land, library, guest telephone and laundry.*
Spiritual Help: *Personal talks, limited directed study, meditation.*
Guests Admitted to: *Chapel, choir, occasional community work.*
Meals: *Large dining-room and small dining-room serving mainly traditional food. Vegetarian and special diets catered for.*
Special Activities: *Guests organise their own activities.*
Situation: *Quiet and in the countryside.*
Maximum Stay: *Normally a fortnight.*
Bookings: *By telephone or write to the Guestmistress.*
Charges: *£16 per person per weekday, £18 per day at weekends. Students pay two-thirds. Rates for day groups by arrangement.*
Access: *BR: to Carnforth. Some local buses pass the gate. Car: via M6, Exit 35, and A6.*

LINCOLNSHIRE

Lincoln

Edward King House
The Old Palace
Lincoln LN2 1PU   Telephone: 0522 528778

Ecumenical

Once the palace of the Bishops of London, this retreat house stands in the shadow of one of England's greatest cathedrals. A spirituality programme is available as well as personal talks.

Open: *All year except Christmas. Receives men, women, young people, groups and non-retreatants.*
Rooms: *5 singles, 12 doubles.*
Facilities: *Conferences, garden, library, guest lounge, TV and pay phone. Children welcomed.*
Spiritual Help: *Personal talks, meditation.*
Guests Admitted to: *Unrestricted access, except to kitchens and chapel.*
Meals: *Everyone eats together. Traditional food, with provision for vegetarian and special diets.*

Special Activities: *There is a spirituality programme for the year. Send for brochure.*
Situation: *In the city, close to the cathedral and most of the tourist attractions of Lincoln.*
Maximum Stay: *By arrangement.*
Bookings: *By letter or telephone.*
Charges: *£15. 50 B&B, £23 per day for private retreats, £30 full board for groups.*
Access: *By public transport or car.*

MANCHESTER

The Cenacle Retreat House
28 Alexandra Road South,
Manchester M16 8HU   Telephone: 061-226 1241

Roman Catholic

Open: *All year except Christmas. Receives men, women, young people and groups.*
Rooms: *6 singles, 4 doubles.*
Facilities: *Small conferences, garden, library, guest lounge and pay phone.*
Spiritual Help: *Personal talks, group sharing and meditation. Individually guided retreats.*
Guests Admitted to: *Chapel.*
Meals: *Everyone eats together. Traditional food, with provision for vegetarian and special diets.*
Special Activities: *No planned programme or brochure.*
Situation: *Quiet, but in the city.*
Maximum Stay: *Depends on length of retreat.*
Bookings: *By letter with deposit and reference if first-timer.*
Charges: *£18 per person per day.*
Access: *By rail, bus or car – directions supplied.*

'Peace does not dwell in outward things, but within the soul' – Fenelon

Liverpool

The Cenacle
7 Lance Lane
Wavertree
Liverpool L15 6TW   Telephone: 051-722 2271

Roman Catholic

Open: *All year, except 18 December to 3 January. Open only for day re-treats, receiving men, women, young people, groups.*
Facilities: *Disabled, conferences, garden, library, guest lounge, pay phone.*
Spiritual Help: *One-day retreats, personal talks, meditation, directed study and spiritual direction.*
Guests Admitted to: *Chapel.*
Meals: *Very plain.*
Special Activities: *Some planned events.*
Situation: *Quiet, in town.*
Maximum Stay: *One day.*
Bookings: *By letter.*
Charges: *By arrangement.*
Access: *BR: to Lime St station. Buses: Nos. 39, 54, 78, 79. Car: via M62.*

Liverpool

Monastery of Poor Clares
Green Lane
Liverpool L18 2ES   Telephone: 051-722 3059

Roman Catholic

Open: *From 1 May to 30 September. Receives women, girls over 17 and non-retreatant women.*
Rooms: *6 singles, 1 double.*
Facilities: *Small garden, small lounge.*
Spiritual Help: *Talks with Mother Abbess.*
Guests Admitted to: *Chapel.*
Meals: *Midday meal only, serving traditional food; self-catering for all other meals.*
Special Activities: *No planned programme of events.*
Situation: *Quiet but in the city.*
Maximum Stay: *1 week.*
Bookings: *By telephone but must confirm by letter.*
Charges: *£10 per person per day but payment made according to means in special circumstances.*
Access: *BR: to Lime St station. Bus: No. 78.*

New Brighton

Faith House
Yoga and Natural Health Centre
155 Victoria Road
New Brighton
Merseyside L45 9LB   Telephone: 051-639 9402

New Age

At Faith House yoga combines with fat-reducing techniques like Slendertone
– not to mention facials – but then why not? It is certainly pleasant to be
physically pampered as well as spiritually rested. Those not wishing to
receive beauty treatments can learn yoga, meditation and undergo reflexology.
By London standards, the charges are low. There are dance and exercise
classes in a small gym. For some this will seem a retreat, for others not at all,
as they will find it too much part of the mainstream of our contemporary
culture. Be prepared for New Brighton – a rather damp and heavily Victorian
town that has had its day.

Open: *All year. Receives men, women and groups.*
Rooms: *A good number of singles and doubles are available as it is a large,
reconditioned Victorian building.*
Facilities: *Gym, guest lounge, library, TV and pay phone. No pets and no
smoking.*
Spiritual Help: *Yoga, meditation in guided classes, practical advice on
stress management, group sharing and some personal talks.*
Guests Admitted to: *Unrestricted access.*
Meals: *Taken in large dining-room. Traditional food, special diets by
arrangement.*
Special Activities: *Send for brochure.*
Situation: *Old seaside town.*
Maximum Stay: *By arrangement.*
Bookings: *By telephone then letter.*
Charges: *Please enquire as these can vary from £29 per person per day, to
£70 per weekend. Ask what is included in price before booking.*
Access: *BR: to New Brighton. Bus: National Express to Liverpool, then
local bus. Car: to New Brighton.*

Rainhill

Loyola Hall Spirituality Centre
Warrington Road
Rainhill
Prescot
Merseyside L35 6NZ   Telephone: 051-426 4137

Roman Catholic – Ecumenical

This is a Jesuit retreat centre – and that usually means some hard work on prayer, personal introspection, and spiritual growth if you want to undertake an individually guided retreat. In addition to this form of retreat, there are preached ones and special courses for those who work with young adults. The Centre itself is set in a park and consists of a combination of older buildings and functional new ones.

Open: *All year except Christmas week. Receives men, women, young people, families for day events, groups and occasionally non-retreatants.*
Rooms: *45 single plus dormitories.*
Facilities: *Limited for disabled, but lift and chair lift provided, conferences, park, library, guest lounge, TV and video for conferences, pay phone. Children permitted by arrangement,*
Spiritual Help: *Personal talks, group sharing, meditation, directed study. Individually guided retreats in the tradition of St Ignatius Loyola. Courses on spiritual direction, prayer guidance.*
Guests Admitted to: *Unrestricted access.*
Meals: *Eaten in the guest house. Varied, traditional food, with provision for vegetarian and special diets.*
Special Activities: *Planned programme of events, including conferences, courses on spiritual direction, lecture programme, parish retreats. Send for brochure.*
Situation: *In the village.*
Maximum Stay: *30 days.*
Bookings: *By letter or telephone*
Charges: *£21 per person per day, reduced rates for students and unwaged.*
Access: *For rail and bus, see the programme. Car: via M62, Exit 7 to Prescot.*

' There is no wealth but life' – John Ruskin

Alnwick

Alnmouth Friary
Alnmouth
Alnwick
Northd. NE66 3NJ   Telephone: 0665 830213

Anglican

The Society of St Francis Friars offers support and accommodation for those who do not necessarily need a retreat of a religious nature but who are desperate for a quiet break. However, they are unable to deal with those who are suffering from mental instability or are heavily dependent on drugs or alcohol. The Friary is situated on the coastline, with beautiful Northumberland scenery and the Scottish borderlands near by.

Open: *All year except for about 4–5 weeks. Receives men, women, young people, families, groups and non-retreatants.*
Rooms: *4 singles, 5 doubles.*
Facilities: *Lift for the disabled, conferences, camping by arrangement, garden, library, TV, guest lounge and pay phone. Children welcome.*
Spiritual Help: *Personal talks, group sharing as part of guided weekends, meditation and directed study if needed.*
Guests Admitted to: *Chapel, work of the community.*
Meals: *Everyone eats together. Traditional food, with provision for vegetarian and special diets.*
Special Activities: *Planned programme of events. Send for brochure.*
Situation: *Rather busy, but on the coast, edge of village, close to countryside.*
Maximum Stay: *Normally 1 week.*
Bookings: *By letter.*
Charges: *No fixed charge – about £10 per person per day.*
Access: *BR: to Alnmouth, 1 mile away. Bus: from Alnmouth to the Friary. Car: via A1.*

Belsay

Harnham Buddhist Monastery
Harnham
Belsay
Northd. NE20 OHF   Telephone: 0661 881612

Buddhist

This is a Thai monastery where visitors are always welcome but accommodation is only available by prior arrangement. The monks teach at various Buddhist groups and visit schools and prisons. Being a monastic community, the sexes are segregated except for families with small children. If you can't make it to the monastery but feel you might like to attend one of their study or meditation groups elsewhere, then write and ask for information about them.

Open: *All year except January, February and September. Receives men, women, young people, groups and families.*
Rooms: *1 double and 2 dormitories.*
Facilities: *Library, guest lounge and pay phone. Limited number of children are welcome.*
Spiritual Help: *Personal talks, group sharing, meditation and directed study.*
Guests Admitted to: *Shrine room and work of the community. The monastic quarters are not open to guests.*
Meals: *Everyone eats together. Wholefood – vegetarians catered for, but no provision for special diets.*
Special Activities: *There is a calendar published 3 times a year about forthcoming events, ceremonies and retreats. One of the requirements for staying is the willingness to follow the schedule and live by the 8 precepts. (See information for guests in the brochure.)*
Situation: *Very quiet, in the countryside.*
Maximum Stay: *No fixed time.*
Bookings: *By letter or telephone.*
Charges: *By donation.*
Access: *By bus or car – directions and map in brochure.*

Berwick on Tweed

Marygate House
Holy Island
Berwick on Tweed
Northd. TD15 2SD   Telephone: 0289 89246

Ecumenical

Marygate House is situated on an island famous in Christian history and even today a place of pilgrimage and tourism. The centre is very quiet in winter but busy and popular in the summer.

Open: *All year except Christmas and New Year. Receives men, women, young people, families and groups.*
Rooms: *4 singles, 4 doubles, plus dormitories.*
Facilities: *Conferences, garden, library, guest lounge and pay phone. Children and pets welcomed.*
Spiritual Help: *Possible personal talks, meditation and directed study.*
Guests Admitted to: *Unrestricted access to all areas, including chapel of silence.*
Meals: *Everyone eats together. Mostly simple, traditional food with*

provision for vegetarian and special diets. Facilities for silent meals, which are taken separately. No self-catering.
Special Activities: *No planned programme of events.*
Situation: *Very quiet in winter, rather busy in summer.*
Maximum Stay: *2 weeks.*
Bookings: *By letter or telephone.*
Charges: *Approximately £12 per person per day.*
Access: *By rail or bus is possible but by car is best. Enquire when you book.*

Hexham

Throssel Hole Priory
Carrshield
Hexham
Northd. NE47 8AL   Telephone: 0434 345204

Buddhist

Since the time of Buddha many schools of Buddhism have developed. This monastery and centre of the Soto Zen School of Buddhism practises Serene Meditation. A variety of services for lay Buddhists is available, including naming ceremonies for children; cemetery plot and memorial services; and spiritual counselling by letter or telephone. There is a quarterly journal and a mail-order service offering books, taped lectures, meditation benches and cushions. Priests run retreats and make public talks outside the monastery. There is a sub-priory in Reading and about 30 affiliated Serene Meditation groups around the country.

Open: *All year except for periods in May and December. Receives men and women over 18 years. Families only received on specific weekends. Group educational visits from schools and colleges, by arrangement. Non-retreatants taken for tours of the monastery and may join in ceremony on the first Sunday of the month.*
Rooms: *Dormitory sleeps 30 – sexes are separated.*
Facilities: *Garden, park for retreatants, library, guest lounge. Children welcome at the ceremony on the first Sunday of the month.*
Spiritual Help: *Classes led by senior monk – private spiritual guidance on request. Full instruction given in meditation. Guidance is also given for private study/reflection.*
Guests Admitted to: *The ceremony hall, lay common-room and community work in most areas.*
Meals: *Taken together – vegetarian food.*
Special Activities: *By arrangement, with a special programme. Send for the brochure.*
Situation: *In the countryside.*
Maximum Stay: *3 months – longer by arrangement.*
Bookings: *Application form.*

Charges: *By donation.*
Access: *BR: from Newcastle, or Carlisle to Hexham. Bus: from Newcastle to Hexham and Allendale. Car: via M6 or A1 to Bishop Auckland.*

YORKSHIRE (EAST)

Doncaster

Pilgrim House
1 Highfield Road
Bawtry
Doncaster
E. Yorks. DN10 6QN   Telephone: 0302 710587

Anglican

A large bungalow owned and run by a retired Anglican deaconess who is pleased to help with spiritual guidance and directed study. There is a small chapel, a study room and a pleasant garden.

Open: *All year. Receives men, women, young people, groups, religious, non-retreatants, but no families.*
Rooms: *4 singles, 3 doubles.*
Facilities: *Disabled, conferences, chapel, shrine room, garden, library, guest lounge and TV.*
Spiritual Help: *Personal talks, group sharing, meditation, directed study.*
Guests Admitted to: *Unrestricted access.*
Meals: *Everyone eats together or alone, as they prefer. Traditional food and vegetarians catered for.*
Special Activities: *Only a few – ask when you write.*
Situation: *Quiet, in a small town.*
Maximum Stay: *6 weeks.*
Bookings: *By letter or telephone.*
Charges: *Send for details.*
Access: *BR: to Doncaster. Bus: to Bawtry – bungalow is 10 minutes' walk from centre.*

Sheffield

Whirlow Grange Diocesan Conference Centre
Eccleshall Road South
Sheffield S11 9PZ   Telephone: 0742 363173

Anglican

The Centre occupies a grey-stone house on a rise on the outskirts of Sheffield, near Peak District beauty spots. The place is rather institutional, but it has comfortable rooms and facilities. There are healing seminars, sacred-dance group weekends and Franciscan directed retreats.

Open: *All year except Christmas and New Year. Receives men, women, young people, families, groups and non-retreatants.*
Rooms: *19 singles, 10 twin-bedded rooms, dormitories. A few caravans are available.*
Facilities: *Disabled, conferences, garden, nearby park, library, guest lounge, TV and pay phone.*
Spiritual Help: *Personal talks, group sharing, occasional meditation and directed study.*
Guests Admitted to: *Unrestricted access to all areas, including chapel.*
Meals: *Everyone eats together. Good home-cooking, with provision for vegetarian and special diets.*
Special Activities: *Planned programme of events. Send for brochure.*
Situation: *Quiet and on the outskirts of the city. Peak District National Park within easy reach.*
Maximum Stay: *Any time within reason.*
Bookings: *By letter or telephone.*
Charges: *Send for details.*
Access: *By rail, bus or car (via A625).*

YORKSHIRE (NORTH)

Ampleforth

Ampleforth Abbey
Ampleforth
N. Yorks. YO6 4EN   Telephone: 04393 225 (Monastery)
                                            04393 440 (The Grange)
                                            04393 405 (Redcar Farm)
Roman Catholic

The facilities at this large and busy monastery include single rooms for men guests. In addition there is the Grange, a large guest-house for men, and Redcar Farm – about three miles away – which offers a barn and a camping site, particularly suitable for young people. The Abbey is a good place to stay for personal study and reflection within the overall setting of a monastic community.

Open: *All year except July to mid-August and over Christmas and New Year. The Grange is closed during Easter week. Receives men and women.*
Rooms: *10 singles for men in the monastery; 16 singles, 5 doubles in the Grange; barn and camping at Redcar Farm.*
Facilities: *Church, guest lounge, library, bookstall, garden, plenty of places to walk.*
Spiritual Help: *No planned programme, but ask when you book.*
Guests Admitted to: *Abbey church, monastery grounds.*
Meals: *Served in refectory for those staying in monastery; food also served at the Grange, with DIY for drinks. Self-service at Redcar Farm.*
Special Activities: *None.*
Situation: *Quiet, in the countryside.*
Maximum Stay: *By arrangement.*
Bookings: *By letter to the Warden at the Grange or to the Guestmaster at the monastery.*
Charges: *Monastery by donation, Grange on application.*
Access: *BR and coach: to York, 23 miles away. Bus: ask about local public transport when you book. Car: via B1363 from York.*

Hovingham

Church House
Scackleton
Hovingham
N. Yorks. YO6 4NB   Telephone: 0653 628474

New Age – Non-religious

Attached to the main farmhouse is an attractive cottage, modernised but with some features of a traditional Yorkshire cottage. Yoga and spinning instruction are available. The owner has been using organic-gardening methods on her smallholding for several years.

Open: *All year. Receives men, women, families and groups up to 5.*
Rooms: *2 singles, 1 double.*
Facilities: *Garden, TV. Children and pets welcomed.*
Spiritual Help: *Meditation, yoga, asana, pranayama.*
Guests Admitted to: *All areas.*
Meals: *Wholefood, with provision for vegetarian and special diets.*
Special Activities: *Yoga, spinning and organic-gardening instruction.*
Situation: *Quiet, in a village in the countryside.*
Maximum Stay: *By arrangement.*
Bookings: *By telephone or letter.*

Charges: *Send for details.*
Access: *By car to York, or will collect from York or Malton stations.*

Scarborough

Wydale Hall
Brompton by Sawdon
Scarborough
N. Yorks. YO13 9DG   Telephone: 0723 85270

Interdenominational

Open: *All year. Receives men, women, young people, families, groups and non-retreatants.*
Rooms: *10 singles, 16 doubles, plus family rooms.*
Facilities: *Conferences, chapel, garden, library, guest lounge, bar, bookstall, TV and guest pay phone. Children welcome.*
Spiritual Help: *Retreat groups should bring their own conductor.*
Guests Admitted to: *Unrestricted access to all areas, including chapel.*
Meals: *Everyone eats together. Traditional food, with provision for vegetarian and special diets.*
Special Activities: *No planned programme of events.*
Situation: *Quiet and in the countryside. Old house with formal terraces at the front. When guests are keeping silent, the staff endeavour to remain as quiet as possible and during meals only appear to clear and serve – guests' ease and comfort is the main priority.*
Maximum Stay: *1 week.*
Bookings: *By letter or telephone.*
Charges: *Send for details.*
Access: *BR: to Scarborough. Buses: from Scarborough. Car: Wydale Hall is 1 mile north of A170.*

Skipton

Parcevall Hall
Appletreewick
Skipton
N. Yorks. BD23 6DG   Telephone: 075672 213

Anglican – Ecumenical

This is an Elizabethan manor-house whose interior is filled with oak and atmosphere. Legends and history abound, and the nine acres of garden are said to have been admired by the late Queen Mary. A traditional place for either a private retreat or participation in the programme of events.

Open: *All year. Receives men, women, groups, non-retreatants, sometimes young people and families.*
Rooms: *5 singles, 10 doubles.*
Facilities: *Disabled, conferences, garden, library, guest lounge, TV and pay phone.*
Spiritual Help: *Retreat guidance by arrangement.*
Guests Admitted to: *Chapel, garden.*
Meals: *Everyone eats together. Traditional food, with provision for vegetarian and special diets.*
Special Activities: *Programme of events. Send for brochure.*
Situation: *Very quiet, in the countryside.*
Maximum Stay: *1 week.*
Bookings: *By letter.*
Charges: *See brochure.*
Access: *By car. Not accessible by public transport.*

Tadcaster

Hazlewood Castle
Tadcaster
N. Yorks. LS24 9NJ   Telephone: 0937 832738

Roman Catholic

Hazlewood Castle, formerly the home of the Vavasour family for over 800 years, is a bit forbidding, but the guest house in a converted stable-block is very comfortable. Situated in 70 acres of woodland, it is ideal for peaceful walks and reflection. The Carmelite Friars offer a varied programme of events and workshops, including preached retreats, Christian Zen meditation, personally directed sessions to develop your spirituality, and a course on lifestyle to give young adults the experience of a variety of prayer forms.

Open: *All year except Christmas and New Year. Receives men, women, young people, families with children, groups, and non- retreatants.*
Rooms: *16 singles, 9 doubles and 6 rooms with 3 beds.*
Facilities: *Very limited for disabled, conferences, garden, park, library, guest lounge, TV and pay phone.*
Spiritual Help: *Personal talks, group sharing, meditation and directed study.*
Guests Admitted to: *Chapel, and work of the community.*
Meals: *Everyone eats together. Traditional food, with provision for vegetarian and special diets.*
Special Activities: *Programme with planned events. Send for brochure.*
Situation: *Surrounded by woodland.*
Maximum Stay: *By arrangement.*
Bookings: *By letter.*
Charges: *By arrangement.*

Access: *BR: to Leeds or York. Bus: No. 843 from York. Car: via A1, midway between Leeds and York on the A64.*

Thirsk

Holy Rood Convent
10 Sowerby Road
Thirsk
N. Yorks. TO7 1HX   Telephone: 0845 522580

Ecumenical

When you go to this convent, you will be involved in the daily rhythm of prayer and worship, as guests are expected to join the community in the Divine Office in chapel and in the Eucharist, which is celebrated daily either there or in the local church.

Open: *All year except Christmas, Easter and mid-September. Receives men and women.*
Rooms: *2 singles.*
Facilities: *Garden, library and guest lounge.*
Spiritual Help: *Personal talks.*
Guests Admitted to: *Chapel.*
Meals: *Everyone eats together. Plain cooking, DIY for tea and coffee.*
Special Activities: *No planned programme.*
Situation: *Quiet and in the village.*
Maximum Stay: *1 week.*
Bookings: *By letter to Guest Sister.*
Charges: *To cover costs – please enquire when booking.*
Access: *BR: to Thirsk $1^1/_2$ miles away. Bus: to Thirsk, then 10 - minute walk. Car: via A61 to B1448, or A19 and A168.*

Whitby

St Oswald's Pastoral Centre
Woodlands Drive
Sleights
nr. Whitby
N. Yorks. YO21 1RY   Telephone: 0947 810496

Anglican

Open: *All year except Christmas and August. Receives men, women, young people, families, groups and non-retreatants.*
Rooms: *5 singles, 2 doubles, plus a hermitage.*
Facilities: *Garden, library, guest lounge, TV and guest telephone.*

Spiritual Help: *Personal talks, meditation if needed. Leaders are available for group retreats.*
Guests Admitted to: *Unrestricted access except to community quarters.*
Meals: *Everyone eats together. Traditional food, with provision for vegetarian and special diets. Self-catering available.*
Special Activities: *Planned programme of events. Send for the brochure.*
Situation: *Very quiet, in the countryside near to the moors.*
Maximum Stay: *Normally 10 days.*
Bookings: *By letter or telephone.*
Charges: *£15 per person per day suggested.*
Access: *By car is best.*

York

St Bede's Monastery
23 Blossom Street
York YO2 2AQ   Telephone: 0904 610443

Roman Catholic

St Bede's was founded in 1987 as a joint venture by the Middlesborough Diocese and the Ampleforth monks. It is a base for ecumenical work right in the heart of York and next door to Bar Convent Museum and Youth Centre. All the rooms are modern in style with practical furnishings. The programme is that of a pastoral centre and so there are events and talks throughout most of the year.

Open: *All year except Christmas. Receives men only.*
Rooms: *4 singles.*
Facilities: *Chapel, non-residential conferences, garden, TV, bookstall.*
Spiritual Help: *Personal talks, sharing in community prayer, daily Mass.*
Guests Admitted to: *Unrestricted access.*
Meals: *Traditional food, eaten together.*
Special Activities: *Programme of events. Send for brochure.*
Situation: *Rather busy and in the city.*
Maximum Stay: *No restrictions.*
Bookings: *By letter.*
Charges: *By donation.*
Access: *By rail, bus or car to York.*

Ilkley

Myddelton Lodge
Langbar Road
Ilkley
W. Yorks. LS29 OEB   Telephone: 0943 607887

Roman Catholic – Non-denominational

The centre faces south, overlooking the town of Ilkley and the Ilkley Moors, with easy access to the Dales. There are a range of retreats on offer, including retreats for schools and for the disabled, plus their parents and helpers.

Open: *All year. Receives individuals and all groups.*
Rooms: *20 singles, 20 doubles.*
Facilities: *Disabled, conferences, chapel, garden, park, library, guest lounge, TV and pay phone. Children welcomed. Pets permitted.*
Spiritual Help: *Personal talks, group sharing, meditation, directed study.*
Guests Admitted to: *Unrestricted access to all areas, including chapel.*
Meals: *Everyone eats together. Home-cooking, with provision for vegetarian and special diets.*
Special Activities: *Planned programme of events. Send for brochure.*
Situation: *Very quiet, good grounds, beautiful countryside, good walking. The centre has a welcoming and homely atmosphere.*
Maximum Stay: *Unlimited.*
Bookings: *By letter or telephone.*
Charges: *£18 per person per 24 hours; special rates for children and teenagers.*
Access: *By rail, bus or car. Ask for details when applying.*

Wakefield

St Peter's Convent
Dovecote Lane
Horbury
Wakefield
W. Yorks. WF4 6BB   Telephone: 0924 72181

Anglican

The community has recently moved out of the large convent building into what was their guest house, but comfortable rooms are still available for guests.

Open: *All year except August. Receives men, women, young people, families and non-retreatants.*
Rooms: *4 singles.*

Facilities: *Garden, library, guest lounge and guest telephone. Children welcome if accompanied.*

Spiritual Help: *Personal talks, meditation, opportunity to share the worship of the community, Divine Office and daily Mass. Use of the chapel for personal prayer.*

Guests Admitted to: *Chapel, choir, guest quarters within the Convent.*

Meals: *Taken in the dining room. Traditional food, with provision for vegetarian and special diets.*

Special Activities: *No planned programme of events.*

Situation: *Quiet and in the village.*

Maximum Stay: *2 weeks.*

Bookings: *By letter.*

Charges: *Send for details.*

Access: *BR: to Wakefield. Bus: Nos. 26 and 27 from Wakefield.*

'Glance at the sun. See the moon and stars. Gaze at the beauty of earth's greenings. Now, think' – Hildegarde of Bingen

Wales

Corwen

Coleg Y Groes
The College
Corwen
Clwyd LL21 OAU   Telephone: 0490 2169

Christian

Two women deacons in the Church of Wales and a pastoral counsellor run this big, comfortable house nestling in a quiet spot between church and mountainside near the River Dee. There are counselling and prayer for healing, and individual needs are catered for in an environment that aims to convey the peace of Christ.

Open: *Most of the year. Receives men, women, young people, families, small groups and non-retreatants.*
Rooms: *Singles and doubles are available.*
Facilities: *Garden, library, guest lounge and TV. Children welcome, dogs permitted by previous arrangement.*
Spiritual Help: *Personal talks, directed study, guided prayer for individuals.*
Guests Admitted to: *Guest accommodation only.*
Meals: *Taken in the guest house. Good, varied home-cooking, with provision by arrangement for vegetarian and special diets but not for vegans. Meals served on tray in room for those keeping silence.*
Special Activities: *A few planned events. Send for the leaflet.*
Situation: *Very quiet, secluded, in the countryside but near main road.*
Maximum Stay: *Unrestricted.*
Bookings: *By telephone or letter.*
Charges: *Send for price list.*
Access: *BR: nearest station is Wrexham. Infrequent bus service. Car: house is just off A5.*

Corwen

Vajraloka Buddhist Meditation Centre
Blaen-ddol House
Treddol
Corwen
Clwyd LL21 OEN   Telephone: 0490 81406

Buddhist

Apart from running a few retreats during the year for women, Vajraloka is principally a men's Buddhist centre. Its sole purpose is to provide facilities for the practice of meditation, and it is open to newcomers as well as the more experienced meditators. If you have done a month or so of meditation, then you can come on most of the courses here. The Centre is set in the beautiful countryside of North Wales and it is a very peaceful place. Remember to bring loose clothing for meditation.

Open: *All year round. Receives men, sometimes women.*
Rooms: *2 singles, 3 doubles, dormitory.*
Facilities: *Shrine room, garden, library, pay phone.*
Spiritual Help: *Meditation, directed study. On all retreats the community teaches a creative approach in meditation workshops.*
Guests Admitted to: *Unrestricted access.*
Meals: *Everyone eats together. Vegetarian food, with provision for vegan and macrobiotic diets..*
Special Activities: *Planned programme of events – send for the brochure. One of very few single-sex Buddhist meditation centres in Europe where meditation continues throughout the year.*
Situation: *Very quiet, beautiful countryside.*
Maximum Stay: *3 months.*
Bookings: *By letter or telephone.*
Charges: *Standard rate £19 per person per night; concessionary tariff of £12 per night.*
Access: *By rail, bus or car, but ask when you book as the route is a little complicated.*

Hawarden

Poor Clares Monastery
Ty Mam Duw
Upper Aston Hall Lane
Hawarden
Clwyd CH5 3EN   Telephone: 0244 531029

Roman Catholic

Open: *All year. Receives women, married couples, priests, young people, groups and families, but no holiday-makers.*
Rooms: *4 singles, 2 doubles.*
Facilities: *Disabled, conferences, garden, guest lounge and guest telephone. Children permitted under supervision.*
Spiritual Help: *Personal talks, meditation.*
Guests Admitted to: *Chapel. (Gate closes early.)*
Meals: *Meals taken in the guest house. Traditional food, with provision for vegetarian and special diets. Self-catering facilities.*
Special Activities: *No planned programme of events.*
Situation: *Quiet, in the village.*
Maximum Stay: *Unlimited.*
Bookings: *By letter with a reference.*

Charges: *By donation.*
Access: *BR: to Chester. Ask about buses when you book.*

St Asaph

St Beuno's Spiritual Exercise Centre
St Asaph
Tremeirchion
Clwyd LL17 OAS   Telephone: 0745 583444

Roman Catholic

This is a leading Jesuit centre of spirituality for the teaching and study of the spiritual exercises of St Ignatius Loyola. These famous exercises are a series of Scripture-based, Christ-centred meditations and contemplations designed to help each retreatant to discover his or her 'hidden self'. There are courses designed to last six or eight days, others which are given in eight-day periods over three months, and the full course of spiritual exercises involving a continuous period of some 30 days. The Ignatian exercises are among the most famous and rigorous of all spiritual retreats. You should first read up about this form of retreat and perhaps discuss it with your spiritual adviser or priest before deciding to go. Highly recommended.

Open: *As published in programme. Receives men, women, young people and groups.*
Rooms: *40 singles.*
Facilities: *Limited for disabled, garden, library, guest lounge and pay phone.*
Spiritual Help: *Personal talks, group sharing, meditation, directed study.*
Guests Admitted to: *Unrestricted access.*
Meals: *Traditional food, with provision for vegetarian and special diets.*
Special Activities: *Send for brochure.*
Situation: *Quiet, and in the countryside.*
Maximum Stay: *According to programme.*
Bookings: *By letter.*
Charges: *Send for details.*
Access: *By rail to Rhyl, otherwise by car.*

Cardigan

Robin and Rachel Holtom
Glanhelyg
Llechryd
nr. Cardigan
Dyfed SA43 2NJ   Telephone: 023 987 482

New Age

Glanhelyg is a rambling old private country-house, built in Victorian times. Some of the courses on offer include painting, basket weaving, Rudolf Steiner eurythmy, Celtic healing, a sweat-lodge weekend for women, reflecting American-Indian traditions, the use of astrology in relationships, and a look at Christianity in the New Age. The approach aims at personal growth and development. For example, students on painting courses are encouraged to explore new ways of seeing rather than imitate established painting techniques. All meals are organic vegetarian.

Open: *All year. Receives men, women, young people, families, groups and non-retreatants.*
Rooms: *Singles and doubles are available.*
Facilities: *Disabled, conferences, camping, garden, library and guest lounge. Children welcome.*
Spiritual Help: *Directed study. Painting courses a speciality in summer, with circle dance and yoga in the winter.*
Guests Admitted To: *Unrestricted access.*
Meals: *Everyone eats together. Food is vegetarian, with provision for special diets. Self-catering facilities in guest house.*
Special Activities: *Planned programme of events. Send for brochure.*
Situation: *Quiet and in the countryside.*
Maximum Stay: *Unlimited.*
Bookings: *By telephone or letter.*
Charges: *£15 per person per day, B&B and evening meal. Reduced fees for unwaged or those with low income.*
Access: *BR: to Cardigan. Easy by bus – see brochure map.*

Llandeilo

Tipi Valley
Cwmdn
Llandeilo
Dyfed   Telephone: None

New Age – North American Indian

Tipi Valley is a scattered community of 60 or so families living in tipi lodges of the type used by North American Indians. This area of Wales is truly rural in a secret, rocky, green way, with beautiful tracts of bracken, deep forest valleys and lanes without traffic. Rain is never very far away. Tipi Valley qualifies as a place of retreat because of its isolation, lack of obvious structure, prevailing silence, guest lodge and rituals that are more or less based on American Indian spirituality. These rituals consist of simple communal chanting and dancing to earth spirits. There can be much nakedness, so if you are over-modest then be warned. The sweat-lodge is a low willow-frame, covered in cloth, that works like a pitch-dark sauna. It is incredibly hot and you can only bear it if you keep chanting. When you have had enough, run a short distance to a mountain pool and dive in – the effect is purging, therapeutic and rather magical. To stay here you must come equipped for camping. The guest lodge provides cover and a cooking-hearth. You will be expected to cut and gather reeds for the tipi floor, collect wood, and cook in rotation with others. Bring rain-gear and good boots. While Tipi Valley is not for the unfit or the highly conservative, it is also not exclusively a young people's place. All ages seem equally attracted to the lifestyle, which is unique in Britain.

Open: *All year. Receives men, women, groups and families, including children.*
Rooms: *Sleeping places are arranged when you arrive. A large tipi serves as the guest lounge.*
Facilities: *No modern facilities at all.*
Spiritual Help: *Chanting, Indian sweat-lodges, rituals linked to nature.*
Guests Admitted to: *Everywhere in valley, while respecting the privacy of others.*
Meals: *Bring your own food. Most of the resident community is vegetarian.*
Special Activities: *No planned programme.*
Situation: *7 miles from nowhere, among hills in a hidden valley. Very quiet and deeply rural.*
Maximum Stay: *Probably as long as you like.*
Bookings: *None required.*
Charges: *None.*
Access: *Bus or train to Swansea, then local bus to Llandeilo. From there walk, hitch, or take a taxi 7 miles to Cwmdn. Rest awhile because next you climb 5 miles into the hills. Local residents will give you directions if you get lost.*

Rhandirmwyn

Nantymwyn Retreat of the Visitation
Rhandirmwyn
Dyfed SA20 0NR   Telephone: 0550 6247

Anglican – Ecumenical

This old Welsh farmhouse is run as a retreat centre by an Anglican priest and his wife for all who wish to make a private retreat in a warm, welcoming and relaxing environment. Occasionally parish groups also stay here. Divine Office daily and the Eucharist every other day help to maintain a spiritual atmosphere for all. There is a smallholding and garden, in which retreatants are welcome to help if they want. In this way, you can achieve a balance between prayer and physical work – a combination that contemplative monasteries have found over the centuries brings a deepening of spirituality. The house is in a very beautiful part of the Cambrian Mountains and the surroundings are delightful – but if all you are after is a cheap holiday, then go somewhere else.

Open: *All year. Receives men and women.*
Rooms: *Can accommodate 6, more if absolutely necessary.*
Facilities: *Chapel, garden, smallholding, library, lounge and TV.*
Spiritual Help: *Personal talks if required. Some directed study if you ask.*
Guests Admitted to: *More or less unrestricted access.*
Meals: *Everyone eats together, dining from garden produce.*
Special Activities: *No planned programme.*
Situation: *In the countryside, very peaceful.*
Maximum Stay: *By arrangement.*
Bookings: *By letter.*
Charges: *Please enquire when you write.*
Access: *By car via A40 or A483 to Llandovery, then up Towy Valley.*

GWENT

Monmouth

Society of the Sacred Cross
Tymawr Convent
Lydart
Monmouth
Gwent NP5 4RN   Telephone: 0600 860244

Anglican

Lots of vegetables and fruit are grown by the sisters here, so the food is fresh, if plain, and you will feel well looked after in this house, which has views across a lush valley of green fields.

Open: *All year except October. Receives men, women, young people, groups and non-retreatants.*
Rooms: *8 singles, 3 doubles.*
Facilities: *Garden, park, library, guest lounge and guest telephone. Pets permitted occasionally.*
Spiritual Help: *Personal talks.*

Guests Admitted to: *Chapel, work of the community.*
Meals: *Very plain food taken in the guest house, with provision for vegetarian and special diets. Self-catering facilities.*
Special Activities: *No planned programme of events.*
Situation: *Very quiet, in the countryside.*
Maximum Stay: *2 weeks.*
Bookings: *By letter or telephone.*
Charges: *£12 per person per night, full board; £5 per night, self-catering.*
Access: *By car is best. House is 4 miles south of Monmouth.*

GWYNEDD

Dolgellau

Carmelite Monastery
Cader Road
Dolgellau
Gwynedd LL40 1SH   Telephone: 0341 422546

Roman Catholic

Open: *All year. Receives women.*
Rooms: *Only limited space, but guest priests and sisters who wish to make a retreat can use the bungalow. This is also available to women considering the Carmelite life.*
Facilities: *Small garden, TV on request.*
Spiritual Help: *Personal talks if requested, meditation and directed study.*
Guests Admitted to: *Chapel.*
Meals: *DIY facilities only.*
Special Activities: *No special activities or planned programme.*
Situation: *Quiet and in the countryside, with opportunities for walks in the mountains.*
Maximum Stay: *1 week.*
Bookings: *By telephone but confirm by letter.*
Charges: *On request.*
Access: *By rail to Machynlleth station, then by bus or car.*

Llanrwst

Christian Conference, Retreat & Holiday Centre
Pencraig Arthur
Llanddoged
Llanrwst
Gwynedd LL26 ODZ   Telephone: 0492 640959

Interdenominational

The Reverend John Farrimond, a Methodist minister, had just got Pencraig Arthur going as a retreat centre when he was called to work elsewhere. He hopes in a few years to run it again, offering personal talks and guided retreats. Meanwhile it is available on a self-catering basis and guests must look after themselves and the house. It is located on the edge of Snowdonia National Park so there is excellent walking. Perhaps a good place for a small, self-motivated group who want to go on a renewal retreat outside the monastic, church, or warden-run retreat-centre settings.

Open: *By arrangement. Receives men, women, young people, families, groups and non-retreatants.*
Rooms: *1 single, 6 doubles, 1 caravan.*
Facilities: *Conferences, garden, guest lounge, TV and guest telephone. Children welcomed.*
Spiritual Help: *None at this time.*
Guests Admitted to: *Unrestricted access.*
Meals: *Self-catering.*
Special Activities: *None at this time.*
Situation: *Very quiet, in the countryside.*
Maximum Stay: *By arrangement.*
Bookings: *By telephone or letter.*
Charges: *By arrangement.*
Access: *By car only.*

Pwllheli

'Croesfryn'
Bryncroes
nr. Sarn
Pwllheli
Gwynedd LL53 8EY   Telephone: 071-359 1394
                                              for enquiries
Buddhist

This retreat centre belongs strictly to the Mahayana Buddhist tradition of Lama Tsong Kha Pa (Gelug). There is a resident Tibetan monk who is a qualified meditation master, and he can give personal guidance in Buddhist meditation by prior arrangement.

Open: *All year. Receives men, women, young people, families, groups and religious.*
Rooms: *About 10 singles, plus dormitories, hermitage, hostel and caravans.*
Facilities: *Camping, garden, library, guest lounge and TV.*
Spiritual Help: *Personal talks, group sharing, meditation and directed study.*
Guests Admitted to: *Shrine room and the work of the community.*
Meals: *DIY facilities only.*
Special Activities: *Group retreats at Christmas, Easter and in the summer.*
Situation: *Very quiet and in the countryside. Distant views across Lleyn Peninsula.*
Maximum Stay: *By negotiation.*
Bookings: *By letter to Jamyang Meditation Centre, 10 Finsbury Park Road, London N4 2JZ.*
Charges: *Low.*
Access: *By car.*

POWYS

Brecon

Coleg Trefeca
Trefeca
Talgarth
Brecon
Powys LD3 OPP   Telephone: 0874 711423

Presbyterian Church of Wales

The centre consists of a group of 18th-century buildings and a modern block, standing in five acres of grounds set in the Brecon Beacons National Park. Short retreats, ecumenical activities, holiday weeks for older folk and young people are on offer, as well as courses in Myers-Briggs, Christian pastoral counselling, study for lay preachers, and Jewish-Christian consultation. The programme brochure is in both Welsh and English. A good place for a stimulating retreat, mixing with other like-minded people.

Open: *All year. Receives men, women, young people, families, groups and non-retreatants.*
Rooms: *19 twin-bedded.*
Facilities: *Conferences, garden, library, guest lounge, TV and guest pay phone. Children and pets welcomed.*
Spiritual Help: *Personal talks if requested.*
Guests Admitted to: *Unrestricted access.*

Meals: *Everyone eats together. Very plain food, with provision for vegetarian and special diets.*
Special Activities: *Planned programme, though groups, churches and secular organisations may follow their own programme.*
Situation: *Very quiet, in an area of outstanding natural beauty. 10 miles from Brecon and an ideal centre for those who wish to walk, climb, ponytrek, or simply admire the views.*
Maximum Stay: *Unrestricted.*
Bookings: *By telephone but confirm by letter.*
Charges: *Very reasonable, varying according to personal situation.*
Access: *By car.*

Brecon

Llangasty Retreat House
Brecon
Powys LD3 7PJ   Telephone: 087 484 250

Anglican

This isolated and large stone house, hidden away from roads and the busy world, is run by the Sisters of Charity. It is comfortable, cheerful and overlooks a marvellous lake.

Open: *All year except mid-December to 1 February. Receives men, women, young people, families, groups and non-retreatants.*
Rooms: *10 singles, 3 doubles.*
Facilities: *Conferences, garden, library, guest lounge, direct- dialling telephone. Children welcomed.*
Spiritual Help: *Personal talks.*
Guests Admitted to: *Chapel.*
Meals: *Everyone eats together. Traditional food, with provision for vegetarian and special diets.*
Special Activities: *Painting and prayer courses are held once or twice a year.*
Situation: *Very quiet, in the countryside.*
Maximum Stay: *By arrangement.*
Bookings: *By telephone but confirm by letter.*
Charges: *£13 + VAT per person for 24 hours.*
Access: *By car to Brecon.*

'He leads me beside the waters of peace' – Psalm 23

Builth Wells

The Skreen
Erwood
Builth Wells
Powys LD2 3SJ   Telephone: 098 23 210

Ecumenical

The Skreen enjoys a reputation for being a place where you may search, explore, share, be silent, worship and be at peace with yourself. There are no individual retreats but there is a programme of residential courses and workshops. These may include an introduction to women mystics of the past and present; making and using icons; praying through music and dance; and an exploration of St John's Gospel. The house is beautifully situated above the River Wye, near a small village.

Open: *All year except Christmas, New Year and August. Receives men and women, sometimes children.*
Rooms: *2 singles, 5 doubles, 2 rooms with 3 beds and a cottage for 2.*
Facilities: *Chapel, garden, library and guest lounge.*
Spiritual Help: *Organised retreats.*
Guests Admitted to: *Unrestricted except to private sitting-room.*
Meals: *Everyone eats together. Wholefood, with provision for vegetarian and special diets. Cottage is self-catering.*
Special Activities: *Planned programme of events. Send for brochure.*
Situation: *Quiet.*
Maximum Stay: *As per programme.*
Bookings: *By letter or telephone.*
Charges: *£17.50 per person for 24 hours.*
Access: *Car-route directions in the brochure.*

Knighton

The Bleddfa Trust
Centre for Caring and the Arts
The Old School
Knighton
Powys   Telephone: 054 47 540

Interdenominational

Here is an exciting and different place to go for spiritual and personal development. John Hencher, who runs the monthly workshops on self-knowledge and self-development, is called 'Director of Caring', which seems a wonderfully thought-provoking title to possess in this age of materialism. These workshops are meant to open new horizons of spirituality and self-awareness. For example, they might be on 'light' or 'hope', and from these simple words the day unfolds at Bleddfa into a new awakening of the spirit, leading to better insight into yourself. Such days of group sharing are especially useful for those who may think that they have already fully explored the creative dimensions of their personal spirituality. The Bleddfa Trust runs a gallery in the Old School which has gained a national reputation for the quality of its art and craft exhibitions, all of which are mounted with great sensitivity by the director, John Cupper. There is a small book-and-gift shop, and you may take tea or a herbal tisane seated outside in a charming herb garden. Highly recommended.

Open: *All year. Receives men and women.*
Rooms: *Guests stay in local B&B accommodation.*
Facilities: *Various meeting rooms, Old School gallery, bookshop.*
Spiritual Help: *A monthly workshop is held on the first Saturday of each month from 10. 30 a.m. to 5. 00 p.m. Personal talks, group sharing, meditation.*
Guests Admitted to: *Centre and gardens.*
Meals: *Bring your own food.*
Special Activities: *Send for brochure.*
Situation: *In wonderful countryside with distant views.*
Maximum Stay: *For length of course or events.*
Bookings: *By letter.*
Charges: *Usually £12 per person per day.*
Access: *By car only.*

Llangunllo

The Samatha Centre
Greenstreete
Llangunllo
Powys LD7 1SP   Telephone 061-881 0038

Buddhist (Therevada Tradition)

Greenstreete Farm was purchased by the Samatha Trust in 1987 for use as a residential meditation centre. It consists of a big farmhouse set in 88 acres of land. The setting is lovely, with views in all directions of green pastures and rising hills. There are streams and woods with secluded places where small huts have been built for use by meditators wanting solitude. Everyone is welcome here to learn this gentle and effective way of meditation.

Open: *May to October. Receives men and women.*
Rooms: *8 singles, camping.*
Facilities: *Shrine room, small library.*
Spiritual Help: *Personal talks, group sharing, directed study, and individual instruction on Samatha meditation.*

Guests Admitted to: *Unrestricted access everywhere.*

Meals: *Everyone eats together. Traditional food. Provision for vegetarians, and special diets, within reason.*

Special Activities: *Send for the programme.*

Situation: *Deep in the countryside, and very quiet.*

Maximum Stay: *By arrangement.*

Bookings: *By letter or telephone.*

Charges: *£15 per day or £100 per week.*

Access: *BR: to Llangunllo station which is less than a mile away. It is an easy walk to the Centre. By car from Knighton in Powys to Llangunllo, then through the village and the Centre will be seen on a hill to the left. The entrance is sign-posted.*

'God is beauty' – St Francis of Assisi

Scotland

Hawick

Chisholme House
Roberton
nr. Hawick
Roxburgh TD9 7PH   Telephone: 0450 88215

New Age – Beshara School of Esoteric Education

Beshara means 'good news'. It is reputed to be the word the angel Gabriel used when he announced the coming of Christ to Mary. The idea of the Beshara School is to strive towards an understanding of the unity of existence. This study of spiritual awareness is quite demanding as it encompasses many traditions, ranging from Judaic, Christian and Far Eastern to classical texts. The house itself is Georgian, the accommodation almost luxuriously comfortable, and the food imaginatively prepared. The staff and students are helpful, relaxed and welcoming. Courses run from 10 days to six months. Guests can choose to participate in the end-of-day meditational practice where names of gods are chanted. For those who are genuinely spiritually minded and who do not want anything denominational, church structured, or based on a single spiritual tradition, then Chisholme is a good place to try.

Open: *All year. Receives men, women, young people, families, groups and non-retreatants.*
Rooms: *2 singles, 6 doubles, dormitory, special bedroom for the disabled and another 2 under construction.*
Facilities: *Disabled, camping by arrangement.*
Spiritual Help: *Personal talks, meditation, directed study.*
Guests Admitted to: *Unrestricted access in main building, meditation room.*
Meals: *Everyone eats together. Traditional food, some home-produced. Vegetarians and medical diets catered for.*
Special Activities: *Annual open day, lectures. Some people come just to work in the large garden. Brochure available.*
Situation: *Very quiet, in the countryside.*
Maximum Stay: *By arrangement.*
Bookings: *By letter.*
Charges: *£20 per person per day; 9-day course £200; 6-month course £2,800. Special rate for the disadvantaged.*
Access: *BR: to Carlisle, then by bus. Bus: to Hawick, then by taxi. Car: via M6, A7.*

'Prayer has been man's unceasing cry to God.
It is the most universal evidence that there is in him something
higher than his natural life' – Abbot Vonier

Hawick

Whitchester Christian Guest House & Retreat Centre
Borthaugh
Hawick
Roxburgh TD9 7LN   Telephone: 0450 77477

Interdenominational

Open: *All year. Receives men, women, families, groups and non-retreatants.*
Rooms: *1 single, 8 doubles.*
Facilities: *Disabled, conferences, large gardens, library, guest lounge, TV and pay phone. Children welcomed, pets permitted by arrangement.*
Spiritual Help: *Personal talks, meditation, directed study.*
Guests Admitted to: *Unrestricted access to all areas, including chapel.*
Meals: *Taken in the guest house. Traditional Scottish wholefood, with provision for vegetarians and special diets.*
Special Activities: *Staff's daily worship is open to guests.*
Situation: *Very quiet.*
Maximum Stay: *6 weeks.*
Bookings: *By letter or telephone.*
Charges: *Send for tariff.*
Access: *By rail, bus or car (A7).*

CENTRAL

Dunblane

Scottish Churches House
Kirk Street
Dunblane
Perthshire FK15 OAJ   Telephone: 0786 823588

Interdenominational

This is a conference centre, belonging to all the mainline churches in Scotland, but daily retreats are organised for individuals. These usually take place during Lent, autumn and Advent.

Open: *All year except August. Receives men, women, groups and non-retreatants over 18 years of age.*
Rooms: *12 singles, 20 doubles.*
Facilities: *Conferences, library, guest lounge, direct-dialling pay phone.*
Spiritual Help: *Group sharing.*
Guests Admitted to: *Unrestricted access to all areas, including chapel.*
Meals: *Everyone eats together. Wholefood, with provision for vegetarian*

and special diets.
Special Activities: *No planned programme of events.*
Situation: *Quiet but in the town.*
Maximum Stay: *1 week.*
Bookings: *By telephone or letter.*
Charges: *By arrangement.*
Access: *By rail, bus or car.*

DUMFRIES and GALLOWAY

Castle Douglas

Loriestone Hall Peoples' Centre
Loriestone
Castle Douglas
Dumfriesshire DG7 2NB   Telephone: 06445 275

New Age

Book well in advance for a retreat at this Victorian baronial 'pile', situated some six miles from the village of Loriestone. The place is a labyrinth of passages, staircases and rooms, all rather dark, dank and crumbling – none the less it is one of the more beautiful Scottish spiritual centres. Around the imposing imitation castle is a green estate verging on the great forest of Galloway. The small community of 25 or so people is joined by about 60 guests each week during the summer. Meals are vegetarian and vegan – among the most imaginative of their kind of any retreat house. Courses at the Centre vary tremendously, ranging from sexuality and ecology to psychological and physical therapies. Accommodation is basic – take a sleeping-bag and some warm clothes, unless it is a hot summer. An interesting place for a working retreat of a non-religious yet meditative nature.

Open: *Summer. Receives men, women, young people, groups, and families by arrangement. No disabled children. Casual visitors are not welcomed.*
Rooms: *Dormitories to accommodate up to 80 people.*
Facilities: *Conferences, camping by arrangement, garden, park, library, guest lounge, TV and pay phone.*
Spiritual Help: *Group sharing, meditation.*
Guests Admitted to: *Unrestricted.*
Meals: *Wholefood vegetarian. Vegans catered for.*
Special Activities: *Send for brochure.*
Situation: *Very quiet, in the countryside. The 200-acre estate is a government-designated environmentally sensitive area.*
Maximum Stay: *2 weeks.*
Bookings: *By letter or telephone.*
Charges: *£12 per person per night. £150 for a 2-week working retreat.*

From £150 for weekly courses.
Access: *BR: to Dumfries. Bus: to Castle Douglas – the Post Bus runs twice daily to Loriestone Hall. Car: via M6, then A75, A713, followed by B795 to Loriestone.*

Langholm

Samye Ling Tibetan Centre
Eskdalemuir
nr. Langholm
Dumfriesshire DG13 OQL   Telephone: 03873 232

Buddhist

The Centre was founded in 1907, the first British Tibetan monastery to be set up following the Cultural Revolution. Lamas regularly visit in summer and guests may request interviews. Unless on retreat, guests stay in separate accommodation from the retreat centre. All guests may participate in temple meditation, prayer and work. The atmosphere is lively and warm. There is a full-time community, consisting mostly of young people who obviously derive peace and pleasure from being at the Centre and lend the place an atmosphere of calm. They work at the dairy and farm. There is also a foundry, weaving and painting shops, a pottery and printing press. The Centre leaves one with an impression of New Age ideas combined with very genuine Tibetan Buddhism. A stimulating place, there is plenty to do and a wonderful landscape to explore.

Open: *All year. Receives men, women, young people, single-parent families and non-retreatants. Disabled received by arrangement.*
Rooms: *6 singles, 8 doubles, 5 dormitories, plus space for tents, owner-occupied caravans.*
Facilities: *Conferences, camping, garden, small library and pay phone. Children welcome.*
Spiritual Help: *Personal talks, informal group-sharing encouraged, meditation. Weekend courses in therapy, massage, holistic practice. Also 10-year study courses divided into 3 blocks. Full retreats by arrangement. Courses also run for 2 weeks at Christmas, 1 month at Easter and 3 months over summer (July – September).*
Guests Admitted to: *Temple, shrine room, craft work of the community, building projects and general projects. Guests are asked to work for 2 hours a day.*
Meals: *Everyone eats together. The food is vegetarian, with provision for special diets by arrangement.*
Special Activities: *Planned programme of events. Send for the brochure.*
Situation: *Quiet, busy in summer.*
Maximum Stay: *As arranged.*
Bookings: *By letter or telephone.*

Charges: *Send for details.*
Access: *All routes difficult. BR and bus to Lockerbie, then by taxi for 14 miles.*

'Prayer is an encounter and a relationship, a relationship which is deep, and this relationship cannot be forced either on us or on God'
– Metropolitan Anthony of Sourozh

EDINBURGH

House of Prayer
8 Nile Grove
Edinburgh EH10 4RF   Telephone: 031-447 1772

Christian – Interdenominational

Located in one of Scotland's few moneyed and middle-class suburban areas, the House of Prayer embraces all denominations and tries to promote an unsensational Christian spiritualism. Meditation is encouraged and there is a chapel with regular services. Rooms are clean and bright, and surrounding the house is a fine garden. This place is more for the traditionally inclined older Christian than the young seeker – but there are plenty of up-to-date courses in the programme, from 30-day retreats and prayer days for women, to lectures on that most gifted of poets, Gerard Manley Hopkins.

Open: *All year. Receives men, women, groups up to 10. No children.*
Rooms: *10 singles.*
Facilities: *Chapel, conferences, garden, library, guest lounge and guest telephone.*
Spiritual Help: *Personal talks, group sharing, meditation, directed study, chapel services.*
Guests Admitted to: *Unrestricted access.*
Meals: *Everyone eats together. Traditional food. Vegetarians catered for by prior arrangement. No special diets.*
Special Activities: *Retreats tend to operate as courses unless a private retreat is specified. Day events are open to non-residents.*
Situation: *Quiet suburb.*
Maximum Stay: *30 days.*
Bookings: *By letter or telephone.*
Charges: *£17 per person per day. Concessions if you are poor.*
Access: *By rail or car to Edinburgh. Local buses: Nos. 11, 15, 16, 23, C11, C1 from Waverley station.*

St Peter's Pastoral & Retreat Centre
33 Briar Road
Newlands
Glasgow G24 2TU   Telephone: 041-633 0484

Roman Catholic – Ecumenical

Glorious Glasgow, with its clean streets and polite young people, can boast
the magnificent Burrell Art Collection, theatres and garden festivals that are
all on your doorstep if you stay here – and St Peter's is happy for you to use
its facilities for either a retreat or a holiday break.

Open: *All year except Christmas and New Year and 3 weeks in July/August.*
Receives men, women, young people, families, groups and non-retreatants.
Rooms: *38 singles, doubles and 3-bedded rooms.*
Facilities: *Disabled, conferences, garden, guest lounge, TV and pay phone.*
Children welcomed.
Spiritual Help: *Only as arranged by retreatants themselves.*
Guests Admitted to: *Chapel, small oratory.*
Meals: *Everyone eats together. Traditional varied menu, with provision for*
vegetarian and special diets.
Special Activities: *Planned programme of events. Send for brochure.*
Situation: *Quiet, extensive grounds – lovely for short walks or a quiet time.*
15 minutes' drive from city centre.
Maximum Stay: *By arrangement.*
Bookings: *By telephone – confirm by letter.*
Charges: *Send for the separate tariff as charges vary widely.*
Access: *By rail, bus or car to Glasgow.*

GRAMPIAN

Aberdeen

St Margaret's Convent
17 Spital
Aberdeen AB2 3HT   Telephone: 0224 632648

Scottish Episcopal

Open: *All year round except short periods spring and autumn. Receives*
men, women, non-retreatants.
Rooms: *2 singles, 2 doubles.*
Facilities: *Small garden, small library, TV.*
Spiritual Help: *Personal talks, directed study when Chaplain available.*
Guests Admitted to: *Chapel.*

Meals: *Everyone eats together. Very plain food with provision for vegetarian and special diets.*
Special Activities: *No planned programme of events.*
Situation: *Rather busy, in the city. The convent is situated on a high ridge above the road and can be reached only by a steep path and steps.*
Maximum Stay: *2 weeks.*
Bookings: *By letter.*
Charges: *Realistic donation.*
Access: *BR: Aberdeen, then taxi. Car: Aberdeen.*

Elgin

Pluscarden Abbey
Elgin
Moray IV30 3UA   Telephone: 034 389 257
                                                       (no calls after 7.30 p.m.)
Roman Catholic

Pluscarden Abbey is at the foot of a steep hill, surrounded by dense, Caledonian-pine forest and pastureland. The vale of St Anres is quite the most extraordinarily beautiful glen to be found in northern Scotland's farmland. Roe-deer proliferate, along with buzzards and red squirrels, while Highland cattle roam in the forests. The Abbey is a 13th-century Benedictine monastery, repopulated in 1948 by the Benedictines, who are restoring it. Notable is the stained glass designed by the monks – to my mind one of the few successful marriages of modern and medieval aesthetics. The monastery counts about 30 monks – now famous for their Latin plain-chant Masses, which have been recorded for distribution on both sides of the Atlantic. The Benedictine tradition of hospitality is well observed. Guests may attend all worship, but a rule of silence has to be respected. However, the Guestmaster is happy to converse and may invite you to join in the work – mainly gardening, log-cutting or assistance in the kitchen. Guest facilities are strictly limited. Highly recommended.

Open: *All year except over Christmas. Receives men, women, families, groups, religious and non-retreatants.*
Rooms: *7 singles for men, 10 for women only, 2 doubles for women.*
Facilities: *Garden, library with permission, guest lounge and pay phone. Not suitable for the disabled,*
Spiritual Help: *Personal talks, worship and prayer, Divine Office. People in need may ask for guidance from the Guestmaster or Abbot.*
Guests Admitted to: *Chapel, choir and men may share in some work of the community.*
Meals: *Meals for men in refectory; DIY for women in guest house. Very plain food, mainly vegetarian.*
Special Activities: *No planned programme of events.*
Situation: *Very quiet, in the Vale of St Andrews.*

Maximum Stay: *2 weeks.*
Bookings: *By letter.*
Charges: *By donation, according to your means.*
Access: *BR: to Elgin. Bus: runs on school days. Car: direct route from Elgin, about 6 miles away.*

Findhorn

Minton House
Findhorn
Moray IV36 0YY   Telephone: 0309 30819

Non-religious

While following the general philosophy of the Findhorn Community (see next entry), this is a separate organisation. Guests are able to share in some of the Findhorn events and facilities.

Open: *All year. Receives men, women, young people, families, groups and non-retreatants.*
Rooms: *3 singles, 4 doubles, dormitory for 4.*
Facilities: *Conferences, garden, library, guest lounge and pay phone. Children welcomed. Pets permitted by arrangement only.*
Spiritual Help: *Meditation, massage counselling, Alexander Technique, healing sessions.*
Guests Admitted to: *Shrine room, work of community.*
Meals: *Everyone eats together. Vegetarian wholefood – special diets catered for.*
Special Activities: *Planned programme of events. Send for brochure. Also concerts, dances, theatre and recitals.*
Situation: *On the shores of Findhorn Bay, lovely landscape.*
Maximum Stay: *By arrangement.*
Bookings: *By letter or telephone.*
Charges: *Available on application.*
Access: *BR: to Forres, then by taxi. Bus: from Inverness to Forres, then Findhorn. Easy by car.*

Forres

Findhorn Foundation Community
Forres
Morayshire IV36 OYY   Telephone: 0309 30203

New Age

The Community or Foundation was founded in 1962 with one family living in a caravan. Nature spirits, or 'devas', are said to have allowed them to raise vegetables and exotic flowers from a barren soil of sand and gravel. A permanent community of 150–200 now lives near the gardens, next to which an area of wilderness has been left for the 'devas' – out of bounds to humans. Enthusiasm, harmony and love are the precepts by which the Community purports to work, and there is a strong emphasis on meditation. Hard work is demanded from all paying guests, including those attending courses. Courses of all descriptions run throughout the year. The idea behind this is to create a 'spiritual school', led by 'focalisers' who teach anything from T'ai Ch'i to ecology. Art, graphic design and 'sacred dance' are also popular pursuits here.

Such is the popularity of Findhorn among New Age believers that it is hard to get accommodation unless you book months in advance. The place is generally quite crowded. Indeed, about 5,000 people visit Findhorn annually.

Findhorn is not for the poor. Actual retreats are run in a secondary centre in Iona (not part of the 'Iona Community', which is a separate organisation). They cost £95 per week and run from 14 July to 8 September. Before booking the retreat, you must complete an 'experience week' or 'living the life we choose' course (costing £180–£240). Another island retreat on Erraid, near Iona, is available on the same terms.

Findhorn is not a place for a private retreat as understood in the Christian or Buddhist traditions, but for anyone wishing to view at first hand the more material rather than the strictly spiritual side of the 'New Age' movement, Findhorn offers an interesting insight.

Open: *All year. Receives men, women, young people, groups, families and non-retreatants.*

Rooms: *Camping, caravans.*

Facilities: *Disabled, conferences, garden, park, library, guest lounge, TV and pay phone. Children welcomed.*

Spiritual Help: *Personal talks, group sharing, meditation, directed study.*

Guests Admitted to: *Unrestricted access except to private houses and rooms for course study.*

Meals: *Everyone eats together. Traditional food, with provision for vegetarians. Self-catering in caravans.*

Special Activities: *Planned programme of events – send for the brochure. Spontaneous folk-music entertainment in evenings.*

Situation: *Quiet, but crowded in summer. Near village, on estuary peninsula, miles of sand-dune walking. RAF base next door – can be noisy.*

Maximum Stay: *According to course length.*

Bookings: *By letter or telephone.*

Charges: *Send for details.*

Access: *By rail to Inverness, then to Forres. Car route easy.*

Beauly

Tigh Na Bruaich
Struy
by Beauly
Inverness IV4 7JU   Telephone: 046 376 254

New Age

This is a centre for alternative healing set in the Highlands and run by a therapist in natural healing. Her approach to individual well-being is fourfold: concern for spirituality, chemical make-up (including food intake), the body and the emotions. The centre serves as a base for other New Age practitioners who offer courses in McTimoney Chiropractic, touch for health, the use of crystals, meditation and rebirthing.

Open: *All year. Receives men, women, young people, families and groups.*
Rooms: *Single rooms and a cottage.*
Facilities: *Garden, library and direct-dialling guest telephone.*
Spiritual Help: *Personal talks, group sharing and directed study. Individual sessions or group work with other practitioners. Guidance in meditation and stress release.*
Guests Admitted to: *Unrestricted access, help with gardening.*
Meals: *Everyone eats together. Wholefood, with provision for vegetarian and special diets.*
Special Activities: *Courses exploring the self through nature; meditation courses; individual daily sessions for a week or longer. Send for brochure.*
Situation: *Very quiet and situated in a beautiful wooded glen in the Highlands. The grounds cover 5 acres.*
Maximum Stay: *2 weeks.*
Bookings: *By letter or telephone.*
Charges: *£350 per person per week, £50 per day, £30 for an approximately 2-hour session.*
Access: *BR: to Inverness – they will collect you.*

Fort Augustus

St Benedict's Abbey
Fort Augustus
Inverness-shire PH32 4DB   Telephone: 0320 6444

Roman Catholic

The buildings are rather heavy Victorian Gothic and less attractive than one might expect. However, there are some interesting features – a Roman plaque, Loch Ness, and a dungeon, now an underground chapel. School playing-fields and a garden surround the Abbey. Despite the size of the building (which covers about 15 acres), only about 30 monks inhabit the place. It is in a beautiful state of repair and upkeep, but one gets the impression that this is a dwindling institution. Because of its location on the tourist route of the Great Glen, the Abbey is always stretched to provide guest accommodation. Those wishing for a retreat in this busy centre should visit in the winter months only, which is during the school term so expect some degree of noise. The monks are cultured, courteous and excellent conversationalists. The prospective retreatant would be well advised to visit the monastery a few times to get to know some of the monks before staying with them, otherwise one might miss the understated but very deep warmth of the brethren.

Open: *All year. Receives men and non-retreatants.*
Rooms: *10–12 singles.*
Facilities: *Chapel, garden, park, library, guest lounge and pay phone.*
Spiritual Help: *Sacrament of Reconciliation daily, Mass.*
Guests Admitted to: *Chapel, choir and work of the community.*
Meals: *Everyone eats together. Food is largely vegetarian.*
Special Activities: *No planned programme of events.*
Situation: *Quiet, in the town. Stunning views of Loch Ness and Monadhliath Mountains.*
Maximum Stay: *By arrangement.*
Bookings: *By letter.*
Charges: *By arrangement.*
Access: *Easy access by bus.*

Garve

Scoraig Samadhan
Scoraig Peninsula
Dundonnell
by Garve
Wester Ross IV23 2RE   Telephone: 085 483 260

New Age – Non-denominational

The word 'samadhan' means 'the answer', and the founder of this private centre is Sundara Forsyth, a Shiatsu practitioner. Visitors can expect a long journey no matter how they travel, but the rewards are many – not least the peace and quiet of a remote coastland and the wildlife that abounds there, including a large herd of rare indigenous mountain goats. The centre contains a light, modern room for meditation and courses. Bedrooms are comfortable and every bed has a thick duvet. In addition to Shiatsu, individual instruction in rebirthing and movement ritual are offered. Courses in weaving, spinning, painting and drawing, and an introduction to homoeopathy are also available.

Open: *All year. Receives men, women, young people, groups and non-retreatants.*
Rooms: *4 singles, 4 doubles, 1 twin-bedded room, hostel.*
Facilities: *Conferences, camping, garden, library, guest lounge, TV and guest telephone. No children or pets.*
Spiritual Help: *Personal talks, group sharing, meditation, directed study.*
Guests Admitted to: *Unrestricted access, farm chores and daily routines of household.*
Meals: *Everyone eats together. Food is almost always vegetarian but sometimes seafood and venison are provided.*
Special Activities: *Planned programme. Send for brochure.*
Situation: *Wilderness – remote, beautiful and peaceful. Walking, boating and fishing available.*
Maximum Stay: *Open-ended.*
Bookings: *By letter.*
Charges: *3-day workshop £150, week workshop £250. Ask for rates for individual instruction.*
Access: *70 miles from Inverness to Badluarach, where you leave the car. Boatman will ferry you to Samadhan. Westerbus on Monday, Wednesday, Saturday to Badcaul, where you will be met. Via post-boat or on foot from Badrallagh.*

LOTHIAN

Haddington

Sancta Maria Abbey
Nunraw Guest House
Haddington
East Lothian EH41 4LW   Telephone: 062 083 223

Roman Catholic

More people want to stay at this Cistercian monastery and guest house than can be accommodated, so don't be disappointed if it is full. The surrounding countryside is very beautiful and the monastery runs a large agricultural establishment. This is a place of silence and deep spirituality, where you may truly put aside the burdens of everyday living and open yourself to the benefits of silence and solitude.

Open: *All year except Christmas and November. Receives men, women, young people, families and groups.*
Rooms: *4 singles, 6 doubles, dormitories.*
Facilities: *Park, library, guest lounge and direct-dialling pay phone. Children welcomed.*
Spiritual Help: *Personal talks.*

Guests Admitted to: *Chapel.*
Meals: *Traditional food, taken in the guest house. Vegetarian and special diets catered for.*
Special Activities: *No planned programme of events.*
Situation: *Very quiet and in the countryside.*
Maximum Stay: *5 days.*
Bookings: *By letter.*
Charges: *By arrangement.*
Access: *By car.*

Musselburgh

Carberry Tower
Residential Conference Centre
Musselburgh
Midlothian EH21 8PY   Telephone: 031-665 3135

Church of Scotland

Carberry Tower is a very Scottish country-house with delightful public rooms and a good library. The programme is extensive and includes youth weekends, open and midweek courses, and Bible study.

Open: *All year. Receives men, women, young people, families and children, groups, religious and non-retreatants.*
Rooms: *19 singles, 42 doubles, plus caravans.*
Facilities: *Conferences, camping, garden, park, library, guest lounge, TV and pay phone.*
Spiritual Help: *Groups participate in a scheduled programme, or they arrange their own. No direction for individuals.*
Guests Admitted to: *Unrestricted access.*
Meals: *Everyone eats together. Traditional food, with provision for vegetarian and special diets.*
Special Activities: *Lots of activities, including 70 courses a year. Send for brochure.*
Situation: *Very quiet but busy because of guests. Set in 30 acres of parkland with fine trees.*
Maximum Stay: *Up to 1 month.*
Bookings: *Telephone first but confirm by letter.*
Charges: *See brochure.*
Access: *See good map and directions in brochure.*

Biggar

Skirling House
Skirling
Biggar ML12 6HD   Telephone: 089 96 274

Buddhist

Although this is a big place, it has an atmosphere conducive to meditation and spiritual renewal. Everyone is welcome, and those on individual retreat set their own schedule. The programme of events is still evolving as it is a new centre, but already some courses are being led by well-known people such as the abbots of Chisthurst Monastery and Harnham Vihara. Workshops cover such topics as 'mindfulness of the body', and yoga and work retreats are available. Remember to take loose clothing and blankets or a sleeping-bag.

Open: *All year. Receives men, women, young people, families by arrangement. Groups and non-retreatants received only if contemplative reflection is intended.*
Rooms: *3 singles, 1 double, dormitories, barn. Bring your own blankets, towel, hot-water bottle.*
Facilities: *Conferences (provided they are compatible), garden, library and guest lounge.*
Spiritual Help: *Please discuss with the manager, as there is a resident counsellor available.*
Guests Admitted to: *Shrine room, work of the community (gardening).*
Meals: *Everyone eats together – vegetarian food. Self-catering possible.*
Special Activities: *Planned programme of events. Send for the brochure.*
Situation: *Quiet, with lovely walks in the beautiful countryside.*
Maximum Stay: *Unlimited.*
Bookings: *By letter – please send s.a.e.*
Charges: *Currently £9 per person per night but under review, so please enquire.*
Access: *By rail, bus or car – directions in brochure.*

Isle of Cumbrae

The College
Millport
Isle of Cumbrae KA28 OHE   Telephone: 0475 530353/530082

Anglican

Open: *All year – closed December and January. Receives men, women, young people, groups and non-retreatants.*
Rooms: *14 singles, 2 doubles, 4 twin-bedded rooms.*
Facilities: *Conferences, garden, library, guest lounge and pay phone.*

Spiritual Help: *Personal talks, meditation and directed study.*
Guests Admitted to: *Unrestricted access to all areas, including chapel.*
Meals: *Everyone eats together – the food is traditional.*
Special Activities: *No planned programme of events.*
Situation: *Very quiet.*
Maximum Stay: *Unlimited*
Bookings: *By letter.*
Charges: *On request*
Access: *By rail plus Cal-mac Ferry.*

Isle of Iona

The Iona Community
The Abbey
Isle of Iona
Argyll PA76 6SN   Telephone: 06817 404

Christian – Ecumenical

The Iona Community is an ecumenical movement of ordained and lay Christians and welcomes more than 150,000 visitors to this ancient, holy island every year. It was on Iona that St Columba in AD 563 began his mission to bring Christianity to Scotland. The 13th-century Benedictine abbey and church have now been restored. There is an extensive programme of courses, events and retreats.

Open: *All year except January and February. Receives men, women, young people, families and groups.*
Rooms: *3 single, 13 double and a dormitory.*
Facilities: *Disabled, garden, common room and pay phone.   Children welcome. This is not a conference centre.*
Spiritual Help: *Guests are expected to join the community life.*
Guests Admitted to: *Unrestricted.*
Meals: *Everyone eats together. Food is mainly vegetarian.*
Special Activities: *Guests share chores, join in worship, concerts, workshops, discussions.*
Situation: *Quiet, near village, set on an island in Inner Hebrides.*
Maximum Stay: *Usually 1 week.*
Bookings: *Send for booking form.*
Charges: *Send for details.*
Access: *Train from Glasgow to Oban, then ferry to Isle of Mull, bus or car 37 miles across Mull, finally a ferry to Iona.*

Isle of Iona

Bishop's House
Isle of Iona
Argyll PA76 6SJ   Telephone: 06817 306

Scottish Episcopal Church

Devoid of many of the distractions of the 20th century, Iona is a good place to rediscover simplicity and to feel some unity with nature and creation. It has been steeped in Christian prayer for 14 centuries. Bishop's House is both a place for retreat and for those who may wish to take a very quiet break in a Christian environment. There is a resident chaplain and the house runs 'open week' retreats for those coming as individuals.

Open: *March to October. Receives men, women, young people, families with children over 9 years, groups.*
Rooms: *4 singles, 3 doubles, 6 twin-bedded rooms.*
Facilities: *Conferences, garden, small library, guest lounge and guest telephone.*
Spiritual Help: *Personal talks, meditation and directed study.*
Guests Admitted to: *Unrestricted access everywhere.*
Meals: *Everyone eats together. Good, varied home-cooking, with provision for vegetarian and special diets.*
Special Activities: *Most guests come in parish parties and often bring their own chaplain and organise their own programme. Planned programme of events – send for brochure.*
Situation: *Very quiet.*
Maximum Stay: *No restrictions.*
Bookings: *By letter or telephone.*
Charges: *See the brochure.*
Access: *No easy way. (See entry for Iona Community, page 188.)*

Largs

Benedictine Monastery
5 Mackerston Place
Largs
Ayrshire KA30 8BY   Telephone: 0475 687320

Roman Catholic

A quiet and comfortable place where you will be left to structure your own day or follow the prayer rhythm of the nuns. With no organised retreats or programmes, this is a retreat house designed for the world-weary whose spiritual energies are at a low ebb.

Open: *All year. Receives women.*
Rooms: *Single and double rooms are available.*
Facilities: *Library, chapel.*
Spiritual Help: *Divine Office, daily Mass.*
Guests Admitted to: *Chapel.*
Meals: *DIY for breakfast. Lunch and supper served. Traditional food.*
Special Activities: *None.*
Situation: *Quiet.*
Maximum Stay: *By arrangement.*
Bookings: *By letter.*
Charges: *By arrangement or donation.*
Access: *BR: to Largs from Glasgow. Car: follow Clyde coastal route from Glasgow.*

TAYSIDE

Crieff

St Ninian's Centre
Comrie Road
Crieff
Perthshire PH7 4BG   Telephone: 0764 3766

Interdenominational

A former church, St Ninian's has been adapted into a modern residential centre, providing a wide range of courses, retreats, renewal weekends and refreshment breaks. The little town of Crieff is situated in pretty countryside and has much to offer in the way of parks and nature trails for walking, and local sports facilities, including fishing.

Open: *All year except Christmas. Receives men, women, young people, families and groups.*
Rooms: *22 singles, 14 doubles, dormitory.*
Facilities: *Conferences, library, guest lounge, TV and guest pay phone. Children welcomed, guide dogs permitted.*
Spiritual Help: *Group sharing and directed study. Staff assist at mission-training and renewal conferences that are held for elders, lay preachers, church groups and youth groups.*
Guests Admitted to: *Chapel.*
Meals: *Everyone eats together. Traditional food, with provision for vegetarian and special diets.*
Special Activities: *Planned programme of events. Send for brochure.*
Situation: *In the town, near countryside and with good views. Central for shops and park.*
Maximum Stay: *2 weeks.*

Bookings: *By letter.*
Charges: *Send for tariff.*
Access: *By rail, bus or car via Perth and Stirling.*

Perth

St Mary's Mission & Renewal Centre
St Mary's Monastery
Kinnoull
Perth PH2 7BP   Telephone: 0738 24075

Roman Catholic

This is a large, rather institutional retreat centre overlooking Perth and enjoying peaceful seclusion. There is plenty of accommodation here, and retreat and renewal courses (one lasting six weeks) are available for both lay guests and religious. Individuals are welcome throughout the year.

Open: *All year. Receives men, women, young people, families, groups and religious.*
Rooms: *22 singles, 14 doubles.*
Facilities: *Disabled, conferences, camping, garden, library, guest lounge, TV and guest pay phone (0738 36487). Children welcomed. No pets.*
Spiritual Help: *Personal talks, group sharing, directed study and special renewal courses.*
Guests Admitted to: *Access to most areas, including chapel.*
Meals: *Everyone eats together. Traditional food, with provision for vegetarians and special diets.*
Special Activities: *Planned events and courses. Send for brochure.*
Situation: *Quiet, above the city.*
Maximum Stay: *By arrangement.*
Bookings: *By letter or telephone.*
Charges: *Enquire when requesting brochure or booking to stay.*
Access: *BR to Perth, bus thereafter. By car to Perth city, then via Hatton Road to St Mary's Monastery.*

'It is rare to find anyone who is truly reasonable, for we are usually diverted from the path of reason by self-love' – St Fancis de Sales

Northern Ireland

Columbanus Community of Reconciliation
683 Antrim Road
Belfast BT15 4EG   Telephone: 0232 778009

Most of the guests at Columbanus are interested in the religious and socio-
political situation in Northern Ireland. They use this place as a base from
which to explore such implications and as a means of informing themselves
on a personal basis. Using this experience they hope to create change in their
own cultural and church environments. Programmes can be arranged for
groups. This is very much an ecumenical community, comprising Roman
Catholic, Anglican and Presbyterian members, all of whom share the aims
and ministry of reconciliation.

Open: *All year except 3 weeks in August. Receives men, women, young
people, groups and non-retreatants.*
Rooms: *1 single, 2 doubles, dormitories.*
Facilities: *Door ramps for the disabled but no sleeping facilities. Small
conferences, large garden, nearby park, library, guest lounge, TV and direct-
dialling telephone.*
Spiritual Help: *Community prayers – morning and evening and for anyone
around at lunch-time. Spiritual direction can sometimes be offered to
individuals.*
Guests Admitted to: *Unrestricted access for individuals.*
Meals: *Eaten together in dining room. Tasty, wholesome food, with
provision for vegetarians. Self-catering for groups.*
Special Activities: *Occasional lectures – faith, history, ecumenics.*
Situation: *In the city, rather busy.*
Maximum Stay: *Unlimited.*
Bookings: *By letter.*
Charges: *Sample rates: £12 per person, full board; £6 B&B; £2. 50 lunch;
£3. 50 dinner.*
Access: *Buses: Nos. 1, 2, 3, 4, 5, 6, 45 from City Hall.*

*'There is no thought, feeling or desire within us which cannot become the
substance of prayer' – Gerald W. Hughes*

Republic of Ireland

Beara

Dzogchen Beara
Allihies
West Cork   Telephone: 027 730 32

Tibetan Buddhist

This is a developing meditation and retreat centre for Buddhist study and practice. It is 400 feet up on the cliffs above Bantry Bay, with a vast panorama of the Atlantic Ocean. Guests stay in self-catering houses and studios. Dzogchen Beara is under the spiritual direction of Sogyal Rinpoche, a lama, scholar and meditation master. Born in Tibet, he has been living in the West for some 15 years.

Open: *All year. Receives men, women, young people, families, groups and non-retreatants.*
Rooms: *Singles and doubles available in 6 separate holiday- houses.*
Facilities: *Conferences. Children and pets welcomed.*
Spiritual Help: *Meditation.*
Guests Admitted to: *Shrine room.*
Meals: *Self-catering.*
Special Activities: *Programme of planned events – send for brochure. Near famous gardens. Good sporting facilities in vicinity, offering tennis, riding, sailing, fishing and golf.*
Situation: *Very quiet.*
Maximum Stay: *Unlimited.*
Bookings: *By telephone or letter.*
Charges: *£10 per person per night.*
Access: *By bus or car from Cork.*

Montenotte (Cork)

St Dominic's Priory and Retreat Centre
Ennismore
Montenotte
Cork   Telephone: 021 502520

Roman Catholic

'Get up and make your way to the potter's house: there I shall let you hear what I have to say.' (Jeremiah 18:2) This is a good line of Scripture to bear in mind, if you find a weekend course entitled 'pottery meditations' too curious. Other stimulating courses on offer here from the resident Dominican community include charismatic retreats for lay guests and religious, retreats for retired lay people, and reflexology and meditation workshops.

Open: *All year except 24 December to 6 January. Receives men, women, young people, groups and non-retreatants.*
Rooms: *40 singles, 6 doubles, dormitories for 50, hermitage, barn.*
Facilities: *Limited for disabled, conferences, garden, park, library, guest lounge and direct-dialling pay phone.*
Spiritual Help: *Personal talks, group sharing, meditation and directed study.*
Guests Admitted to: *Almost unrestricted access to all areas, including chapel, choir, shrine room, some work of the community.*
Meals: *Taken in the guest house. Traditional food, with provision for vegetarian and special diets. Self-catering facilities available.*
Special Activities: *Planned programme of events. Send for brochure.*
Situation: *Quiet, in the countryside, but can be rather busy. With 30 acres of grounds and spectacularly situated gardens, the Centre feels as though it is in open countryside, but is only 3 miles from the city centre.*
Maximum Stay: *Unlimited.*
Bookings: *By telephone but confirmation by letter required.*
Charges: *£19 per person per 24 hours, full board. Self-catering and dormitory rates available on application.*
Access: *By rail to Cork. Bus: No. 8 from city centre. Car: see map in brochure.*

DUBLIN

Dublin

Dominican Retreat & Pastoral Centre
Tallaght
Dublin 24   Telephone: Dublin 515002

Roman Catholic

There are good facilities here for the disabled, as well as accommodation with DIY cooking facilities for those wishing to make a silent retreat in the 'poustinia' tradition. Although in the town, it is quiet and there is a garden and park.

Open: *All year except Christmas. Receives men, women, young people, families and groups.*
Rooms: *28 singles, 5 doubles.*
Facilities: *Good facilities for disabled and conferences, chapel, choir, garden, park, guest lounge, TV and pay phone.*
Spiritual Help: *Personal talks, group sharing, meditation.*
Guests Admitted to: *Unrestricted access everywhere, including chapel, choir.*
Meals: *Everyone eats together. Traditional food, with provision for vegetarian and special diets.*

Special Activities: *Planned programme of events. Send for brochure.*
Situation: *In town, but quiet.*
Maximum Stay: *1 week.*
Bookings: *By letter or telephone.*
Charges: *£22 per person per day, full board.*
Access: *Bus: No. 77 or 77a from centre of Dublin.*

'If a care is too small to be turned into a prayer, it is too small to be made into a burden' – Corrie ten Boom

KERRY

Ardfert

Ardfert Retreat Centre
Ardfert
County Kerry   Telephone: 066 34276

Roman Catholic

Officially opened in 1981, the Centre is staffed by Presentation Sisters and a priest director, and serves some 54 parishes. While this is a place for group bookings, individuals wishing to join any Saturday or Sunday parish-group retreat are welcome to do so by prior arrangement with the secretary of the Centre. There is a new lending-library service for books and videos on Christian topics.

Open: *All year. Receives men, women, young people, religious – but you must be part of a group.*
Rooms: *31 singles.*
Facilities: *A diocesan retreat centre in constant use by parish groups and schools.*
Guests Admitted to: *Almost unrestricted access.*
Spiritual Help: *Personal talks, group sharing and meditation.*
Meals: *Available for groups but not for individual visitors. Wholefood.*
Special Activities: *Send for brochure.*
Situation: *Very quiet, in the countryside.*
Maximum Stay: *According to the programme.*
Bookings: *By letter.*
Charges: *See brochure, as these vary from £19 per person per day to £36 per weekend.*
Access: *Train and bus to Tralee. Car: Centre is 5 miles north of Tralee.*

Murroe

Glenstal Abbey
Murroe
County Limerick   Telephone: 061 386103

Roman Catholic

Glenstal, founded in 1927 on the site of a medieval abbey, has a tradition of involvement in arts and crafts, in the areas of sculpture, metalwork, wood-turning and pottery, and runs a nearby school. This is a large and active community, perhaps one of the very few who can say that guests may be admitted to the choir 'if room is available'. In most monasteries today there are more empty choir- stalls than filled ones at Divine Office. In 1975, the Abbey founded a new monastic community in Nigeria and these links with Africa have been strengthened over the years.

Open: *All year except Christmas. Receives men, women, young people and sometimes non-retreatants.*
Rooms: *8 singles, 2 doubles.*
Facilities: *Conferences by arrangement, park and gardens, small library and pay phone.*
Spiritual Help: *Personal talks if requested.*
Guests Admitted to: *Chapel and choir, if room is available.*
Meals: *Some meals taken with monastic community, others in the parlour. Traditional food – arrangements can be made for vegetarian or special diets. Tea- and coffee-making facilities.*
Special Activities: *No planned programme of events.*
Situation: *Very quiet and in the countryside.*
Maximum Stay: *7 days.*
Bookings: *By letter.*
Charges: *£20 per person per day suggested.*
Access: *Rail from Dublin, buses infrequent. Car: Abbey is 12 miles from Limerick, off the Dublin Road.*

TIPPERARY

Roscrea

Mount St Joseph Abbey
Roscrea
County Tipperary   Telephone: 0505 21711

Roman Catholic – Ecumenical

Almost 300 boys attend secondary school here, and this active and large community of Cistercian monks have made no less than three new foundations since the war – one each in Ireland, Scotland and Australia. The Abbey is set in quiet countryside and the atmosphere is conducive to prayer and relaxation. The monastic choir and liturgy is deeply rich and inspiring.

Open: *All year except Christmas. Receives men, women, young people individually, groups and non-retreatants.*
Rooms: *12 singles, 5 doubles, 7 twin-bedded rooms.*
Facilities: *Conferences, limited library, guest lounge and pay phone.*
Spiritual Help: *Personal talks, meditation can be made privately in prayer room in the guest house or in the church.*
Guests Admitted to: *Chapel.*
Meals: *Everyone eats together in the guest house – traditional food.*
Special Activities: *No planned programme of events.*
Situation: *In quiet countryside.*
Maximum Stay: *2 weeks.*
Bookings: *By letter or telephone.*
Charges: *£15 per person per day.*
Access: *By rail or car from Dublin. Bus: to Roscrea town – guest house 3 miles away.*

'Earth and heaven are in us' – Mahatma Gandhi

France

The majority of retreat places in France are Roman Catholic monasteries and convents with a few notable exceptions such as Taizé, which is a world-famous ecumenical community to which thousands of young men and women go each year.

The listing is divided alphabetically by the department in France with the department number after it. For example: Calvados (14). Then, on the left-hand side, comes the name of the town or city, followed by the name and address of the retreat centre. The name of the town or city is provided in order to help locate the centre on a map – it does not always correspond exactly with the postal address of the centre. A brief line or two is given to describe each centre: where the gender of the retreatants is not specified, this indicates that both sexes are welcome.

When applying, please do not telephone but write in the first instance. Do not assume members of the community will speak English. However, if you must write in English, someone will probably answer your letter.

AIN (01)

Le Plantay
Abbaye Notre-Dame-des-Dombes
Le Plantay
01330 Villars-les-Dombes   Telephone: 74 98 14 40
Roman Catholic. Receives individual retreatants.

ALLIER (03)

Chantelle
Abbaye Saint-Vincent
03140 Chantelle   Telephone: 70 56 62 55
Roman Catholic. Receives lay brothers, individual and group retreatants.

Dompierre-sur-Besbre
Abbaye de Sept-Fons
03290 Dompierre-sur-Besbre   Telephone: 70 34 50 92
Roman Catholic. 27 rooms for individual retreatants and couples.

Moulins
Monastère de la Visitation
65, rue des Tanneries
03000 Moulins   Telephone: 70 44 27 43
Roman Catholic. 2 rooms for private retreatants.

ALPES-MARITIMES (06)

Carros
Communauté des Carmélites
06510 Carros-Village   Telephone: 93 29 10 71
Roman Catholic. 7 rooms for retreats of 3 to 10 days.

Lérins (Iles de)
Abbaye de Lérins
B.P. 157
06406 Cannes Cedex   Telephone: 93 48 68 68
Roman Catholic. 35 rooms for retreats of up to 5 days.

ARDÈCHE (07)

Saint-Étienne-de-Lugdarès
Abbaye de Notre-Dame-des-Neiges
07590 Saint-Étienne-de-Lugdarès   Telephone: 66 46 00 68
Roman Catholic. Open all year to all individuals and groups.

AUBE (10)

Troyes
Carmel de Notre-Dame-de-Pitié
1164, route d'Auxerre
Saint-Germain
10120 Saint-André-les-Vergers   Telephone: 25 82 20 19
Roman Catholic. Several rooms for individual retreats.

AUDE (11)

Azille
Monastère Sainte-Claire
Azille
11700 Capendu   Telephone: 68 91 40 24
Roman Catholic. Open to all – limited number of rooms.

Prouilhe
Monastère Sainte-Marie
Prouilhe
11270 Fanjeaux   Telephone: 68 91 40 24
Roman Catholic. Open to all, for weekends or retreats of up to 2 weeks.

AVEYRON (12)

Espalion
Abbaye Notre-Dame-de-Bonneval
12500 Espalion   Telephone: 68 91 40 24
Roman Catholic. Board and lodging for retreats and meditation.

Mur-de-Barrez
Monastère Sainte-Claire
2, rue de la Berque
12600 Mur-de-Barrez   Telephone: 65 66 00 46
Roman Catholic. Receives individuals, and families with children.

Saint-Sernin-sur-Rance
Monastère Notre-Dame-d'Orient
12380 Saint-Sernin-sur-Rance   Telephone: 65 99 60 88
Roman Catholic. Receives young and not so young, laymen and lay-
women, priests, monks, nuns.

BOUCHES-DU-RHÔNE (13)

Aix-en-Provence
Monastère du Saint-Sacrement
Notre-Dame-de-la-Seds
2, avenue Jean-Dalmas
13090 Aix-en-Provence   Telephone: 42 64 44 36
Roman Catholic. Receives groups of young people or adults in the
daytime or evening only.

Jouques
Abbaye Notre-Dame-de-Fidélité
13490 Jouques   Telephone: 42 57 80 17
Roman Catholic. Receives individuals or groups.

Marseille
Carmel Notre-Dame
81, chemin de l'Oule
Montolivet
13012 Marseille   Telephone: 91 93 59 10
Roman Catholic. Receives individuals – please apply in writing.

Simiane-Collongue
Monastère de Saint-Germain
Saint-Germain
13109 Simiane-Collongue   Telephone: 42 22 60 60
Roman Catholic. Receives retreatants seeking silence and prayer.

Tarascon
Abbaye Saint-Michel-de-Frigolet
13150 Tarascon-sur-Rhône   Telephone: 90 95 70 07
Roman Catholic – a place of herbs and beauty. Open for retreats,
holidays, and study. Apply in writing.

CALVADOS (14)

Bayeux
Monastère de la Sainte-Trinite
48, rue Saint-Loup
B.P. 93
14402 Bayeux Cedex   Telephone: 31 92 02 99
Roman Catholic. Receives individuals and groups for a maximum stay of
2 weeks – apply in writing.

Caen
Monastère des Carmélites
51, avenue Clemenceau
14000 Caen   Telephone: 31 93 66 63
Roman Catholic. Receives individual retreatants.

Juaye-Mondaye
Abbaye de Mondaye
Juaye-Mondaye
14250 Tilly-sur-Seulles   Telephone: 31 92 58 11
Roman Catholic. Open all year (excluding last week in August) to all
individuals and groups, except unaccompanied children, for stays of 1 day
up to 1 week.

Lisieux
Abbaye Notre-Dame-du-Pré
39, avenue du Six-Juin
14100 Lisieux   Telephone: 31 31 32 63
Roman Catholic. Open to all, but to men by recommendation.

CHARENTE (16)

Montmoreau-Saint-Cybard
Abbaye Sainte-Marie-de-Maumont
Juignac
16190 Montmoreau-Saint-Cybard   Telephone: 45 60 34 38
Roman Catholic. Open to individuals or groups for stays of up to 10 days.

CHARENTE-MARITIME (17)

La Rochelle
Monastère Sainte-Claire
6, rue de Gué
17000 La Rochelle   Telephone: 46 34 35 21
Roman Catholic. Open to all women.

Saint-Palais-sur-Mer
Monastère de Béthanie
67, route de Courlay
17420 Saint-Palais-sur-Mer   Telephone: 46 23 12 19
Roman Catholic. Receives individuals and families.

CHER (18)

Bourges
Carmel
6, rue du Puits-Noir
18000 Bourges   Telephone: 48 24 34 04
Roman Catholic. Open for individual retreats.

CORRÈZE (19)

Aubazine
Monastère de la Théophanie
Aubazine
19190 Beynat   Telephone: none
Roman Catholic. Several rooms for individual retreats – apply in writing only.

CORSE (20)

Erbalunga
Monastère des Bénédictines du Saint-Sacrement
20222 Erbalunga   Telephone: 95 33 22 32
Roman Catholic. Open from 1 June to 20 September for stays of 2 to 3 weeks. References required before first stay.

COTE-D'ÔR (21)

Flavignerot
Carmel
Flavignerot
21160 Marsannay-la-Côte   Telephone: 80 42 92 38
Roman Catholic. Receives men and women.

Flavigny-sur-Ozerain
Monastère Saint-Joseph-de-Clairval
Flavigny-sur-Ozerain
21150 Venaray-les-Laumes   Telephone: 80 96 22 31
Roman Catholic. Open only to men and young people.

CÔTES-DU-NORD (22)

Saint-Brieuc
Carmel
55, rue Pinot-Duclos
22000 Saint-Brieuc   Telephone: 96 94 22 95
Roman Catholic. Receives women for individual retreats.

DORDOGNE (24)

Bergerac
Carmel du Sacré-Coeur
79, rue Valette
24100 Bergerac   Telephone: 53 57 15 33
Roman Catholic. Open only to women retreatants.

Échourgnac
Abbaye Notre-Dame-de-Bonne-Espérance
Échourgnac
24410 Saint-Aulaye   Telephone: 53 80 36 43
Roman Catholic. Open to all retreatants.

Nans-sous-Sainte-Anne
Prieuré Saint-Benoît
Nans-sous-Sainte-Anne
25330 Amancey   Telephone: 81 86 61 79
Roman Catholic. 7 rooms for private retreats.

DRÔME (26)

Aiguebelle
Abbaye Notre-Dame-d'Aiguebelle
Montjoyer
26230 Grignan   Telephone: 75 98 52 33
Roman Catholic. Receives men for retreats.

Crest
Monastère Sainte-Claire
53, rue des Auberts
26400 Crest   Telephone: 75 25 49 13
Roman Catholic. Receives men for stays of up to 10 days.

Grignan
Prieuré de l'Emmanuel
26230 Grignan   Telephone: 75 46 50 37
Roman Catholic. Receives women individually or in groups.

Triors
Monastère Notre-Dame-de-Triors
26750 Romans-sur-Isère   Telephone: 75 71 43 39
Roman Catholic. Receives men only.

EURE (27)

Le Bec-Hellouin
Abbaye Notre-Dame-du-Bec
Le Bec-Hellouin
27800 Brionne   Telephone: 32 44 86 09
Roman Catholic. Open to men individually or in groups.

EURE-ET-LOIR (28)

Chartres
Monastère de la Visitation
24, avenue d'Aligre
28000 Chartres   Telephone: 37 21 40 40
Roman Catholic. Receives men only.

Landivisiau
Monastère de Kerbenéat
Plounéventer
29230 Landivisiau   Telephone: 98 20 47 43
Roman Catholic. Receives men individually or in groups.

Le Relecq-Kerhuon
Carmel de Brest
88 bis, boulevard Clemenceau
29219 Le Relecq-Kerhuon   Telephone: 98 28 27 93
Roman Catholic. 3 rooms for men only.

GARD (30)

Uzès
Carmel
7, avenue Louis-Alteirac
30700 Uzès   Telephone: 66 22 10 62
Roman Catholic. Open to women only for individual retreats.

GARONNE (HAUTE-) (31)

Blagnac
Monastère Notre-Dame-des-Sept-Douleurs
et de Sainte-Catherine-de-Sienne
60, avenue Général-Compans
31700 Blagnac   Telephone: 61 71 47 80
Roman Catholic. Receives men only – individually or in groups.

Lévignac
Abbaye Sainte-Marie-du-Désert
Bellegarde-Sainte-Marie
31530 Lévignac   Telephone: 61 85 61 32
Roman Catholic. 25 rooms for retreatants.

Muret
Carmel
La Combe-Sainte-Marie
67, chemin Lacombe
31600 Muret   Telephone: 61 51 03 67
Roman Catholic. Receives women only for individual retreats.

GERS (32)

Auch
Carmel
12, rue Pelletier-d'Oisy
32000 Auch   Telephone: 62 63 04 76
Roman Catholic. Receives women only for individual retreats.

Saramon
Monastère Cistercien de Sainte-Marie-de-Boulaur
32450 Saramon   Telephone: 62 65 40 07
Roman Catholic. Receives women and families only.

GIRONDE (33)

Auros
Abbaye de Sainte-Marie-du-Rivet
33124 Auros   Telephone: 56 65 40 10
Roman Catholic. Receives families and priests.

Bordeaux
Monastère de la Visitation
47, cours Marc-Nouaux
33000 Bordeaux   Telephone: 56 44 25 72
Roman Catholic. Receives women only.

HÉRAULT (34)

Le Bousquet-d'Orb
Monastère Orthodoxe Saint-Nicolas
La Dalmerie
34260 Le Bousquet-d'Orb   Telephone: 67 23 41 10
Roman Catholic. Receives men only.

Roqueredonde
La Borie Noble
38650 Roqueredonde   Telephone: 67 44 09 89
*Ecumenical – a Gandhian Ark Community, living a non-violent way of
life. Open all year round – receives men, women, young people, families
and groups.*

Saint-Mathieu-de-Tréviers
Communauté de la Transfiguration
34270 Saint-Mathieu-de-Tréviers   Telephone: 67 55 20 62
Roman Catholic. 40 rooms (20 doubles) for women only.

ILLE-ET-VILAINE (35)

Plerguer
Notre-Dame-de-Beaufort
Plerguer
35540 Miniac-Morvan   Telephone: 99 48 07 57
Roman Catholic. Receives men only – individually or in groups.

INDRE (36)

Fontgombault
Abbaye Notre-Dame-de-Fontgombault
Fontgombault
36220 Tournon-Saint-Martin Telephone: 54 37 12 03
Roman Catholic. Receives men only.

Pellevoisin
Monastère de Marie, Mère de Miséricorde
36180 Pellevoisin Telephone: none
Roman Catholic. 12 rooms for women only.

ISÈRE (38)

Voiron
Monastère de la Visitation
Notre-Dame-du-May
38500 Voiron Telephone: 76 05 26 29
Roman Catholic. Receives young women and married women only.

JURA (39)

Ougney
Abbaye d'Acey
Vitreux (Ougney)
39350 Gendrey Telephone: 84 81 04 11
Roman Catholic. Receives men individually – 15 rooms.

LANDES (40)

Aire-sur-l'Adour
Carmel
6, rue Maubec
B.P. 25
40800 Aire-sur-l'Adour Telephone: 58 71 82 18
Roman Catholic. Receives women only.

LOIRE (42)

Pradines
Abbaye Saint-Joseph-et-Saint-Pierre de Pradines
Pradines
42630 Régny Telephone: 77 64 80 06
Roman Catholic. Receives men only – individually or in groups.

LOIRE (HAUTE-) (43)

Langeac
Monastère de Sainte-Catherine
2, rue de Pont
43300 Langeac Telephone: 71 77 01 50
Roman Catholic. Receives women only.

Le Puy
Monastère Sainte-Claire
2, rue Sainte-Claire
43000 Le Puy   Telephone: 71 09 17 47
Roman Catholic. Receives men only.

                              LOIRE-ATLANTIQUE (44)

La Meilleraye-de-Bretagne
Abbaye Notre-Dame-de-Melleray
La Meilleraye-de-Bretagne
44520 Moisdon-la-Rivière   Telephone: 40 55 20 01
Roman Catholic. Receives men only.

Nantes
Monastère Sainte-Claire
20, rue Molac
44000 Nantes   Telephone: 40 20 37 36
Roman Catholic. Receives men only for individual retreats.

                                         LOIRET (45)

Saint-Jean-de-Braye
Monastère des Bénédictines de Notre-Dame-du-Calvaire
65, avenue de Verdun
B.P. 4
45801 Saint-Jean-de-Braye   Telephone: 38 61 43 05
Roman Catholic. Receives young women, women and families without
small babies.

                              MAINE-ET-LOIRE (49)

Angers
Prieuré de Notre-Dame-du-Calvaire
8, rue Vauvert
49100 Angers   Telephone: 41 87 76 28
Roman Catholic. Receives women only – individually or in small groups.

Bégrolles-en-Mauges
Abbaye de Bellefontaine
Bégrolles-en-Mauges
49122 Le May-sur-Evre   Telephone: 41 63 81 60
Roman Catholic. Receives men and mixed groups.

Saint-Georges-des-Gardes
Abbaye Notre-Dame-des-Gardes
Saint-Georges-des-Gardes
49120 Chemillé   Telephone: 41 62 91 13
Roman Catholic. Receives women, couples, mixed groups and young
people.

Avranches
Carmel
59, boulevard du Luxembourg
50300 Avranches   Telephone: 33 58 23 66
Roman Catholic. Receives men and women.

Le Mont-Saint-Michel
Communauté de l'Abbaye
B.P. 3
50116 Le Mont-Saint-Michel   Telephone: 33 60 14 47
Roman Catholic. Receives men and women.

Saint-James
Prieuré Saint-Jacques
50240 Saint-James   Telephone: 33 48 31 39
Roman Catholic. Receives men and women.

Saint-Pair-sur-Mer
Carmel
213, route de Lézeaux
50380 Saint-Pair-sur-Mer   Telephone: 33 50 12 00
Roman Catholic. Receives individual retreatants.

MARNE (51)

Fismes
Abbaye Notre-Dame-d'Igny
Arcis-le-Ponsart
51170 Fismes   Telephone: 26 78 08 40
Roman Catholic. Open all year for retreats.

Reims
Monastère Sainte-Claire (Soeurs Pauvres)
13, avenue Roger-Salengro
51430 Tinqueux   Telephone: 26 08 23 15
Roman Catholic. Receives women, couples, priests, religious – individually or in groups.

Saint-Thierry
Monastère des Bénédictines
51220 Saint-Thierry   Telephone: 26 03 10 72
Roman Catholic. Limited number of rooms for individuals or groups.

MAYENNE (53)

Craon
Monastère des Bénédictines du Saint-Sacrement
15, rue de la Libération
53400 Craon Telephone: 43 06 13 38
Roman Catholic. Receives group retreatants.

MEURTRE-ET-MOSELLE (54)

Nancy
Monastère de la Visitation
64, rue Marquette
54000 Nancy Telephone: 83 96 63 83
Roman Catholic. Receives women and religious for individual retreats.

MORBIHAN (56)

Bréhan
Abbaye Notre-Dame-de-Timadeuc
Bréhan
56580 Rohan Telephone: 97 51 50 29
Roman Catholic. Receives men and women.

Campénéac
Abbaye-la-Joie-Notre-Dame
Campénéac
56800 Ploërmel Telephone: 97 93 42 07
Roman Catholic. Receives women and group retreatants.

Plouharnel
Abbaye Sainte-Anne-de-Kergonan
56720 Plouharnel Telephone: 97 52 30 75
Roman Catholic. Receives men individually.

MOSELLE (57)

Delme
Abbaye d'Oriocourt Telephone: 87 05 31 67
57590 Delme 87 01 31 67
Roman Catholic. Receives individual retreatants.

NORD (59)

Le Mont-des-Cats
Abbaye Sainte-Marie-du-Mont
Godewaersvelde
59270 Bailleul Telephone: 28 42 52 50
Roman Catholic. Open for silent retreats only.

Moustier-en-Fagne
Prieuré Saint-Dodon
Moustier-en-Fagne
59132 Trelon   Telephone: 27 61 81 28
Roman Catholic. Receives individual retreatants.

Mouvaux
Monastère de la Visitation
192, rue Lorthiois
59420 Mouvaux   Telephone: 20 26 94 34
Roman Catholic. Receives individuals or small groups.

OISE (60)

Beauvais
Monastère du Carmel-Saint-Joseph
62, rue Louis-Prache
60000 Beauvais   Telephone: 44 45 29 70
Roman Catholic. Individual or group retreats.

ORNE (61)

Alençon
Monastère Sainte-Claire
7, rue de la Demi-Lune
61000 Alençon   Telephone: 33 26 14 58
Roman Catholic. 12 rooms for retreatants.

Argentan
Abbaye Notre-Dame
2, rue de l'Abbaye
B.P. 8
61201 Argentan Cedex   Telephone: 33 67 12 01
Roman Catholic. Several rooms for families and retreatants.

Soligny-la-Trappe
Abbaye de la Trappe
Soligny-la-Trappe
61380 Moulins-la-Marche   Telephone: 33 34 50 44
Roman Catholic. Receives men only – individually or in groups.

PAS-DE-CALAIS (62)

Arras
Carmel Notre-Dame-des-Ardents
40, rue Aristide-Briand
Saint-Nicolas
62223 Saint-Laurent-Blangy   Telephone: 21 55 36 21
Roman Catholic. 4 rooms for day retreats or longer.

Béthune
Monastère du Carmel
23, rue Fernand-Fanien
Fouquières-lès-Lens
62232 Annezin   Telephone: 21 68 11 22
Roman Catholic. 4 rooms for retreatants.

Boulogne-sur-Mer
Monastère de la Visitation
9, rue Maquétra
62222 Saint-Martin-Boulogne   Telephone: 21 31 35 88
Roman Catholic. Receives religious, young women and small family groups.

Wisques
Abbaye Saint-Paul
Wisques
62219 Longuenesse   Telephone: 21 95 11 04
Roman Catholic. Receives men only – individually or in groups. Camping available for young people.

PUY-DE-DÔME (63)

Chamalières
Monastère des Clarisses-Capucines
11, avenue de Villars
63407 Chamalières Cedex   Telephone: 73 37 73 11
Roman Catholic. 4 rooms for silent retreats.

Randol
Abbaye Notre-Dame-de Randol
63450 Saint-Amant-Tallende   Telephone: 73 39 31 00
Roman Catholic. Receives men (individually or in groups) in the monastery itself; families and women (individually or in groups) in houses in the village.

PYRÉNÉES-ATLANTIQUES (64)

Anglet
Monastère des Bernardines
64600 Anglet   Telephone: 59 63 84 34
Roman Catholic. Receives women only.

Orthez
Monastère Sainte-Claire
35, rue Saint-Gilles
64300 Orthez   Telephone: 59 69 46 55
Roman Catholic. Several rooms for quiet stays.

Urt
Abbaye Notre-Dame-de-Belloc
64240 Urt Telephone: 59 29 65 55
Roman Catholic. Receives women only for individual retreats.

PYRÉNÉES (HAUTE-) (65)

Lourdes
Carmel Notre-Dame-de-Lourdes
17, route de Pau
65100 Lourdes Telephone: 62 94 26 67
Roman Catholic. Receives men and women for day retreats and in the summer months for longer stays.

Tournay
Abbaye Notre-Dame
65190 Tournay Telephone: 62 35 70 21
Roman Catholic. Receives men and women.

RHIN (BAS-) (67)

Rosheim
Monastère des Bénédictines du Saint-Sacrement
1, rue Saint-Benoît
67560 Rosheim Telephone: 88 50 41 67
Roman Catholic. Receives men and women all year round.

RHIN (HAUT-) (68)

Landser
Monastère Saint-Alphonse
Landser
68440 Habsheim Telephone: 89 81 30 10
Roman Catholic. Receives women, and young people in groups.

Oelenberg
Abbaye de Notre-Dame-d'Oelenberg
68950 Reiningue Telephone: 89 81 91 23
Roman Catholic. Receives men and women – individually or in groups.

Sigolsheim
Monastère de Marie-Médiatrice
5, rue Oberhof
68240 Sigolsheim Telephone: 89 78 23 24
Roman Catholic. Receives women only.

Autun
Carmel
1, rue Chaffaut
71400 Autun Telephone: 85 52 01 29
Roman Catholic. Receives men and women.

Mazille
Carmel de la Paix
Mazille
B.P. 10 Telephone: 85 59 09 78
71250 Cluny 85 59 03 57
*Roman Catholic. Receives men, women, groups and families with
children.*

Paray-le-Monial
Monastère de la Visitation
13, rue de la Visitation
71600 Paray-le-Monial Telephone: 85 81 09 95
Roman Catholic. Receives men and women.

Taizé
Communauté de Taizé
71250 Taizé Telephone: 85 50 18 18
*Ecumenical. Receives men, women and especially young people. Very
popular and crowded in summer. Highly recommended.*

Venière
Abbaye Notre-Dame
Venière
71700 Tournus Telephone: 85 51 05 85
Roman Catholic. Receives men and women – individually and in groups.

SARTHE

Rouillon
Carmel
Vaujoubert-Notre-Dame
72700 Rouillon Telephone: 43 24 17 68
Roman Catholic. Receives men, women and groups of young people.

Solesmes
Abbaye Saint-Pierre-de-Solesmes
72300 Sablé-sur-Sarthe Telephone: 43 95 03 08
Roman Catholic. Receives men only.

SAVOIE (73)

Saint-Pierre-d'Albigny
Monastère de la Visitation
Clos Minjoud
73250 Saint-Pierre-d'Albigny   Telephone: 79 28 50 12
Roman Catholic. Receives women only.

Tamié
Abbaye Notre-Dame de Tamié
Plancherine
73200 Albertville   Telephone: none
Roman Catholic. Receives men and women.

SAVOIE (HAUTE-) (74)

Annecy
Monastère de la Visitation
11, avenue de la Visitation
74000 Annecy   Telephone: 50 45 20 30
Roman Catholic. Receives women only.

Thonon-les-Bains
Monastère de la Visitation
Marclaz
74200 Thonon-les-Bains   Telephone: 50 70 34 46
Roman Catholic. Receives men, women and families (but without young babies).

SEINE (PARIS) (75)

Paris
Abbaye Sainte-Marie
3, rue de la Source
75016 Paris   Telephone: 45 25 30 07
Roman Catholic. Receives men only.

Monastère de Bethléem
Notre-Dame-de-la-Présence-de-Dieu
2, rue Mesnil
75116 Paris   Telephone: 45 01 24 48
Roman Catholic. Receives men and women.

Monastère de l'Adoration-Réparatrice
39, rue Gay-Lussac
75005 Paris   Telephone: 43 26 75 75
Roman Catholic. Receives men and women for individual retreats.

Monastère de la Visitation
68, avenue Denfert-Rochereau
74014 Paris   Telephone: 43 27 12 90
Roman Catholic. Receives women only.

Mont-Saint-Aignan
Carmel
1, rue Lefort
Gonssolin
76130 Mont-Saint-Aignan   Telephone: 35 71 18 14
Roman Catholic. Receives men and women.

Saint-Wandrille-Rançon
Abbaye Saint-Wandrille
76490 Caudebec-en-Caux   Telephone: 35 96 23 11
Roman Catholic. Receives men and women – individually or in groups.

Brou-sur-Chantereine
Prieuré St Joseph
1, avenue Victor-Thiebaut
77177 Brou-sur-Chantereine   Telephone: 60 20 11 20
*Roman Catholic. Receives all in guest house for individual or group
retreats.*

Faremoutiers
Abbaye Notre-Dame-et-Saint-Pierre
Faremoutiers
77120 Coulommiers   Telephone: 64 04 20 37
Roman Catholic. Receives men and women.

Jouarre
Abbaye Notre-Dame-de-Jouarre
6, rue Montmorin
77640 Jouarre   Telephone: 60 22 06 11
Roman Catholic. Receives women only.

Bonnelles
Monastère des Orantes-de-l'Assomption
Chemin de Noncienne
78830 Bonnelles   Telephone: 30 41 32 76
Roman Catholic. Receives men and women – individually or in groups.

Niort
Carmel du Mystère-Pascal
157, rue de Strasbourg
79000 Niort   Telephone: 49 24 18 72
Roman Catholic. Receives men, women and young people.

TARN (81)
Dourgne
Abbaye Saint-Benoît-d'en-Calcat
81110 Dourgne   Telephone: 63 50 32 37
Roman Catholic. Receives men and women – individually or in groups.

TARN-ET-GARONNE (82)
Verdun-sur-Garonne
Abbaye Saint-Pierre
Mas-Grenier
82600 Verdun-sur-Garonne   Telephone: 63 02 51 22
Roman Catholic. Receives men and women – individually or in groups.

VAR (83)
Cotignac
Prieuré-la-Font-Saint-Joseph-du-Bessillon
83570 Cotignac   Telephone: 94 04 63 44
Roman Catholic. Receives women only.

Saint-Maximin-La-Sainte-Baume
Monastère Sainte-Marie-Madeleine
Route de Barjols
83470 Saint-Maximin-La-Sainte-Baume   Telephone: 94 78 04 71
Roman Catholic. Receives men and women.

VAUCLUSE (84)
Montfavet
Monastere Sainte-Claire-de-Notre-Dame-des-Miracles
La Verdière
B.P. 28
84140 Montfavet   Telephone: 90 31 01 55
Roman Catholic. Receives men and women.

VENDÉE (85)
Chavagnes-en-Paillers
Carmel de la Fouchardière
Chavagnes-en-Paillers
85250 Saint-Fulgent   Telephone: 51 42 21 80
Roman Catholic. Receives men and women.

La Roche-sur-Yon
Monastère Sainte-Claire-de-Saint-Joseph
36, rue Abbé-Pierre-Arnaud
85000 La Roche-sur-Yon   Telephone: 51 37 10 13
Roman Catholic. Receives couples and women.

Les Sables-d'Olonne
Monastère de la Passion
1, rue du Petit-Montauban
La Chaume
85100 Les Sables-d'Olonne   Telephone: 51 95 19 26
Roman Catholic. Receives men and women.

VIENNE (86)

Ligugé
Abbaye Saint-Martin
86240 Ligugé   Telephone: 49 55 21 12
Roman Catholic. Receives men, women and groups of young people.

Poitiers
Abbaye Sainte-Croix   Telephone: 49 37 51 18
86280 Saint-Benoît   49 88 57 33
Roman Catholic. Receives men and women.

Saint-Julien l'Ars
Prieuré de Notre-Dame-du-Calvaire
86800 Saint-Julien l'Ars   Telephone: 49 56 71 01
Roman Catholic. Receives women only.

VIENNE (HAUTE-) (87)

Le Dorat
Carmel Nazareth
10, rue Saint-Michel
87210 Le Dorat   Telephone: 55 60 73 65
Roman Catholic. Receives men and women.

VOSGES (88)

Ubexy
Abbaye Cistercienne Notre-Dame-de-Saint-Joseph-d'Ubexy
88130 Charmes   Telephone: 29 38 04 32
Roman Catholic. Receives men and women, and young people in groups.

YONNE (89)

La Pierre-qui-Vire
Abbaye Sainte-Marie
de-la-Pierre-qui-Vire
89830 Saint-Léger-Vauban   Telephone: 86 32 21 23
Roman Catholic. Receives men and women – individually or in groups.

Sens
Monastere de la Nativité
105, rue Victor-Guichard
89100 Sens   Telephone: 86-65-13-41
Roman Catholic. Receives men and women – individually or in groups.

Lepuix-Gy
Prieuré Saint-Benoît-de-Chauveroche
Lepuix-Gy
90200 Giromagny   Telephone: 84 29 01 57
Roman Catholic. Receives men and women for individual retreats.

Évry
Monastère de la Croix
Cours Monseigneur-Romero
91000 Évry   Telephone: 64 97 22 72
Roman Catholic. Receives men and women.

Limon Vauhallan
Abbaye Saint-Louis-du-Temple
Limon Vauhallan   Telephone: 69 41 16 19
91430 Igny   69 41 00 10
Roman Catholic. Receives men and women.

Soisy-sur-Seine
Communauté de l'Épiphanie
Avenue du Général-de-Gaulle
91450 Soisy-sur-Seine   Telephone: 60 75 32 59
Roman Catholic. Receives men and women – individually and in groups.

Vanves
Prieuré Sainte-Bathilde
7, rue d'Issy
92170 Vanves   Telephone: 46 42 46 20
*Roman Catholic. Receives men and women – individually or in small
groups.*

The National Retreat Centre
24 South Audley Street
London W1Y 5DL   Telephone: 071-493 3534

The Inter-faith Network for the United Kingdom
5-7 Tavistock Place
London WC1H 9SS   Telephone: 071-387 0008

World Congress of Faiths
The Inter-faith Fellowship
28 Powis Gardens
London W11 1JG   Telephone: 071-727 2607

Buddhist Society
58 Ecclestone Square
London SW1 1PH   Telephone: 081-834 5858

London Buddhist Centre
51 Roman Road
London E2 OHU   Telephone: 081-981 1225

Amaravati Buddhist Centre
Great Gaddesden
Hemel Hempstead
Herts. HP1 3BZ   Telephone: 044 284 2455

The Islamic Centre
146 Park Road
London NW8 7RG   Telephone: 071-724 3363

National Council of Hindu Temples
559 St Alban's Road
Watford
Herts. WD2 6JH   Telephone: 0923 674 168

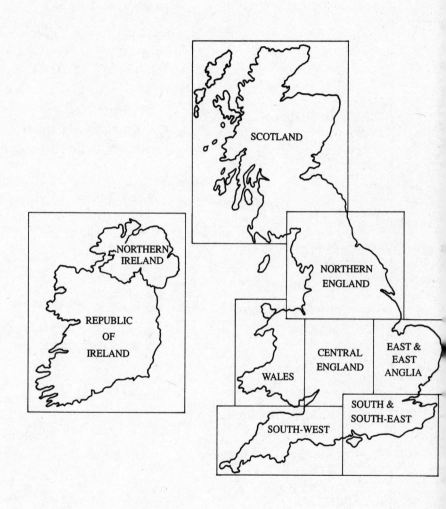

SCOTLAND

NORTHERN IRELAND

NORTHERN ENGLAND

REPUBLIC OF IRELAND

EAST & EAST ANGLIA

CENTRAL ENGLAND

WALES

SOUTH & SOUTH-EAST

SOUTH-WEST

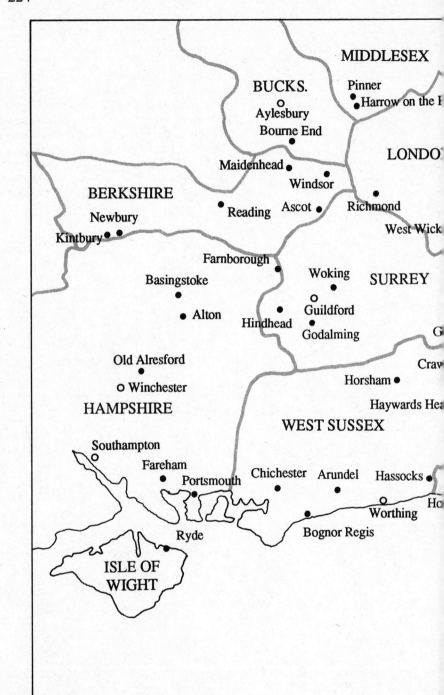

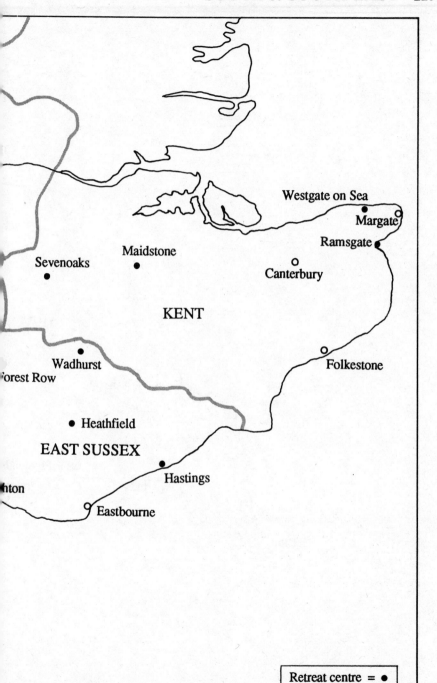

Westgate on Sea

Margate

Ramsgate

Maidstone

Sevenoaks

Canterbury

KENT

Wadhurst

Folkestone

orest Row

Heathfield

EAST SUSSEX

Hastings

hton

Eastbourne

Retreat centre = ●
Main town   = ○

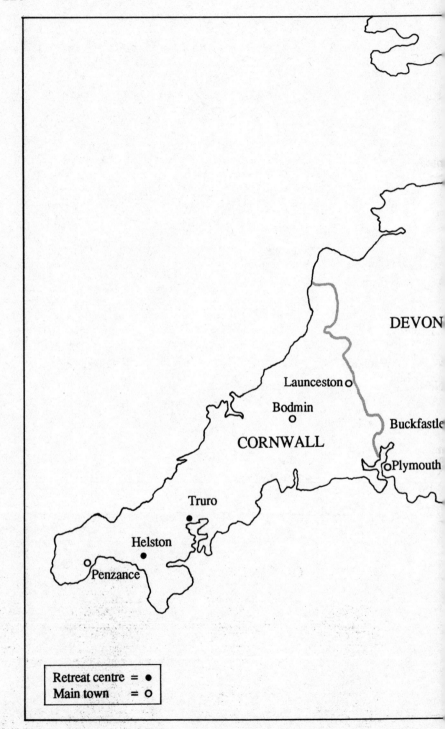

Launceston ○

Bodmin
○

DEVON

Buckfastle

CORNWALL

○ Plymouth

Truro
●

Helston
●

○
Penzance

Retreat centre	= ●
Main town	= ○

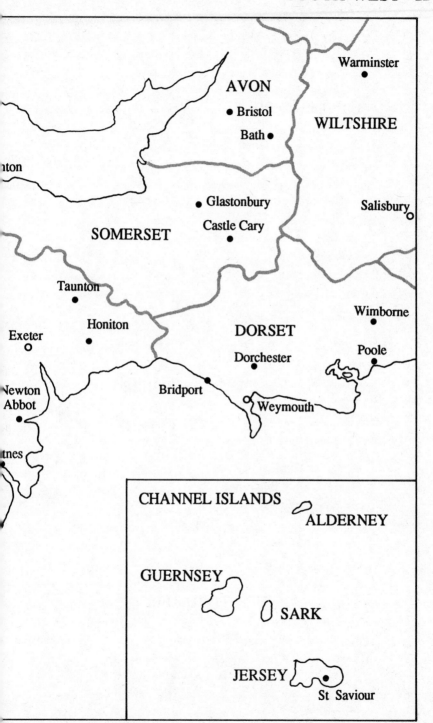

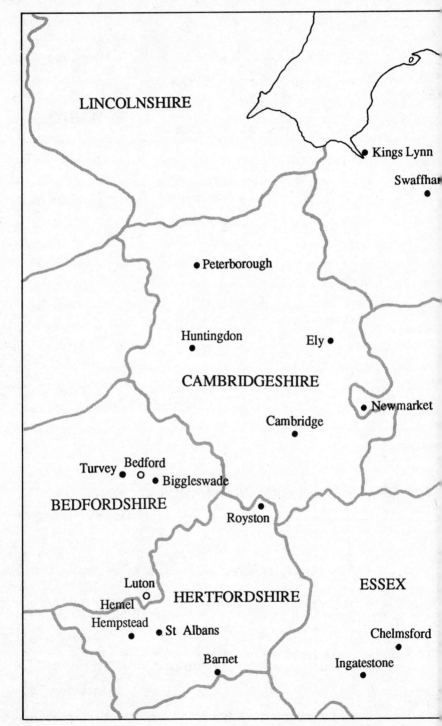

LINCOLNSHIRE

Kings Lynn

Swaffhar

Peterborough

Huntingdon

Ely

CAMBRIDGESHIRE

Newmarket

Cambridge

Turvey Bedford

Biggleswade

BEDFORDSHIRE

Royston

Luton

Hemel

Hempstead

HERTFORDSHIRE

St Albans

ESSEX

Chelmsford

Barnet

Ingatestone

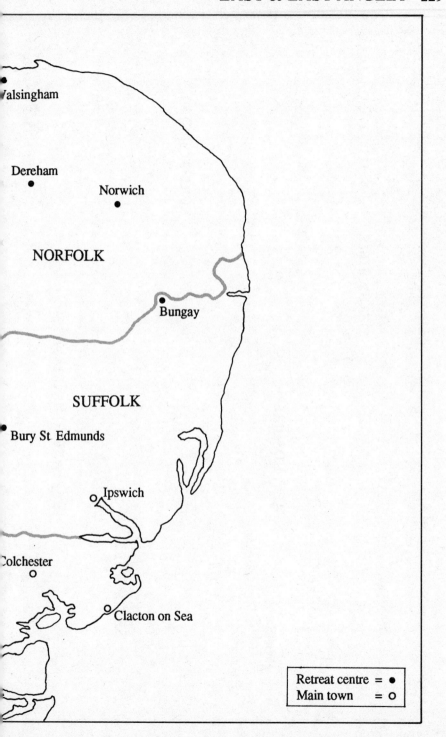

Walsingham

Dereham

Norwich

NORFOLK

Bungay

SUFFOLK

Bury St Edmunds

Ipswich

Colchester

Clacton on Sea

Retreat centre = ●
Main town = ○

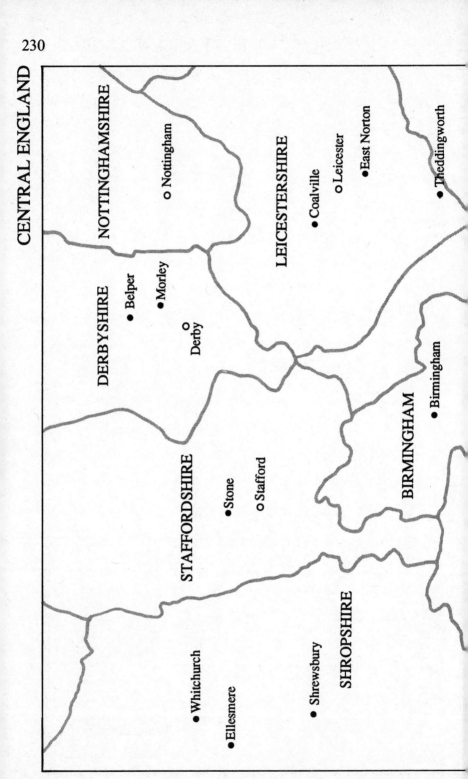

CENTRAL ENGLAND

NOTTINGHAMSHIRE

o Nottingham

LEICESTERSHIRE

● Coalville

o Leicester

● East Norton

● Theddingworth

DERBYSHIRE

● Belper

● Morley

o Derby

BIRMINGHAM

● Birmingham

STAFFORDSHIRE

● Stone

o Stafford

SHROPSHIRE

● Whitchurch

● Ellesmere

● Shrewsbury

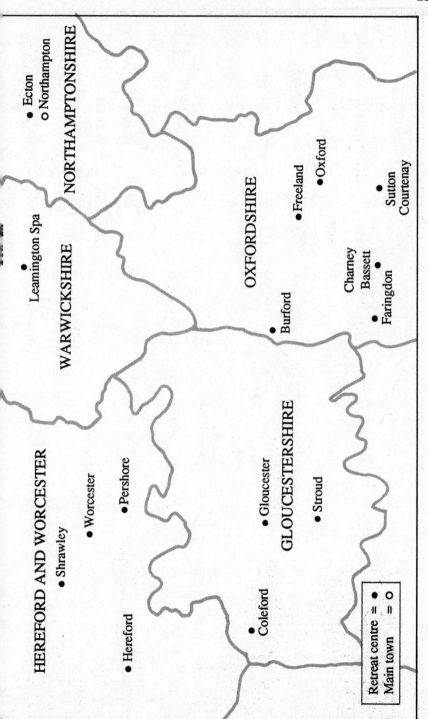

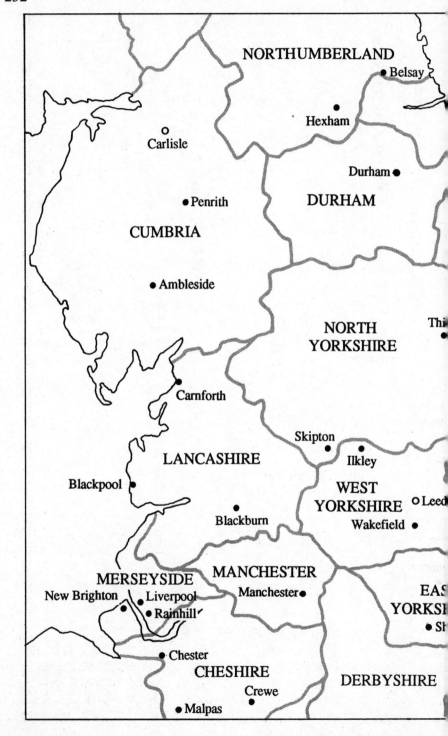

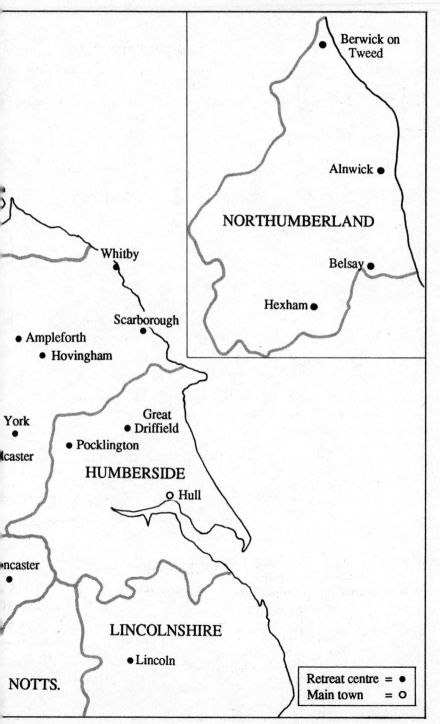

Berwick on
Tweed

Alnwick ●

NORTHUMBERLAND

Belsay ●

Hexham ●

Whitby

Scarborough

● Ampleforth
● Hovingham

York
●

Great
● Driffield

●caster

● Pocklington

HUMBERSIDE

○ Hull

●ncaster
●

LINCOLNSHIRE

● Lincoln

NOTTS.

Retreat centre = ●
Main town   = ○

WALES

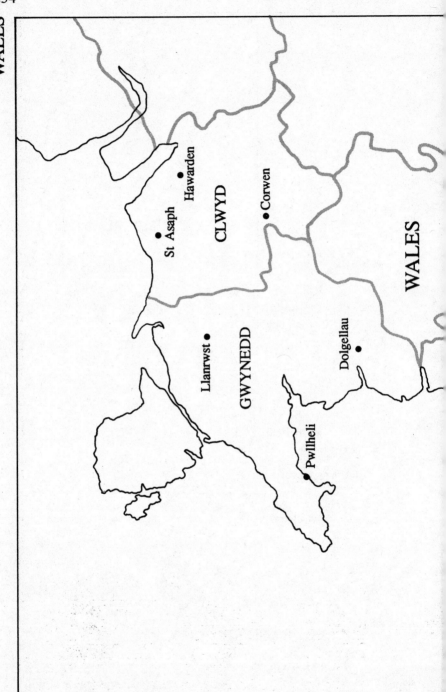

WALES

CLWYD

Hawarden

St Asaph

Corwen

GWYNEDD

Llanrwst

Dolgellau

Pwllheli

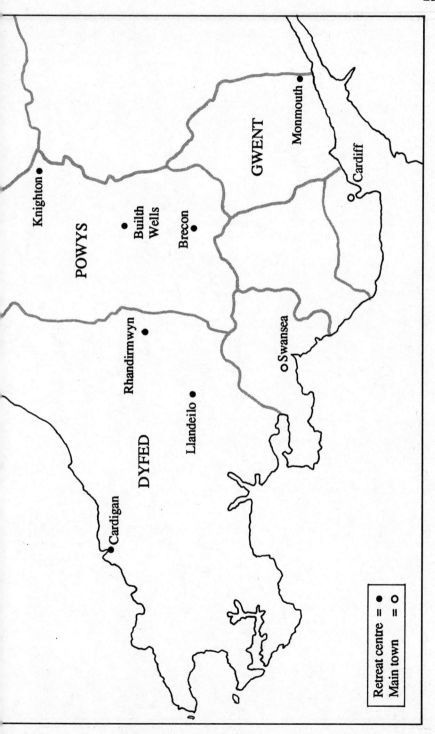

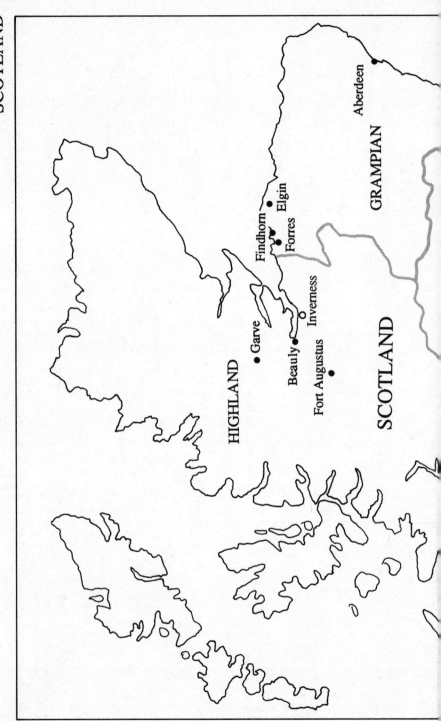

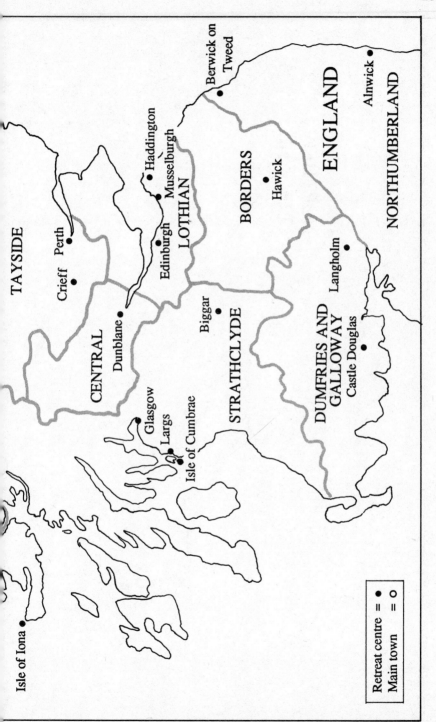

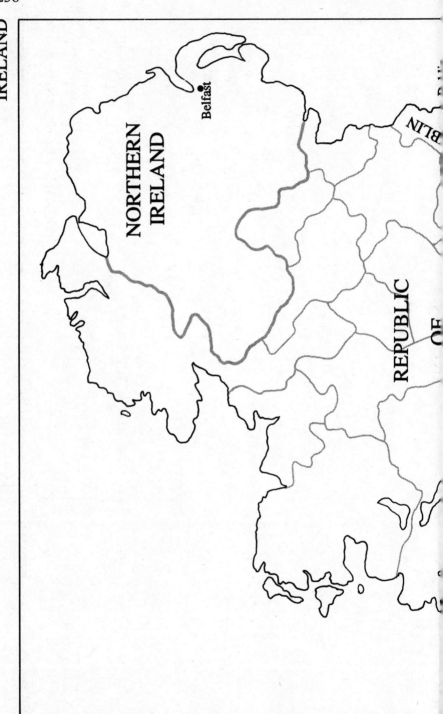

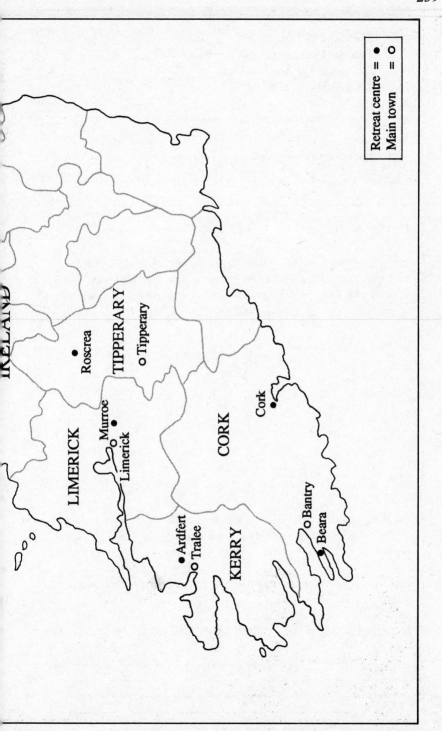

Retreat centre = ●
Main town = ○

IRELAND

TIPPERARY
Roscrea ●
○ Tipperary

LIMERICK
Murroe ●
○ Limerick

CORK
Cork ●

○ Bantry
Beara ●

KERRY
Ardfert ●
○ Tralee

To: The Good Retreat Guide
       Random Century House
       20 Vauxhall Bridge Road
       London SW1V 2SA

I visited the following retreat place on ----------------------- 19 ------

Establishment Name --

Address --

Post Code ---------------------- Telephone ----------------------------

In the space below, please describe what the retreat was like and give any other details you feel to be relevant. For example, what you thought of the rooms and meals, the situation, atmosphere, spiritual help offered, special activities and charges.

From my personal experience I recommend this retreat centre for inclusion in/exclusion from future editions of *The Good Retreat Guide*.

I am not connected in any way with this retreat centre other than as a guest.

Name and address (BLOCK CAPITALS, PLEASE)

Signed --